The Dragon's Blood

The Dragon's Blood

Feminist Intertextuality
in Eudora Welty's *The Golden Apples*

Rebecca Mark

University Press of Mississippi *Jackson*

97 96 95 94 4 3 2 1

Library of Congress Cataloging-in-Publication Data

Mark, Rebecca.
The dragon's blood : feminist intertextuality in Eudora
Welty's The golden apples / Rebecca Mark.
p.   cm.
Includes bibliographical references (p.) and index.
ISBN 0-87805-661-0 (alk. paper)
1. Welty, Eudora, 1909–   Golden apples.   2. Feminism
and literature—United States—History—20th
century.   3. Women and literature—United States—
History—20th century. 4. Intertextuality.   I. Title.
PS3545.E6G636   1994
813'.52—dc20   93-29518
                                                              CIP

British Library Cataloging-in-Publication data available

To Albert and Elizabeth Mark

Such a composition has nothing to do with eternity,
the striving for greatness, brilliance—
only with the musing of a mind
one with her body, experienced fingers quietly pushing
dark against bright, silk against roughness,
pulling the tenets of a life together
with no mere will to mastery,
only care for the many-lived, unending
forms in which she finds herself.

—Adrienne Rich, "Transcendental Etude"
in *Dream of a Common Language*

At around age six, perhaps, I was standing by myself in
our front yard waiting for supper, just at that hour in a
late summer day when the sun is already below the
horizon and the risen full moon in the visible sky stops
being chalky and begins to take on light. There comes
the moment, and I saw it then, when the moon goes
from flat to round. For the first time it met my eyes as a
globe. The word "moon" came into my mouth as though
fed to me out of a silver spoon. Held in my mouth the
moon became a word.

—Eudora Welty, *One Writer's Beginnings*

Contents

Acknowledgments

This book was conceived in California, developed in Minnesota at the boundary waters of the Mississippi, and is flowing out to the sea from the southern port of New Orleans. Many people have inspired, encouraged, and advised me during the journey of writing this book. I would like to thank my teachers, Barbara Charlesworth Gelpi, Myra Jehlen, Arnold Rampersad, and Albert Gelpi; my colleagues at Stanford University, Denise Albanese, Joel Brattin, Kathy Cirksena, Ed Cohen, Maria Damon, and Gertrude Palmer; my colleagues at St. Olaf College, Susan Albertine, David Booth, and Carol Holly; my colleagues at University of Minnesota, Ruth Ellen Joeres, Amy Kaminsky, Naomi Schemen, and Janet Spector; and my colleagues at Tulane University, Dan Balderston, Janice Carlisle, Jane Carter, Hope Glidden, Marsha Houston, Amy Koritz, Cynthia Lowenthal, Joe Roach, J. L. Simmons, Teresa Soufas, Teresa Toulouse, Molly Travis, and Maryann Valiulis. I am indebted to the community of Welty scholars particularly Suzanne Marrs, Gail Mortimer, Noel Polk, Peggy Prenshaw, Louise Westling, Ruth Weston, Patsy Yeager, and my editor Seetha Srinivasan, who have consistently challenged and inspired me. Grants from the Bush Foundation, the Newcomb Foundation and Tulane University provided me with invaluable time in 1988 and 1991 to complete this manuscript. I am grateful for the expert editing of Diane Mark-Walker, Cathe Mizell-Nelson, and Gwen Duffy, and the tireless word-processing of Sandy Haro. I would particularly like to express my appreciation of Barclay Barrios who spent painstaking hours as my research assistant.

I thank my heart sisters Nanc Allen, Mary Ann Brown, and Pat Tunmer; my soul sisters Mary Wood and Julee Raiskin; my "twin" sister Lisa Rofel; my spirit sister Linda Chrisman; my sister in struggle Linda Gardner; my friends Jeff Lockman and Mark Townsend; and my healers, Joann Loulan, Emily Conrad Da' Oud, Susan Harper, Maureen McManus, and Orisia Haas, who gave me the support to continue writing. I also want to acknowledge how lucky I have been to have the constant and unconditional love of my family, Albert and Elizabeth Mark, Charles and Diane Mark-Walker, Andrew Mark and Victoria Hux, Katherine Lee and Lyndon Lee and Alice, Alex, Madeline, and Sam.

Most of all I would like to thank Eudora Welty. After meeting you, and recognizing the genius of your mind, the depth of your passion, the magnificence of your wit, the expansive quality of your heart, the honesty and coherence of your personal vision, and the unqualified sweep of your imagination, I was determined to tell the world that you are a genius of the twentieth century. For the expression of regeneration, the poetic resonance, the constellation of hope which *The Golden Apples* is for me, I thank you.

The Dragon's Blood

I

Scissors and Pins

Feminist Intertextuality

It is no secret that *The Golden Apples* resonates with mythical allusions, but critics are just beginning to recognize the extent to which Eudora Welty uses every kind of cultural artifact from folktales, literary texts, fairy tales, and oral narratives to musical scores, popular songs, advertisements, children's rhymes, and newspaper articles to challenge dominant literary conventions. While a school of largely reductionist "myth-critics" has developed in response to *The Golden Apples*,[1] until quite recently we have not examined in detail the artistic and political significance of the extraordinary intertextuality in this text. A detailed analysis of the interplay of cultural motifs in *The Golden Apples* not only alters our explication of Welty's fiction, it also allows us to reevaluate her relationship to such literary giants as Sir James Frazer, James Joyce, and William Faulkner. While I applaud the work of feminist critics who situate Eudora Welty in a women's literary tradition and who have argued that she shares many narrative strategies, character types, and themes with Virginia Woolf, Willa Cather, Elizabeth Bowen, and Elizabeth Spencer, as well as early nineteenth-century women writers,[2] this study is more concerned with Welty's confrontation with, and transformation of, patriarchal myths and masculinist texts.

As many critics have pointed out, "June Recital" and "Sir Rabbit" include allusions to William Butler Yeats, but few have noticed that "Moon Lake" echoes Sir James Frazer, "The Whole World Knows" answers William Faulkner, and "Music from Spain" responds to James Joyce. While "Shower of Gold" and "The Wanderers" depend more directly on Greek and Celtic mythological and classical references, they also challenge the basic masculinist, and what Irving Howe describes as the nihilistic, tenets of modernism. In alluding to these literary forefathers, Welty is not paying homage, nor is she simply influenced by these masters; she is instead parodying, battling, and above all transforming the subtext of masculine superiority embedded in their texts. This implicit and explicit critique of a Western heroic tradition has gone virtually unnoticed, not only because critics have tried to analyze the literary allusions and the mythological allusions in isolation from one another, not only because no one could imagine a nice southern lady doing such a thing, but primarily because no one has consistently applied a close feminist textual and intertextual analyses to this collection of stories.

By feminist intertextuality I mean not merely resonances or allusions but a process that achieves a dialogic interchange of symbol and metaphor between masculinist and feminist texts. Such interchange allows for the transformation of previously codified meanings, types, and representations. When we explicate *The Golden Apples* from a position of feminist intertextuality, we reveal a coherent strategy. What many critics have interpreted in *The Golden Apples* as problematic references, which at best create a dreamlike atemporality and at worst create confusion, can be seen as a detailed rewriting of the Western myth of the literary hero in all his manifestations: as fertility god in pagan ritual; as triumphant conqueror in early Greek and Celtic myth; as saviour in Christian theology; as defeated, lost, or cynical hero in early modernism.

In the process of writing what later became *The Golden Apples*, Welty first addressed the heroic myth as it revealed itself in modern texts and then progressed backwards historically to confront the vaunting hero Perseus and, further, to recover literary fragments of the fertility god. She began with two of the most pervasive myths of sexual domination: rape, in "The Whole World Knows," and the silencing of the woman artist in "June Recital." She then wrote stories of masculinist and feminist resurrection—"Music from Spain" and "Moon Lake"—and finally stories that allow for a sexual meeting at the crossroads of the masculine and feminine—"Shower of Gold," "Sir Rabbit," and "The Wanderers." In "The Whole World Knows," she establishes and transforms the parameters of the patriarchal narrative as it has been formulated in literary modernism: the narrative of the defeated ego and the accompanying narrative of his degradation of the female.

In quilting together the finished stories, Welty creates a more complex structure, embedding the most violent encounters between masculine and feminine in the middle of the text and surrounding them with more dialogic and transformative images. By introducing the collection with a narrator in "Shower of Gold," Welty gives the text a strong female presence who can lead the feminine through the difficult terrain of "June Recital." By making "Moon Lake," the story of female resurrection, the pivotal text, she asserts that the feminine as well as the masculine can enter the underworld and return, thus equalizing the two halves of the engendered duality. In this way Welty develops a strong feminist presence that can stand up to Ran's rage in "The Whole World Knows" and embrace the masculine journey of discovery and resurrection in "Music from Spain." In "The Wanderers," Welty has extended this presence so fully that Virgie can experience a transcendent independence. The new composite female character developed throughout the collection is capable of doing battle with, making love to, becoming, and laughing at the heroic king.

When Welty wrote "The Whole World Knows," she was at a turning point in her career. Although she had successfully completed her first novel, *Delta Wedding*, she had not yet established herself as a major writer. No one really thought, and some still do not think, that she could ever be considered Faulkner's equal. Interestingly enough, the first story Welty wrote at this juncture in her career is a parody of, or at least a direct response to, the Quentin section of *The Sound and the Fury*. But to stop at this point, to answer only William Faulkner, a fellow Mississippian and southern writer, would be to circumscribe her sphere of power. Instead, by weaving into her text fragments from Greek and Celtic myths and from the works of Beethoven, Yeats, Frazer, Woolf, Eliot, and Joyce, she situates herself not on the margin of literary discourse but at the center, thus destabilizing the categories marginal, regional, and minor. Welty transforms Western narratives of rape, domination, and victimization of the feminine by the masculine into narratives of engagement, battle, confrontation, fertility, sexual exchange between masculine and feminine, finally challenging the very viability of the two terms.

We could consider Welty's intertextuality derivative or assume that she is simply a genius capable of remembering and using hundreds of sources, but by doing so we would overlook the political nature of the work. To view *The Golden Apples* as the work of a single genius, in the language of what Foucault calls "the man-and-his-work-criticism," is to make her writing part of the tradition rather than a subversive undercurrent ("What Is an Author?", 141). Edward Said indicates how developed the discussion of origins has become when he asks us to consider "how many words and ideas in current thought and writing hover about the concept of 'beginnings:' innovation, novelty, originality, revolution, change, convention, tradition, period, authority, influence, to name just a few" (*Beginnings*, 6).[3] Said's list indicates that influence studies have centered around two preoccupations: either the attempt to prove exactly how a particular author differed from predecessors, what was unique, original, revolutionary about the work; or the acceptance of the fact that the cultural tradition (Eliot), influence (Bloom), and discourse

(Foucault) make uniqueness undesirable, unattainable, or meaningless.

There are those who argue that all innovation in art and literature occurs because of the spontaneous invention of genius. Gerald Else, for example, in *The Origin and Early Form of Greek Tragedy*, discounts the argument that tragedy grew out of fertility ritual, claiming that tragedy was the creation of individual men—notably Thespis, Aeschylus, Sophocles, and Euripides. On the other side of the debate, in "Tradition and the Individual Talent," Eliot asserts that what happens to the artist is "a continual surrender of himself as he is at the moment to something which is more valuable . . . a continual self-sacrifice, a continual extinction of personality" (6). Tradition is more valuable than self in Eliot's essay. "Tradition . . . cannot be inherited . . . if you want it you must obtain it by great labor" (4).

Both Else's argument for the dominance of the self and Eliot's for the relinquishing of the self to tradition develop from the same patriarchal model. Neither argument could survive without the underlying belief that great works make great men immortal—whether it is the immortality of an individual or a culture. As Foucault states, "Our culture has metamorphosed this idea of narrative, or writing, as something designed to ward off death" ("What Is an Author?" 142). The etymology of the word "author—L. *aucter*: one who causes to grow" appears to give force to this concept by defining the author as the originator, the genius (genesis) behind the innovation (Klien, *A Comprehensive Etymological Dictionary*). Whereas Foucault's "What Is an Author?" might be seen to deconstruct this hierarchical connection between paternity and authorship, it merely takes authorship away from individuals and gives it back to cultural discourse. It does nothing to alter the violent masculine anxiety over mortality, which is at the root of the discourse: "The work, which once had the duty of providing immortality, now possesses the right to kill, to be its author's murderer" ("What Is an Author?" 142). Foucault's idea is not new, however, but part of the same old structure built upon the necessary castration, annihilation, of a narcissistic ego. If the author supposes that he can gain immortality through his work, he has established an abstract system in which there is an identity "I," which must be maintained by the written word that will represent "I." This structure depends on defining life as identity and identity as the abstract notion of immortality. In this system the work has more power than the individual; it will predate and postdate him. He will be in an antagonistic and jealous relationship to the text. He is dependent on the text, the very world of ecological regeneration that, in his desire to dominate, he has named as other, female, dark, death.

Sandra Gilbert and Susan Gubar, in *Madwoman in the Attic*, observe that "the patriarchal notion that the writer 'fathers' his text just as God fathered the world is and has been so all-pervasive in Western literary civilization that, as Said has shown, the metaphor is built into the very word, 'author,' with which writer, deity, and pater-familias are identified" (4). Gubar and Gilbert connect the act of authorship with dissemination in a masculine sexual economy (i.e., the pen is penis) and try to counter the discourse of paternal authority by developing a language to discuss female authorship. Their theory that the metaphor of literary paternity creates an anxiety of authorship for the female writer has led many critics to try to develop a metaphor of literary maternity.

Susan Friedman argues in "Creativity and the Childbirth Metaphor: Gender Difference and Literary Discourse" that "in contrast to the phallic analogy that implicitly excludes women from creativity, the childbirth metaphor validates women's artistic effort by unifying their mental and physical labour into pro-creativity" (49). While this appears to be a more natural extension of childbirth imagery, if we substitute "mother" for "father," we are still participating in metaphorical supersession. The concept of authorship, as it implies authority over and the fathering of a text, derives its meaning from the assertion that conceiving an idea is analogous to giving birth to a baby. By substituting mother for father we are participating in a biologically determined discourse that limits the ways in which we can imagine the relationship between author and text. We do not need to substitute one parent for another; we need rather to disjoin literary creation from reproduction and childrearing. In an attempt to solve this dilemma, lesbian feminist writers, including Adrienne Rich and Monique Wittig, have advocated the use of the term "lesbian" as a metaphor for feminist creativity. The term "lesbian" has the advantage of retaining erotic power while allowing for feminist autonomy and independence. Farwell describes this dynamic as a "shattering of old images and language, a space in which the woman writer can both oppose patriarchal categories and begin to define a new concept of reality" (117). What Rich has called the "lesbian continuum," or the "lesbian within us," is a powerful political concept but does not solve the problem of influence, allusion, and intertextuality between lesbian texts and patriarchal texts, or between the imagination defined as lesbian and masculine texts.

These feminist literary treatments of influence and tradition have focused on three strategies: (1) the establishment of a distinct women's literary tradition (culminating in the production of such works as *The Norton Anthology of Women's Literature*); (2) the attempt to break completely with the masculinist past (Lorde, 112) and Irigaray's and Cixous's focus on "l'écriture feminine"); and (3) the desire to revise or transform what is perceived as a patriarchal legacy.[4] The problem with the desire to isolate ourselves from the works of the authorial fathers is that we cannot do it. It is an imaginary desire, as imaginary as the masculinist desire to separate from the female other. Although concepts such as "l'écriture feminine" and "women's literary tradition" are necessary contributions to the discussion of feminist imagination, they do not explain the highly intertextual works of Jane Austen, Toni Morrison, Hilda Doolittle, Virginia Woolf, or Eudora Welty. The surgical removal of masculinity or masculinist culture from a text as multivocal as *The Golden Apples* would be not only impossible but dangerous to the life of the text.

This project began in the early eighties when feminist critics were engaged in the archaeological agenda of unearthing previously silenced women writers, the theoretical agenda of defining a space for feminist criticism, and the political agenda of reclaiming the female body. At the same time we were also questioning the very terms "woman," "feminist," and "female." While the continuous process of destabilizing the position of "the women writer" by situating her in historical, cultural, geographic locations is evocative and politically necessary, we must also recognize that the cultural production of woman indicates not an absence but a presence so powerful that the production of countercultural types and representations may take longer to produce change than if the type had been determined by biology alone. In *Epistemology of the Closet*, Eve Sedgwick recognizes the strange tendency of feminist and postmodernist critics to assume that because an identity is constructed it can be easily laid aside like an unfashionable garment: "I remember the buoyant enthusiasm with which feminist scholars used to greet the finding that one or another brutal form of oppression was not biological but 'only' cultural! I have often wondered what the basis was for our optimism about the malleability of culture by any one group or program" (41). Women in most cultures have an identification, if not with a biological imperative, then at least with sets of social and cultural types and definitions. Release from these often damaging definitions and identifications requires a Steinian reorganization of language from the level of letter and punctuation to the conglomerations we call words, metaphors, sentences, paragraphs, narratives, and myths.

While there are numerous ways in which feminist criticism is enlivened by critiques of essentialist and identity politics, by questions concerning the instability of meaning and the problematics of interpretations, in our desire to master the latest theoretical terrain, we often allow ourselves to be distracted from the act of decoding the buried texts that we have so painstakingly resurrected. We have yet to interpret the complex metaphorical sign systems on which many texts by women writers depend. Hélène Cixous's insistence, in "The Laugh of the Medusa," that there were no women writers who inscribed the female body was a perfect example of this blindness. Even in the 1990s the texts of many women writers remain virtually unexamined.

The focus of this exploration on a single text, *The Golden Apples*, endeavors to prove that the detailed interplay of theory and text reveals more subtle and unexplored feminist intertexualities and intersexualities than we have yet realized. I also believe, as Roland Barthes states in his introduction to *S/Z*, that the single text is valid, because "literature itself is never anything but a single text" (12). It is an "entrance into a network with a thousand entrances; to take this entrance is to aim, ultimately, not at a legal structure of norms and departures, a narrative or poetic law, but a perspective (of fragments, of voices from other texts, other codes) whose vanishing point is nonetheless . . . mysteriously opened" (12). Only when we pay attention to the smallest details can we begin to experience the writing as it reweaves the once dominant mythical structures.

In *The Heart of the Story*, Peter Schmidt comments on how long it took Welty to write her stories or "the time these stories took to weave themselves, and the time they need to be read properly, or listened to. Silence and slow time" (xxi). Welty herself reminds us that reading and writing are slow, cumulative processes. Because of this, unlike Barthes, she believes that the text cannot be entered anywhere with the same effect: "Fiction was made of words to travel under the reading eye, and made to go in one sequence and one direction, slowly, accumulating; time is an element. The words follow the contours of some continuous relationship between what can be told and what cannot be told, to be in the silence of reading the lightest of the hammers that tap their way along this side of chaos" (*The Eye of the Story*, 143).

Welty's notion of accumulation, a notion Gertrude Stein explores in her use of repetition in *The Making of Americans*, goes against Barthes's notion of an undetermined plurality.[5] In order to experience the movement of dispersal and recombination and not remain frozen at any one moment, we must pay attention to the most minute alterations, associations, echoes, and allusions while recognizing the constellations and patterns. Welty's revision of Western culture in *The Golden Apples* demands an attention to detail, to a coding in which each word has both representational and metaphorical meanings. In *The Golden Apples*, Welty writes not in the code of one who wants to keep information hidden from an enemy but in the necessary code of one whose experience and artistic vision places her at the locus from which language is emerging into form, where she is murmuring a new tune in response to the cultural myths that communicate literary meaning in Western culture. We only understand her meaning when we hear the interplay between the moment, the physical detail, and the echo, the metaphoric and symbolic resonance, what Welty calls "the double—doubling back"—the process of dispersal and return.

This exploration of Eudora Welty's *The Golden Apples* will argue that Welty's feminist intertextuality could be called intersexuality, precisely because her writing evokes an enlivening of metaphor, character, and symbol or an eroticization of the word. When the word is freed from the violent heroic demand that it represent sword and phallus, it becomes instead the source of a sexual and suggestive renewal that allows new meanings and representations to reveal themselves. Eudora Welty and many other feminist writers dismantle the damaging narrative structures of patriarchal dominance by creating a linguistic practice that permits a constantly evolving relationship between established meaning and emerging meaning. *The Golden Apples* is a text that creates representations that continually revitalize themselves in a response to any dominating or rigidifying force.

Although many critics have labeled Welty's prose feminist, we are just beginning to explicate Welty's unique feminism. It is not an obvious or polemic feminism as her responses in interviews have indicated. In Prenshaw's *Conversations with Eudora Welty*, Welty states: "Writing is a profession outside sex"; (36) her comment on the women's liberation movement: "Noisiness"; (36) and on the meaning of male chauvinism: "No idea" (37). When asked if she thinks women are more, less, or about as emotional as men, Welty answers: "As emotional; more competitive; less passive, rational, sincere; as strong, violent" (34). When asked which women she respects most, she responds, "Georgia O'Keefe, Martha Graham. For reasons plain to all—among them, common to both, an inviolate independence of spirit in pursuing their arts, the wholeness of their gifts of imagination" (35). With an inviolate independence of spirit, Welty's art does not yield readily to the labels or demands of any particular political or critical agenda. Yet in her answers she does not actually reject feminism but reaffirms it, by returning to the independence and spirit at the core of political feminism.

Welty's vision, in as far as it expands the way we can imagine occupying the sign female, is undeniably feminist, as Peggy Prenshaw, Louise Westling, Ruth D. Weston, Patricia Yeager, and, most recently, Peter Schmidt have argued.[6] Following Prenshaw's, Kerr's, and Bolsterli's notion of a world of women in Welty's fiction, Ruth D. Weston contends that Welty has an imagination that "expresses itself in metaphoric structures which reflect the female's connection and/or disjunction with her world" (74). By focusing on the connection and disjunction of the female, we might overlook the ways in which all categories, including masculinity and femininity, are being decentered and, more importantly, how the center itself becomes in the fictional world of Welty's narratives a constantly expanding and shifting metaphorical and intertextual universe in which old notions of disjunction or "woman's world" no longer apply. In fact to assume that there is one female identity and one female world is to greatly diminish the continually evolving and expanding signification that is the radical gift of Welty's feminism. The opening story of *The Golden Apples* begins with a meeting that is at times violent, at times passionate, between many masculine and feminine worlds and the rest of the collection develops around encounters, border crossings and shifting identities, which confuse and liberate our fixed notions of gender and sexuality. By focusing on Welty's debt to a women's tradition in literature, Schmidt's recent book continues the serious historical work that has been revitalizing Welty criticism in the nineties. Unfortunately his division of the female muse into the monstrous Medusa and the more transformative Sibyl, while illuminating, tends to be reductive in that it does not allow for the possibility that the rage and power of the Medusa is as regenerative and creative as the prophetic vision of the Sibyl. Understanding the dynamic in the Perseus and Medusa myth requires recognizing the dynamic between feminist and masculinist texts.

Patricia Yeager explores this more interactive approach to Welty's writing in her article "Because a Fire Was in My Head." Arguing against Margaret Duras's proposal for a separatist feminist writing, Yeager submits that "reinscription of phallocentrism may be a sign not of weakness or plagiarism, but of woman's own ability to signify, that is, her ability to play with, to control, and to restructure patriarchal traditions" (959). This concept of woman as a willing participant, as active arranger of the Western literary text, is an empowering model. Yeager goes on to assert that Welty's "transformations of the canon's 'alien' mythologies" do not fit into any previously discussed theory of influence because Welty "does not deny, repress, or disguise her obligation to Yeats; she emphasizes her own comic resourcefulness by expropriating Yeat's poems in unexpected ways" (964).[7] By proposing an image of the woman writer as satirist, Sarah laughing at God, doubting His prowess, Yeager's theories offer an alternative to the images of female authors as frightened and sick daughters, troubled mothers, mad sisters, distraught lovers, anxious artists, and suicidal muses. But even Yeager's theories, which embrace intertextuality, still maintain the idea of an autonomous author, a controlling force who can consciously appropriate and restructure patriarchal traditions. Yeager's theories neglect to realize that the author is simultaneously appropriating and being appropriated, generating text and becoming the text that she generates.

Julia Kristeva, who brings Barthes's and Foucault's theories of influence, authority, and text together into a coherent discussion of intertextuality, reminds us that "what is being dealt with is a specific dynamics of the subject of the utterance, who consequently, precisely because of this intertextuality, is not an individual in the etymological sense of the term, not an identity . . . this new identity may be the plurality capable of manifesting itself as the plurality of characters the author uses, but in more recent writing, in the twentieth century novel, it may appear as fragments of characters, or fragments of ideology, or fragments of representation" (281).

Following Kristeva's analyses, the identity of the female author does not have to be an identity but rather the voicing of a multiplicity of fragments, all the representational fragments that have joined to create the solid term female or feminine. This does not mean, however, that there is no difference between a male and female author, or a masculine and feminine text. The ability to speak in many voices will be determined by one's, cultural, historical, and experiential framework. Just because a multiplicity of fragments exists does not mean everyone can engage them or desires to. Within this definition of intertextuality lies the possibility that authorial identity is nothing less than the willingness and ability to participate with the many threads of the textual universe. The greater the plurality of characters and fragments one can sustain, the more complex the creation. Eudora Welty writes in her preface to *The Collected Works of Eudora Welty*, "What I do in the writing of any character is to try to enter into the mind, heart, and skin of a human being who is not myself. Whether this happens to be a man or a woman, old or young, with skin black or white, the primary challenge lies in making the jump itself. It is the act of a writer's imagination that I set most high" (xi). Welty makes the jump into ever more complex and difficult skins throughout her career.

In an attempt to release texts from a strict chronological relation, Owen Miller, in his essay "Intertextual Identity," argues for a definition of intertextuality that "would accept the full implications of the reversibility of the focused text and intertext, would challenge us to a greater number of reevaluations of the canon" and "would truly be seen as a relational concept, not a monologue but a dialogue, not a solo but a duet" (36). If we recognize a relational and active model of intertextuality, we become at once the living bodies on which the texts are inscribing and the living bodies doing the inscribing, at once authorial and textual. We do not create the intertextuality; we simply choose to become conscious and to participate in the intertextuality that exists. Through the act of writing we become, like Virginia Woolf in *A Room of One's Own*, the one standing outside the library, the one entering the library, and the one writing the fragments into a temporary whole: temporary because intertextual dialogue will demand reevaluation and textual shifting. Christine Herrman, in *The Tongue Snatchers*, reminds us that when a woman "penetrates—always obliquely—into the mysterious virile world from which she has been so long excluded, the site of so many marvellous adventures recounted in books and films . . . she is struck by the fact that abstraction dominates here, in two guises: system and hierarchy" (42). The vibrations brought about by Kristeva's and Owen's definitions of intertextuality defy system and hierarchy. Woolf's presence becomes the irritating fragment that disturbs the institutional structure of Cambridge University. By including and becoming the fragments of discourse, this subject will liberate whatever it contacts. Frozen form will be enlivened in a direct reversal of the Medusa myth in which living bodies are turned into stone.

Welty achieves a revival of literary modernism by including not only what Kristeva calls fragments of ideology or representation but also what Patrick O'Donnell and Robert Con Davis call "'extraliterary' discourses" or "texts not usually conceived of as texts," namely "voice, culture, violence, portraiture, body, sex" (xxi). Welty invites a multitude of cultural forms into her text, including visual art, music, dance, popular culture, and oral tradition, as well as extra-cultural natural forms such as precipitation, wind, temperature, and human expressions such as gesture, touch, and movement. Through her willingness to participate both with what is considered culture and what has not been considered culture, Welty returns the word to its material/textile-/tactile source, allowing language to be constantly renewed in the mouth, the hand, the ear, the eye—as moon becomes "word" in Welty's mouth in *One Writer's Beginnings*. We can understand this reversal of Midas's and Perseus's touch, the erotic vibration of *The Golden Apples*, by recognizing a difference between the narcissistic art of masculinist immortality, in which the author/father makes love to an abstracted reflection of himself, and the art of human sexuality, in which writing as organic life makes love to itself as organic life.[8]

Welty contends that in the process of reading and writing we "are persuaded by them [words] to be brought mind and heart within the presence, the power, of the imagination. This we find to be above all the power to reveal, with nothing barred" (*The Eye of the Story*, 134).[9] To define the power of the imagination as the power to reveal with nothing barred is to move into Barthes's world of plural and constantly referential texts: "It is a question against all in-difference, of asserting the existence of plurality, which is not that of the truth, the probable, or even the possible" (*S/Z*, 5). While *The Golden Apples* does not posit truths, it differentiates, not only between the proliferation of healthy cells and the proliferation of nuclear bombs, but in the multiple spaces between. A word, character, or narrative is more meaningful the more textured, embodied, and palpable it becomes and more likely to survive the better able it is to shift shape and forms. Ironically, while we think of matter as immovable, in language the material metaphor is in reality more permeable than a linguistic abstraction or conglomeration that can only exist in one form. The moon in the mouth takes on more possible meanings that the autonomous moon.

Barthes's discussion of the differences between work and text explores this concept by introducing a metaphor that is particularly appropriate to Welty—the library:

> . . . the work is concrete, occupying a portion of book-space (in a library, for example) the text, on the other hand, is a methodological field. . . . While the work is held in the hand, the text is held in language: it exists only as discourse . . . the text cannot stop at the end of a library shelf, for example; the constitutive movement of the text is a traversal (traverse: it can cut across a work, several works) . . . the text is that which goes to the limits of the rules of enunciation rationality, readability, and on . . . the text is cloth; textus, from which text derives, means "woven." ("From Work to Text" in *Textual Strategies*, 76)

If we place the materiality of text/textile beside the materiality of the library, we have an example of feminist intertextuality that resonates throughout Welty's fiction.[10] The library is found in at least three places in Welty's texts—in *The Optimist's Daughter* when Laurel is reading the text of her father's library and in two scenes in *One Writer's Beginnings*.[11] The library houses artifacts or works, which are unable to be in dialogue with one another without the textualizing eye of the reader/writer. Welty revitalizes the works into texts as she contextualizes, historicizes, and personalizes them. For example, in *One Writer's Beginnings*, Welty tells us that her mother carried a set of Dickens through fire and flood, that her father only had one book as a child, that the librarian made her go back home and get an extra petticoat if she wanted a book from the library. Every detail brings to the solid object of the book the palpable body and emotion, transforming it from work into text.

Intertextuality resists exclusion, and in the fury of inclusion there is a direct and passionate indictment of the ossification and classification of old hierarchies. In *The Optimist's Daughter*, Laurel looks out the open window of her father's library where she sees that "Miss Adele was hanging something white on the clothes-line. She turned as if intuitively toward the window, and raised her arm to wave. It was a beckoning sort of wave. She beckons with her pain, thought Laurel, realizing how often her father must have stood just here, resting his eyes and looked out at her without ever seeing her" (120). As Laurel moves away from her father's library, and looks out the window, she sees a tabula rasa on which she is designing a new fabric that includes the words from the books on the shelves, the words in her memory, the words spoken between her mother and father, and the extraliterary, the gesture, the hand, the sign of the wave and what is signified by that wave—Miss Adele's erotic love for Laurel's father and the pain she suffered at his not seeing her. All of these become part of the new textile Laurel is weaving. When Laurel is not in Mount Salus, she works in Chicago as a fabric designer. The sexuality and textuality of love and intuition indict the library, as the enlivening view of the reader moves through the open window to the wave.

The library is full of masculinist works, the objects that could be seen to silence Laurel's voice, but by being read and written into Welty's text, they no longer maintain their hierarchical power to silence. In fact we meet all the works in their haphazard, congruent, concurrent, nonlinear, nonchronological place on one man's library shelf. Just as the young Welty in *One Writer's Beginnings* devours books, Laurel brings waves and emotions to bear on books, transforming them from solid objects to moving fragments in the process of her reading/writing. Books can be touched, felt, burned, drowned, eaten. When Laurel finishes in the library, she explores her mother's sewing room, where it is "all dark" and she must "feel about for a lamp" (*The Optimist's Daughter*, 132). It is in this dark place that Laurel, like the woman in Rich's "Transcendental Etude," remembers, putting "together the fallen scraps of cloth into stars, flowers, birds, people, or whatever she liked to call them, lining them up, spacing them out, making them into patterns" (134).

In *Losing Battles*, Miss Lexie cuts Gloria down to size and tells the story of the death of Miss Julia Mortimer as she snips and pins and stitches. The obvious connection between Miss Lexie, lexicographer, the one involved with words and storytelling, and her role as a seamstress reveals the close link Welty saw between the process of writing and the process of weaving or piecing together a fabric of life, a metaphor applied to the three fates who were thought to spin, weave, and cut the thread of life. At the end of Katie's life in "The Wanderers," Virgie is found cutting up and piecing together a plaid dress. The old self is dying, and Virgie is designing a new text, a new costume, for herself. In describing her own writing process Welty tells of editing "with scissors and pins . . . putting things in their best and proper place, revealing things at the time when they matter most" (Prenshaw, *Conversations with Eudora Welty*, 89).

If there is anxiety in Welty's relationship to other texts, it is only the anxiety that she will be faint of heart, that fear will keep her characters from the fullest experience, that by depending, as Judge McKelva does, on the ocular-centrism of failing rational vision, they will exclude the intuitive awareness of the wave across the yard, some barely noticeable presence. The model of feminist creativity, which this textured language begins to release, is not one of anxiety, anger, salvation, or sacrifice; it is instead one of difficult and at times terrifying inclusion, living with excruciating ambiguity.

The author in the patriarchal system of immortality through great works both identifies with and fears the text, which is spun and cut and spun again. By embracing, in Kristeva's words "the plurality of characters," Welty, in her intersubjectivity with Laurel, Miss Eckhart, King MacLain, Virgie, and her other characters not only weaves the text, the writing itself, but she allows herself to be the text being woven. Embodying the dynamics of writing itself, not the identity of a writer, she becomes the fragmented multiplicity of ideology and representation able to be formed temporarily into a new pattern of coherent meaning, only to be again released, fragmented. As text, as the movement of writing, the writer is all that is emerging into form. The text of Miss Adele's wave is as important, has as much meaning, as Gibbons's *The Rise and Fall of the Roman Empire*, and both are cut from the same cloth.

Just as Laurel extends her father's library to include and thus embody human emotion and human body, Welty's texts are performing an act of sexual resuscitation on the modernist and ancient literary traditions. By the time Eudora Welty wrote *The Golden Apples*, modernist writers had produced numerous texts focusing on the crisis of the literary hero. Eliot's *The Waste Land*, Stevens's "The Idea of Order at Key West," Hemingway's *The Sun Also Rises*, Fitzgerald's *The Great Gatsby*, Faulkner's *Light in August*, and Joyce's *Ulysses* bemoan the fact that the conquering, vaunting hero of classical literature fails to evoke meaning in twentieth-century technological society. Even minority writers like Richard Wright have sounded the dirge. All of these writers describe and invent the breakdown of the heroic narrative, a narrative that no longer functions to create dramatic tension, that no longer has the vitality to generate text. The myth of the hero, just like the myth of the author, establishes power by denial, by an exclusion that is an inevitable linguistic suicide. Eventually the word is so far removed from material reality that metaphor no longer functions to enliven or weave texture and text.

When Foucault attempts to show the relationship of author to discourse, he contends that "it would be worth examining how the authority became individualized in a culture like ours . . . at what point we began to recount the lives of authors rather than of heroes, and how this fundamental category of 'the-man-and-his-work-criticism' began" ("What Is an Author?" 41). The life of the hero and the life of the author are synonymous. They both engender the narrative of masculine domination, of a desire for autonomy and immortality. The myth of the Western hero has created persistent and limiting stone tablets, plots, film reels, character types, and tropes. Although this myth shows definite historically marked changes and variations, the elements that remain stable are: (1) the centrality of the one male character; (2) his struggle for immortality with some form of the feminine, who usually endangers his life; (3) his eventual dominance over the feminine and/or his despair at never really being able to achieve this dominance.

There is little doubt that cultural and historical context mediates and transforms the meaning of individual myths or metanarratives, but even given the multiplicity of and variations of the heroic narrative, this myth still survives and propagates itself across cultural and historical barriers. In fact its perseverance in the face of drastic cultural shifts, migrations, and the millennia of political revolutions is testimony to its power and its potential silencing of other stories. De Lauretis, in *Alice Doesn't*, comments, "However varied the conditions of . . . the narrative form in fictional genres, rituals, or social discourses, its movement seems to be that of a passage, a transformation predicated on the figure of a hero, a mythical subject" (113). De Lauretis goes on to suggest that the dominant narrative is based on the centrality of the hero's passage through a female space, his entry into this space and his emergence from this space. The hero myth crosses cultural and historical barriers precisely because it is a myth that supports and helps perpetuate masculine economic and political domination. De Lauretis maintains, "The hero, the mythical subject, is constructed as human being and as male; he is the active principle of culture, the establisher of distinction, the creator of differences. Female is what is not susceptible to transformation, to life or death; she (it) is an element of plot-space, a topos, a resistance, matrix and matter" (119).

The literary hero was once the figure of the young male fertility consort who, not frozen in Cellini's vaunting Perseus, scatters his seed in the winter to bring fertility to mother earth in the spring. In many cultures young males were taken from their mothers and taught to bond with the males of the group. In elaborate puberty rituals these men experienced the death of their old feminine selves and the rebirth of new masculine selves, to become of man born (Webster, 1–33). As this ritual is brought into literature, it becomes the story of the hero's battle with the female who represents the impending change of season and his impending death. The hero either achieves victory over this matrix/matter and returns to glory in his victory or must die a tragic death in the struggle. This narrative is embedded in the stories of Perseus, Gilgamesh, Theseus, Ulysses, Orestes, Oedipus, Hamlet, Ishmael, Quentin, and Stephen Daedalus. In its attempt to insist on the possibility of autonomous male regeneration, this myth has given birth to exquisite literature, but largely because of its biologically impossible claim, it has necessarily met a narcissistic dead end. To the extent that the hero, like the author, is successful in killing off the female (an impossible task), he assures his own death and the death of the narrative. The dominance of this myth in the Western literary tradition means that any woman writer must face a landscape peopled with the fragments of vaunting heroes and frail princesses and must negotiate a labyrinth of types that has little or nothing to do with her experience of herself as a female body. This textual legacy is a literary memory or imprint that she cannot ignore. The threads, fragments, and scraps of these narratives are her text. She has no choice but to pick up the pieces as they fall. While picking up these pieces, Welty evokes queens and goddesses who are as strong as, and can therefore directly engage, these god/heros and frail princesses.

The hero myth, upon which so much of Western literature is based, seeks not to express the totality, the fullness of human experience, but instead to justify and reestablish the narrow vision of the rights of a small elite. Thousands of details have substantiated these narratives, creating conglomerates of plot, character, symbol, and metaphor which have become so firmly established that mention of one part evokes the whole. These "finished works" present themselves not as artifacts but as raw material. Welty comments on this phenomena when she writes: "After all, the constellations, patterns, we are used to seeing in the sky are purely subjective; it is because our combining things, our heroes, existed in the world almost as soon as we did that made us long ago see Perseus up there and not a random scattering of little lights" (*On Short Stories*, 10–11). Welty mentions our heroes and Perseus in her example because it is the hero and specifically Perseus—the hero who kills the female—who has blocked our view of the random scattering. In the last pages of *The Golden Apples*, Welty exposes the depth of her willingness to read and write the text of heroic domination:

> Cutting off the Medusa's head was the heroic act, perhaps, that made visible a horror in life, that was at once the horror in love, Virgie thought—the separateness. She might have seen heroism prophetically when she was young and afraid of Miss Eckhart. She might be able to see it now prophetically, but she was never a prophet. Because Virgie saw things in their time, like hearing them—and perhaps because she must believe in the Medusa equally with Perseus—she saw the stroke of the sword in three moments, not one. In the three was the damnation—no, only the secret, unhurting because not caring in itself—beyond the beauty and the sword's stroke and the terror lay their existence in time—far out and endless, a constellation which the heart could read over many a night. (*CSEW*, 460)[12]

Virgie can see that at one time she might have been the hero and Miss Eckhart the victim of her sword, but she does not need to control the future. The word "perhaps" makes us question the heroic, and the repetition of the word "horror" erodes the term even further. The fact that this is what Virgie thought reveals that the hero has been unsuccessful in decapitating the female. (Earlier in the story Virgie is called the Medusa.) Virgie does not need the immortality of authorship or heroism; she is not a prophet.

Virgie sees the stroke of the sword in three moments—the premeditation, the act itself, and the effects of the act—not the one moment that the picture, the cultural artifact, has frozen and labeled heroic. The Medusa was not a single character but one of the three heads of the Gorgon monster. In killing the Medusa, Perseus separates the female as triple goddess from her past and future aspects, from the Gorgon of life and the Gorgon of birth, condemning her to death in the single image. At the same time, the hero rejects his own regeneration and condemns himself to death at the sight of her eyes. By privileging experience, what Virgie saw and heard over the interpretation of that experience "the heroic act," Welty returns us to the raw human feelings—horror, fear, separateness, terror—the scattering of little lights, out of which the myth grew, and reveals the dynamic creative process that originally gave birth to the frozen picture on the wall. Freed from the limits of the solid object, Virgie's perspective expands to include all space, not a chaotic plurality, but an expansive constellation—endless.

As Virgie looks at the dark picture of Perseus on Miss Eckhart's wall, she thinks, "The vaunting was what she remembered, that lifted arm" (*CSEW*, 460). Vaunting means to boast, extol, glorify, or praise, but Welty does not write about the words passed between Perseus and the Medusa. She does not write about the words that Apollodorus, Homer, Pausanius, Strabo, Hyginus, Horace, Pindar, Polonius, Herodotus, Pliny, Josephus, Clement of Alexandria, Euripides, Plato, and Aeschylus (Graves, *The Greek Myths I*, 242–43), not to mention modern mythologists, have used to extol, glorify, and praise the deeds of Perseus. Instead she focuses on the act itself—the lifted arm, the stroke of the sword which cuts off the Medusa's head, the physical vaunting—the physical body that is at once the lifted arm of the hero, the body of the triple headed Gorgon, and the decapitated head of the Medusa. Face to face with the body, Virgie can see the Medusa as well as Perseus, without turning to stone. She looks not only through the eyes of Perseus, the hero, but through the Medusa's eyes and through her own as well. It is through this triple vision, without the protection of the mirror reflection, that Virgie's gaze explodes the stone image and frees the frozen artifice of decapitation.

The Golden Apples is set in Morgana, a name that suggests the Celtic triple goddess Morrigana, the Arthurian sorceress/ magician Morgan Le Fay, and the Fata Morgana, all three cultural representations of female figures. Morrigana has power over the forces of life and death and over the magical realms of artistic creation. When Welty sets Morgana in the middle of MacLain County—a masculine name combining the Celtic "Mac," "son of," and "Lain," the last syllable of the famous Celtic hero Cuchulain, she creates a female sphere within a larger male sphere. Textually she cuts and pins together fragments of Celtic myth. In Celtic mythology as recorded in the *Tain Bo Cualnge*, the goddess Morrigana and the hero Cuchulain are in direct conflict with one another (Dunn, 161–62). When the goddess Morrigana finds herself sexually attracted to the hero Cuchulain and asks him to make love to her, he tells her that he could not possibly have sex with her because he is worn out from the day's battle and must conserve his strength for the weeks ahead. She offers to help him fight his enemies, but he laughs at the very idea. From this point on, Morrigana turns her power against Cuchulain and battles violently against him. She tells him that she will turn herself into a she-wolf, an eel, and a white heifer with red horns and fight him wherever he goes. Although both the goddess and the hero are severely wounded in these struggles, the goddess knows that the only person who can heal her wounds is the one who has inflicted them. She dresses as an old dairy maid and sits by the side of the road where Cuchulain must pass. When he appears she offers him three glasses of milk. With each glass he blesses the goddess and unwittingly heals the deep scars on her body (Dunn, 177–79).

By inducing the hero to drink woman's milk, Morrigana makes him realize his maternal and sexual connection to the female body, a connection that the myth of his own autonomy has allowed him to reject. Although Welty ultimately seeks the point at which the town of Morgana and the county of MacLain can converge, the act of writing means facing the history of separation, taking hold of the sword of Perseus. It is no coincidence that Eudora Welty first names Morgana "Battle Hill." Not only has the masculine literary tradition created a mythic, all-powerful, god/artist as the male subject, but to do so it has, as De Beauvoir shows us, assigned women to carefully defined roles of otherness. Many feminist literary critics—Millet, Russ, Showalter, Gilbert, Gubar, Heilbrun, and others—have pointed out that the masculine creations of the virgin, the mother, and the whore are reductive projections of fear of the female body as a symbol of mortality—the beauty and the terror. The virgin is simply a nonthreatening, nonphysical ornament for the male hero—the object of his love—while the evil Eve or whore is ready to seduce and kill him. She is the enemy of the hero because she reminds him of his own sexuality, his connection to fertility, and thus his own mortality. The earth mother, matrix/matter, gives birth to the hero and nurtures him but must ultimately be conquered by him as he seeks to escape maternal bonds.

These stereotypes are fragments, stolen and frozen moments of old myths; they are the decapitated heads of ancient representations of womanhood. In matriarchal religions, the virgin, the mother, and the crone, the three aspects of the triple goddess, represented the three phases of a women's life: the premenstrual daughter, the menstruating mother, and the menopausal grandmother. They came to represent the life cycle not only of women but of the whole community. While the author/hero could not kill off the three, he could destroy the cycle of nature by separating the female head from the female body and the female from the other aspects of herself. He could create freeze frames. He could represent female not as change but as stagnation. Ironically he could never really attain artistic self-awareness within this structure because he had defined self in such narrow and ultimately suicidal terms. If self means autonomous self, alone in the world with no mate and no offspring, the hero, like the decapitated Medusa, must die. The hero self, separated from regeneration, from woman and rebirth, from an acceptance and love of his own gender and phallus as a source of human regeneration, is a hollow self, a self turned to stone. Cutting off the Medusa's head, separating the female head from the female body and the female from her life, is a suicidal act for the male warrior. As much as he would like to believe in birth without maternity, it will not work. The literary tradition that develops out of the heroic Perseus myth is murderous and suicidal. When Perseus cuts off the Medusa's head, the sight of this disembodied head turns men to stone.

By setting her collection in the shadow of the Celtic triple goddess Morrigana, who wields power through her ability to take on various forms, including lover, mother, witch, and magician (Kristeva's multiple subjects); who actively heals her body by forcing the hero to recognize and even honor the female goddess; who asserts the fertile and sexual connection between male and female; who never allows the hero to split her mind from her body, Welty transforms the hero myth. She discovers her artistic power in the inter/extratextuality, in the faces of the women in her own community, and the buried female deities that these faces evoke. By freeing these women to speak their minds, Welty's voice and vision can survive the shadows and ghosts of heroic exploitation.

If as feminist, humanist, and Marxist critics of culture, we truly believe that literature can invoke change, that the word has power, that we are not biologically, materially, or culturally determined, and that even a myth as tenacious as the hero myth can be rewoven, then we will see in Welty's experiment the greatest revolutionary act. We will see her willingness to take what has been named, killed, murdered, and tortured under the naming and watch as she allows it to release, to engage in conversation and storytelling, to name itself, to exist in time far out and endless. What Welty achieves in this process is an extraordinary incorporation of old forms in the resurrection of the living material from which these forms grew, revitalizing oppressive cultural myths by including the drive to suicide, the despair of the wasteland, the deconstructed abyss, without identifying with or privileging any of these, empowering only the inclusion and the confluence.

Welty creates a plot that moves from duality and aggression to intersection, convergence, and dialogue at the crossroads; from sun and moon to dusk, daybreak, shadow, storm, haze, eclipse, half moon; from the conventional combination of the hero King MacLain and the princess Snowdie, to the unconventional combinations of Virgie and Miss Eckhart, Cassie and Loch, Loch and Easter, Nina and Easter, Virgie and Katie Rainey, Eugene and the Spaniard, Virgie and Ran, and a thousand other alliances. The following chapters will trace the development of intersubjectivity and intertextuality throughout the collection. By focusing on who is speaking and how they expand the realm of what can be spoken as well as on the myths and literary texts to which they respond, I am exploring the ways in which emerging narratives interrupt, expand, and invert established narratives.

Chapter 2 traces the emerging and intersecting narratives of Snowdie, Katie, King MacLain, and Old Plez as they step across the symbolic boundaries that divide the representation of masculinity and femininity, black and white, old and young to cross-pollinate each other's discourses in "Shower of Gold." Chapter 3, devoted to an explication of "June Recital," centers on the ways in which the matriarchal voice of Miss Eckhart and the mother-daughter relationship of Virgie and Miss Eckhart, Cassie and Mrs. Morrisson, Cassie and Miss Eckhart, and Miss Eckhart and her own mother destabilizes and threatens the established patriarchal and patrilineal dissemination of culture. Chapter 4 explores how the competing narratives of Mattie Will, King Mac-Lain, and Junior Holifield in "Sir Rabbit" dismantle the rape narrative, and how the symbolic universe of "Moon Lake," as expressed through the consciousness of Nina, Easter, and Loch, posits clitoral imagery to diffuse the dominant phallic imagery. In Chapter 5 the multivocal nature of "The Whole World Knows" inverts the myth of male infidelity and female subservience. Chapter 6 is a thorough intertextual exploration of "Music from Spain" in which the interweaving narratives of Eugene, the Spaniard, and Emma directly respond to James Joyce's *Ulysses*. Chapter 7 focuses on Virgie's character in "The Wanderers" as she becomes textualized as a charged field of dramatic fiction. All of the following chapters suggest that each of Welty's stories engages the textual universe of at least one, and often more than one, established canonical text. "Shower of Gold" departs from the Greek myth of Zeus and Danaë; "June Recital" alludes to Yeat's "The Song of Wandering Aengus" and Beethoven's "Für Elise"; "Sir Rabbit" plays with African-American and southern folktales; "Moon Lake" directly evokes Sir James Frazer's *The Golden Bough*; "The Whole World Knows" responds to William Faulkner, particularly the Quentin section of *The Sound and the Fury*; "Music from Spain" transforms James Joyce's *Ulysses*; and "The Wanderers" evokes many Greek and Celtic myths as well as local folklore. In each story Welty allows for an interpollination of text and subtext, a dialogue at the crossroads. As we listen closely to these voices, we can hear a progression in the presentation of the feminine. The female character develops from the weak albino Snowdie to the powerful but thwarted witch Miss Eckhart, to the fully determined woman Virgie, from the jealous Hera to the independent Easter, from the victimized Medusa to the sexually free Venus. *The Golden Apples* invents itself in the writing, each character supporting and making possible the existence of the other—what Cixous calls "beginning one another anew only from the living boundaries of the other" ("The Laugh of the Medusa," 883).

2

Crossing the Distance

Intersecting Narratives of Rape and Fertility in "Shower of Gold"

When asked why she chose the name Morgana for her fictional town, Welty responded that she "always loved the conception of Fata Morgana—the illusory shape, the mirage that comes over the sea" (Prenshaw, *Conversations*, 88). *The Golden Apples* collects in the net of its miragelike textual web the dream representations of the heroic myths of Western culture. In "Shower of Gold" Katie remarks that "once they dressed Snowdie all in white, you know she was whiter than your dreams" (*CSEW*, 265). The dreamlike Snowdie MacLain is the emerging female subject in this story. While King MacLain is also invisible or dreamlike, his invisibility is based not on his emerging identity but on the omnipotence of the myths from which he is constructed. Unlike Snowdie, King provides Katie with a fixed plot and built-in drama. He is not a story waiting to be told but a twice-told story that already has a language, metaphor, intrigue, and accepted meaning. King follows the heroic script to the letter; he sweeps down to marry the helpless princess, he wanders off in search of adventure, he leaves his hat on the banks of the Big Black River and never lets anyone know whether he is alive or dead. He can play with death because he exists as a disembodied masculine representation unchecked by the power of embodied feminine representations. Snowdie cannot find him, and neither Katie nor any of the other women can see him. The town spends nine days looking for his body: "They found everybody else that ever honestly drowned along the Big Black in this neighborhood" (*CSEW*, 266).

As Katie begins to tell her story, she must struggle to keep King's absence from looming as large as Snowdie's presence. The line, "that could have started something, too," can be interpreted literally to mean that King's actions could have inspired more men to desert women. However, the more suggestive interpretation, especially given that this line appears in the first paragraph of the collection, is that, although King's walking out and leaving his hat on the banks of the Big Black could have been the beginning of Katie's (Welty's) story, Katie instead chooses to begin with Snowdie: "That was Miss Snowdie MacLain" (*CSEW*, 263). This narrative at the crossroads is not about the hero's mock suicide, not about his attempt to control life and death, not even about his treatment of his wife. At the same time, neither is it about Snowdie's independence. Instead it is about the tension between the two possible narratives. In direct contrast to the heroic narrative, the text of Snowdie and Katie is dynamic and unpredictable. Even in the first line, Snowdie moves out of the narrator's vision: "That was Miss Snowdie MacLain."

In order to breathe life into the static romance plot, Katie Rainey resuscitates Snowdie MacLain, transforming the frail, pale ingenue of masculine fiction into a thriving and complex character: "You seen she wasn't ugly—and the little blinky lines to her eyelids comes from trying to see. She's an albino but nobody would ever try to call her ugly around here—with that tender, tender skin like a baby" (*CSEW*, 263). In describing Snowdie, Katie uses the negation "she wasn't ugly" instead of the positive "she was beautiful" and "albino" instead of the traditional "fair as the driven snow." Her whiteness is at once presence and potential. As the recovering princess, Snowdie is weak and babylike, trying to remember her own powers of vision and perception, trying to define herself. In this first description we find Katie protecting Snowdie both from the male eye, "but nobody would ever try to call her ugly," and from the intrusion of that eye: "And I guess people more or less expected her to teach school: not marry. She couldn't see all that well, was the only thing in the way, but Mr. Comus Stark here and the supervisors overlooked that, knowing the family and Snowdie's real good way with Sunday School children" (*CSEW*, 265).

Because Snowdie's visionary or imaginative powers are not well developed, she cannot fight the male supervisors, whose "super"-"visors" protect their eyes from damage. They can still overlook, or look over, her, but from the beginning Snowdie thwarts social expectations, even the careerist expectations of the woman of her day. Snowdie does not teach school and she does get married: "Then before the school year even got a good start, she got took up by King MacLain all of a sudden" (*CSEW*, 265). While we could read Snowdie's marriage as the defeat of an independent female character, a more complex interpretation recognizes Snowdie as something other than a victim. If she taught Sunday school for the male supervisors, Snowdie would become the stereotypical old-maid school teacher, isolated in a subservient asexual role within a male-defined religious system. By marrying King MacLain, Snowdie steps onto the battleground. To a woman, male sexuality can mean love, regeneration, or desire—the connection with the fertility consort lover—or it can mean domination and fear—the invasion of the rapist. These two images are never completely separate, so that any attempt to connect then becomes highly charged.

If, in "Shower of Gold," Welty tried to protect her female characters from the male hero, she would only reproduce the autonomy and independence that his myth perpetuates. In reviving her decapitated, raped, and silenced female characters, Welty writes them into a dance with the masculinist text. In order to engage this writing, she must see the male concurrently as rapist, wife beater, oppressor, warrior, hero, king, lost brother, lover, consort, fertility god, and the female as rape victim, wife, mother, sister, lover, goddess, queen, warrior. As Welty strives for this crucial engagement with the text of the male hero, she is constantly aware of the danger inherent in his dual identity; at each point confluence with the masculinist text could mean silence, death, rape, or disappearance for her women characters. Without protection against the assault of the vaunting hero, her female characters, new to the light of day, would be "off at the flicker of an eye" (Woolf, *A Room of One's Own*, 88). The writing in *The Golden Apples* fluctuates between connection and protection, a movement that we can see enacted in Welty's change of titles from "Battle Hill" in the original typescript to "Shower of Gold" in later versions. Battle Hill expresses an irreconcilable conflict between opposing forces, whereas "Shower of Gold," with its reference to the myth of Zeus and Danaë, includes allusions both to masculinist aggression and male fertility.

Welty can write this dance only by creating a character strong enough to embody all of these conflicting meanings. Such presence demands the assertion of self in Katie Rainey's narrative "I." Katie's "I" seems to take back the power of the "I" from Virginia Woolf's Mr. A. in *A Room of One's Own*; Mr. A. can see and write only masculine thoughts, only the male's sexual passions. Woolf objects to the "letter I and the aridity, which, like the giant beech tree, it casts within its shade. Nothing will grow there" (*A Room of One's Own*, 104). Mr. A.'s constant need to assert his superiority, an assertion that takes the form of repeated rape makes Phoebe's (his female character's) emotions and feelings invisible. Without Katie's eye directed on her, Snowdie would remain invisible. Katie churns the snow-white milk into butter, filling Snowdie with substance and movement. Churning stirs things up, causes friction and develops new forms.

Not only does Katie, the dairymaid, create agitation by making the events of Snowdie's and King's life her business, but she mixes herself up with Snowdie. Shocked that King asks Snowdie to meet him in the woods, Katie tells her personal narrative as she tells Snowdie's narrative: "I had two children myself, enduring his being gone, and one to die. Yes, and that time he sent her word ahead: 'Meet me in the woods'" (*CSEW*, 264). "Enduring" could modify either Katie or her children, an ambiguity that makes sense when we begin to suspect (although we never really know) that King, as the omnipresent male stud, fathers many of the MacLain County children. By reminding us that Snowdie and King could have sat inside and talked, she ignores the conventions of drama and disturbs the romantic narrative, offering Snowdie simple, practical options. Katie lets the reader know quite clearly that Snowdie does not have to do exactly what King says. She could have asked, "What for?" (*CSEW*, 264). This is what Katie Rainey claims she would have done. By asking these questions and asserting her own "I" perspective, Katie expands the simple tale of the prince asking the young princess to meet him in the wood to a much more complex tale told from the perspective of the female artist. By allowing us to hear Katie's own emotions and desires, Welty takes us beyond a singular focus on King's sexual prowess.

In the first paragraph Katie expresses her suspicion and hatred of King for what he has done to Snowdie, and in the last line— "Best for him of course. We could see the writing on the wall" (*CSEW*, 264)—the women gossips in the town read his text. In Dan. 5:24 the writing on the wall warns the king of his impending ruin. By reading King's narrative in detail, Katie Rainey becomes the writing on the wall, the cause of the king's downfall. Having reduced King to a vulnerable flesh and blood human being, Katie can see him as sexually attractive rather than sexually dangerous. The second paragraph is romantic and reveals Katie's own desire for King. She could have streaked "like an arrow" to the tree; she could see King by the "light of the moon"; and she wonders how poor Snowdie could stand "crossing the distance" (*CSEW*, 264). In *A Room of One's Own*, Woolf watches Phoebe cross the beach to Alan, but we never hear what Phoebe might be thinking or feeling.

In the first three pages of the story, we learn that King is reputed to be an accomplished stud, but we also hear that "Snowdie was Miss Lollie Hudson's daughter, well known. Her father was Mr. Eugene Hudson, a storekeeper down at Crossroads past the Courthouse, but he was a lovely man. Snowdie was their only daughter, and they give her a nice education" (*CSEW*, 264–65). The word "but" in the second sentence indicates that there is something mysterious in the reference to Crossroads. Why would we think that Mr. Eugene Hudson was not a lovely man? Past the courthouse, which represents law and order, lies the crossroads, a point of intersection, connection, and change. The early goddess religions saw the crossroads as the fertile center of the community, a center symbolized by the goddess Hecate who represented the powers of birth, life, and death.[1] As patriarchal religions took over the symbols of the matriarchal religions, the crossroads became the meeting place of witches and evil spirits. Macbeth meets the three witches, the descendants of the triple goddess, at the crossroads. Katie Rainey is letting us know that a man who works at the crossroads is not necessarily an evil spirit or warlock. In fact, from the woman's perspective, he is the direct opposite of this; he is a lovely man who builds his only daughter a house of her own: "Hudson money built that house, and built it for *Snowdie* . . . they prayed over that" (*CSEW*, 263). At the same time Katie tells us that Hudson gave Snowdie a nice education. Southern polite society uses the word "nice" to refer to a girl who has not slept around or lost her virginity. Since Snowdie has received a nice (i.e., nonsexual education), she knows nothing of male aggression or fertility. The only way for her to break out of the confines of this education, then, is to marry King MacLain, to fall to the shower of gold, to become the albino Danaë.

In the myth of Danaë, Acrisius, her father, goes to the oracle to ask who will succeed him as king. The oracle tells him that he will never give birth to sons, that he will have only the one daughter Danaë and that eventually his grandson will murder him. In the hope of altering this outcome, Acrisius locks Danaë in a "dungeon with brazen doors" and throws away the key (Graves, *The Greek Myths I and II*, 73, 237–45). Despite these attempts to escape his fate, Zeus appears to Danaë in a shower of gold and impregnates her; she gives birth to Perseus. Hoping to destroy the grandson who would eventually kill him, Acrisius puts Danaë and Perseus into a wooden casket and throws them into the sea. A fisherman finds the casket, saves Danaë and Perseus, and takes them to King Polydectes who rears Perseus as his son. When Perseus is grown, Polydectes tries to marry Danaë against her will. Perseus fights to save his mother, offering Poly- dectes a gift of the Gorgon monster's head if he will marry Hippodamia instead (*New Larousse Encyclopedia of Mythology*, 105).

Because Snowdie's father works at the crossroads, because he is a lovely man, because he does not want his daughter to be hurt, he shuts her off, not only from the world of male aggres- sion but inadvertently, mirroring Acrisius, from the world of male fertility. As a character born at the crossroads, she falls as easily and as suddenly as Danaë to the shower of gold. MacLain courts her and she marries him: "I think it was when jack-o'- lanterns was pasted on her window I used to see his buggy roll up right to the schoolhouse steps and wait on her" (*CSEW*, 265). In her portrayal of Snowdie, Katie weaves together textual frag- ments of Cinderella, who is picked up by the king's carriage that later turns into a pumpkin, and of the deposed witch of the crossroads, who would paste jack-o'-lanterns—a symbol of pa- gan religion—in the windows of the Christian Sunday school. By having Snowdie marry King MacLain, Welty not only re- writes the Danaë script but defies the Christian and southern dictates of appropriate behavior for the good white lady.

This circumscribed independence is not enough, however, to rescue Snowdie from limiting representations of the feminine. As King's obedient housewife, confined to the home having babies, and putting "her eyes straight out . . . making curtains for every room and all like that" (*CSEW*, 265), Snowdie would be a very short-lived subject. While an object of the traditional hero myth does not need to see, Snowdie, as the eyes through which Katie/Welty can enter the world of artistic creation, must herself have vision. Because Katie Rainey, representing rain, can churn and talk, she can awaken the lost subject of women's writing—the frozen formless snow, Snowdie MacLain—and bring her back to life as spring rain brings winter back to life, as Demeter brought Persephone back to life. However, Snowdie is also Katie's author. The spring rain follows the winter snow; Katie can only regenerate herself through Snowdie. As Katie gives birth to Snowdie, she gives birth to herself as a storyteller.

Yet Snowdie is more than the potentially fertile snow melting into rain; she is also the abstract color white, the color that is itself at once the absence of color and all color, unknown and therefore both most mysterious and most easily lost. She is concurrently the negation of all representation and the possibility of all representation, a tabula rasa on which any script can be written,[2] the body freed to come to life as writing. The references to skin and little lines suggest Snowdie as the actual paper and the lines of the writing. However, in her manifestation as the newborn child, as the slate or skin for the writing, Snowdie is always at risk of receiving inscription rather than becoming inscription, and Katie, in the anxious state of the new mother, is at risk of inscribing or of allowing the hero to inscribe. Welty keeps Snowdie from this objectified position by creating a multireferential characterization.

Snowdie represents not only Danaë, the victim of Zeus, but Leda, who is raped by Zeus in the form of a white swan and gives birth to twins; Hera, the goddess who gives birth to twins on the new year; the pale moon goddess Eurynome;[3] Epona the powerful white-horse goddess of Celtic mythology;[4] and the white first aspect of the triple goddess. As Danaë or Leda, Snowdie might be read either as a victorious mother or as a rape victim. However, the other fragments of her characterization expand her potential beyond these limited figures. As the goddess Hera, Snowdie is not a patient Griselda but an angry wife who fights for her rights against Zeus.[5] As the moon, she controls the change of seasons and the movement of the tides. As the first aspect of the triple goddess, she is the symbol of the Great Mother, the oldest and most powerful of all gods and goddesses. Snowdie's symbolic and mythological connections do not end with the snow and the moon, with goddesses, dreams, or even the tabula rasa. When Katie comments on King's decision to marry Snowdie, she says: "And like, 'Look, everybody, this is what I think of Morgana and MacLain Courthouse and all the way between'—further, for all I know—'marrying a girl with pink eyes.' 'I swan!' we all say. Just like he wants us to, scoundrel" (*CSEW*, 263–64). Though Katie expresses her anger at these women's exact conformity to King's script, on a symbolic level she actually extends this script, letting us know that what King thinks the women are saying may not be what they are actually saying. Although "I swan" means "I swear" or "I'll be damned" in American southern dialect, in Celtic mythology this phrase refers directly to the swan associated with prophecy and divination and thus means, "I know what will happen" (DeKay, 180–81). In addition, the swan returns us to the myth of the rape of Leda by Zeus. The sexual/textual act of holding the word "swan" in their mouths makes the women participate in the sexual act, just as King wants them to, but in this role they are not passive victims; they can streak to the tree of their own free will. In putting the swan in their mouths Welty reverses the rape of Leda. In both Greek and Celtic religions, the swan is a traditional symbol of artistic creation, divination, and regeneration, able to soar from the earth to the sky and back to the earth. The women become artists as they reverse this myth.[6]

By questioning why Snowdie did not "rage and storm a little—to me, anyway, just Mrs. Rainey" (*CSEW*, 266), Katie names the potential anger in what looks like a calm scene and in so doing she begins to answer her own question. The problem is that Snowdie is still trying to see; she had never "got a real good look at life, maybe. Maybe from the beginning. Maybe she just

doesn't know the *extent*. Not the kind of look I got, and away
back when I was twelve year old or so. Like something was put to
my eye" (*CSEW*, 266). Snowdie had a nice education and a lovely
father, and she has never seen the extent to which men abuse
women. Whether Katie gained sexual awareness at twelve or was
raped, she had "something put to her eye." Many ancient religions marked the eye as the center of women's power over man,
connecting the eye with the vulva, represented in Greek, Indian,
Egyptian, and Balkan religious imagery as a yonic symbol with
an eye in the center of a triangle (Walker, *The Woman's Encyclopedia*, 148–49). If we interpret the Medusa myth in sexual terms, a
man could be turned to stone—that is forced to have an erection
and to give up control of himself—if he looked in the eye, or the
vulva, of the Medusa. Given the long record in myth and literature of the male's association of women's reproductive organs
with death and destruction, it makes sense that the evil eye in
mythology is a symbol of the vulva.[7] Ironically, the trouble with
Katie's analysis is that she does not give us a good look at life. She
does not give us the kind of look that takes one all the way back to
the beginning.

She can only ask the question: Why did Snowdie not rage and
storm a little? The potential to storm exists in both characters—
snow and rain. Katie wants Snowdie to show anger, but Snowdie
is not going to make it so easy for Katie, for Welty, or for the
feminist critic. She is not going to rage and she is not going to
storm. Her self-revelations will be much more subtle because
they are connected not to any present outrage but to the crossroads, the scene of the loss of, and potential rebirth of, women's
power. Katie fights the hero as the enemy of women; Snowdie
loves him as fertility consort. Katie lives in the social and economic world of the present; Snowdie lives in the mythological
world of the past, present, and future, the continuously present
textured/textual space of the writing itself.

Snowdie's identity as the writing itself becomes apparent in
her unwillingness to be what other people want her to be. She

does not wait for King. She does not feel oppressed by her pregnancy. She does not show anger. In almost Bartlebyesque fashion she gives nobody the satisfaction of naming her. She simply does not play a role. In these subtle rebellions, Snowdie moves from subject as topic to subject as artist. Because Katie is really watching, really trying to see, she allows this transformation to take place. Katie does not insist on knowing everything. She talks about scenes in which Snowdie's behavior does not make sense to her as readily as she talks about scenes that she thinks she can explain, and whether she explains or not, she gives us a description: "At her house it was like Sunday even in the mornings, every day, in that cleaned-up way. She was taking a joy in her fresh untracked rooms and that dark, quiet, real quiet hall that runs through her house. And I love Snowdie. I love her" (*CSEW*, 266–67). It is this description of Snowdie's room of her own that enables Katie to see Snowdie as a human being separate from King. She can then say, "I love Snowdie," because for a moment at least she knows that she cannot own Snowdie or be Snowdie. Out of the tabula rasa of the quiet room, Snowdie begins to press the limits of Katie's telling. Snowdie takes on the power to inscribe. When the twins are born, Snowdie does not name them after their father: "It was the only sign she ever give Morgana that maybe she didn't think the name King MacLain had stayed beautiful. But not much of a sign" (*CSEW*, 267). Katie goes on to say that many women never name their children after their husbands; yet the important point is that Katie, the narrator, is receiving signs from Snowdie, her subject. The subject is becoming the writing. Snowdie actively "clapped" the names on the boys (*CSEW*, 267).

The most revealing description of the relationship between Snowdie and Katie occurs after King has made his brief reappearance: "After he'd gone by, Snowdie just stood there in the cool without a coat, with her face turned towards the country and her fingers pulling at little threads on her skirt and turning them loose in the wind, making little kind deeds of it, till I went and got her. She didn't cry" (*CSEW*, 273). Snowdie stands in the cool and becomes the textile of the story, both the goddess pulling the thread of life and the male fertility consort who scatters his seed to the wind. She has power and self-definition as part of a much larger textual universe than the immediate narrative of herself and King. She does not need to cry. Yet in not crying she forfeits the ancient feminine power of the goddess, who weeps in the spring to bring her daughter, and later the fertility consort, back to life.

Katie, still worried about the fragility of her subject, afraid that she will die of the cold, brings her inside, but Snowdie knows that she no longer needs Katie as a narrator: "And so that's why Snowdie comes to get her butter now, and won't let me bring it to her any longer. I think she kind of holds it against me, because I was there that day when he come; and she don't like my baby any more" (*CSEW*, 274). We could interpret this passage to mean that Snowdie is awakening to the extent of what King has done to her, that she finally realizes that King has fathered many other children besides her own, and that Virgie, Katie's baby, is probably King's child. The passage hints at this scenario—and the rest of the collection proves its validity—but these facts do not adequately explain Snowdie's transformation. Katie's analysis of why Snowdie comes after her butter tells us more about Katie's own guilt, authorial control, and desire to be part of the drama than about Snowdie's motives.

In the line preceding these, Katie wishes King would have "hit a stone and fell down running, before he got far from here" (*CSEW*, 274). The statement "And so that's why Snowdie comes to get her butter now" can thus be read as a direct reaction to Katie's wish for King's downfall. Snowdie does not want King to fall. She does not want him to be any less than he is because, through King's mysterious disappearance, she has gained entrance into the mythical sphere of the goddess, and of artistic resurrection. The goddess expects her consort to leave, even to die in the winter so that he can be reborn and revitalize the community in the spring. Snowdie conceives her two sons in the spring. She goes across to get her own butter precisely because she does not accept Katie's interpretation of her life.

Katie, in her position as both reader and author, questions how one can read a text that moves beyond authorial control: "You can talk about a baby swallowing a button off a shirt and having to be up-ended and her behind pounded, and it sounds reasonable if you can just see the baby—there she runs—but get to talking about something that's only a kind of *near* thing—and hold your horses" (*CSEW*, 269). Katie tells us that you can talk about the baby swallowing the button if you can see her, and "there she runs." In her eyes, even this supposedly solid reality is constantly fluctuating and changing; the meaning of the writing is in the movement between the physical things, buttons and babies, and the abstractions of these things. Seeing the baby, even if it runs away, allows Katie to believe in this world and to name it, while she cannot see, thus cannot name or transform, those "kind of near things," the antics of King MacLain, his appearances and disappearances, and Snowdie's relation to them. They are the concealments and suppressions developed in the realm of masculine fantasy and fiction: "My baby girl, Virgie, swallowed a button that same day—later on—and that *happened*, it seems like still, but not this [King's appearance and disappearance]" (*CSEW*, 269).

In order to regain the physical connection that would enable her to bring King into the textured writing, Katie must allow her vision to extend to those far reaches of the male mythical wilderness where King travels. However, the reality is that geographically and economically Katie is confined to her home and to the things around her home; she must depend on men to tell her of King's wanderings. Even when she explains King's appearance on Halloween night, an event that happened right under her nose, she comments: "And if it wasn't for something that come from outside us all to tell about it, I wouldn't have the faith I have that it came about" (*CSEW*, 269). When King appears on the steps of Snowdie's house, Snowdie cannot see and Katie does not look, but the two eagle-eyed boys—the eyes of Jove's sacred bird—who look through their masks are able to observe King. Katie recalls that the twins made "a tremendous uproar with their skates . . . I remember what a hard time Snowdie and me had hearing what each other had to say all afternoon" (*CSEW*, 271). While the masculine energy of the twins makes it hard for Snowdie and Katie to hear each other, the women continue talking and sewing clothes, an activity of the triple goddess in her role as Clotho, the spinner of the thread of life, and the first aspect of the triple goddess (Frazer, 341–76). Sewing these clothes, the two women stitch the boys, who cannot and should not be stopped, into the moving and transforming texture of the writing. By weaving the boys' actions and words into her narrative, Katie actively negates the twins' attempt to silence her: "Sometimes we could grab a little boy and baste something up on him whether or no, but we didn't really pay them much mind, we was talking about the prices of things for winter, and the funeral of an old maid" (*CSEW*, 269). Katie's and Snowdie's talk about winter and the death of an old maid is no accident. King returns on Halloween, the day in Celtic mythology on which autumn turns to winter, when the souls of the dead return to warm themselves by the fire, and when witches "speed on errands of mischief" (Graves, *The Greek Myths I*, 48–49).

In some versions of the triple goddess myth, the third aspect of the triple goddess, the old Maid, cuts the thread of life of the male consort and the first aspect brings him back to life in the spring.[8] However, in earlier versions of the myth, the crone herself dies and is resurrected in the form of the first aspect, in this case the baby Virgie. By not watching what the twins are doing, by basting something up on them "whether or no," by not heeding the masculine aberration, Katie and Snowdie reduce the power of the heroic narrative. As they continue to pay attention to their own work, the sewing, gossiping, and stitching, they discuss the death of the old maid and weave her back into the narrative—resurrecting her with their words.

The young king or fertility consort is sacrificed to the old crone in the fall so that his seed may be scattered to the wind and so that it will return to revitalize the earth in the spring (Frazer, 341–76). Katie remarks, "In the meantime children of his growing up in the County Orphans', so say several, and children known and unknown, scattered-like" (*CSEW*, 264). If we see the story in the shadow of the myth of the fertility consort, then King MacLain, returning home when "little gusts of wind had started blowing" (*CSEW*, 264), is in danger from the movement the wind represents, the mythological powers in his house, Snowdie and Katie as manifestations of the life forces in nature and of the triple goddess, and from his own two sons as the male versions of the new year. It is fall, the time in ancient religion when the king should die.

The twins, Eugene Hudson and Lucius Randall, dressed in Halloween costumes as a "Chinaman" and a "lady with an almost scary-sweet smile on her lips" (*CSEW*, 269), race around King on roller skates. The wheels of the skates and the circle that they form around him suggest the wheel of fate and the natural cycle of birth, life, and death which this wheel represents; the boys frighten King away. As in the myth of Danaë, the father, the old consort, is afraid that his sons, the new young fertility gods, will kill him. In fact, it is always the birth of sons in Greek and Celtic mythology which warns the father of his mortality and thus of his impending doom (Graves, *The Greek Myths I*, 73, 237–45). King leaves home after his sons are born and runs away when he sees them on the porch dressed in masks. If we take a closer look at the twins' masks, their hidden power becomes clear, and we realize that King had reason to be afraid. The layering of face on face indicates the congruent palimpsest of representations evoked by the movement of emerging imitations. Wearing the Chinese mask, Eugene becomes the rising sun of the East, signifying the death of the old sun, his father, whose soul, like the setting sun, moves west in its decline.[9] We know that King is the setting sun, because Katie suggests that King might have looked in the dining room window had they not "shut the West out of Snowdie's eyes of course" (*CSEW*, 270). Katie shuts the sun out of Snowdie's eyes, the sun that would burn her fair skin and damage her vision, but this is also the impregnating sun of the myth of Danaë, the same sun that must give up its power to the moon every night. As the woman with the mask and the milking hat, Lucius must be "the more outrageous of the two" (*CSEW*, 271) to the hero, because he represents woman's power to give birth and thus to continue the natural cycle. The expression on this mask is scary and distorted because it is the reminder of the forgotten and buried female past that is haunting King, the mask of the Gorgon Medusa, and of the male's attempt to mimic and co-opt female power. Life has moved forward without King, who left, some thought, because he was afraid of having "a nestful of little albinos" (*CSEW*, 263). Snowdie has given birth, raised his children, and thus sealed his fate without King's being able to do a thing about it. This is the Danaë myth as told from the female perspective. Although Acrisius locks Danaë in a tower, Zeus still impregnates her. Although King leaves, Snowdie still gives birth and the twins still grow up.

Katie views Snowdie's pregnancy as central to her narration and marks the day the twins were born as the beginning of her involvement in Snowdie's life: "Then, twins. That was where I come in, I could help when things got to there. I took her a little churning of butter with her milk and we took up" (*CSEW*, 264). In giving birth to the twins, Snowdie gives birth to her narrator, Katie Rainey, because she becomes a subject for Katie's narration. The birth of twins is a story in itself, as Snowdie MacLain's act of delivering twins on New Year's Day links her to ancient sources of women's power and thus sustains her as a character outside of King's world. Snowdie recognizes her position and reacts to her pregnancy with a sense of empowerment.

As Snowdie emerges from behind King's shadow and from behind Katie's "I," she is not pure white but golden like butter, not a kitten, but a lion; she does not fit the epithet "poor Snowdie" with which Katie tries to inscribe her. Snowdie's power to give birth transforms her from the weak victim—putting her eyes out struggling against the light—to the lion, who represents the ascending spirit of the sacred year (Graves, *The Greek Myths I*, 73, 237–45). The lion, like the goddess of the May, appears in the spring. Snowdie is pregnant at Easter, the time at which, Christian doctrine teaches, Christ achieves victory over death and, like Dionysus, is reborn from his father, without the active participation of his mother or any other female. Snowdie's pregnancy makes her bold and bright because she is triumphant in the face of the male lie. In this battle the physical fact of her pregnancy wins out over the male myth. No man can escape the natural cycle of birth, life, and death; all men are mortal and of woman born. As Katie looks at Snowdie, she remembers that King is a traveling salesman and that he sells tea and spices. In this description we see King as the young fertility god or Christ figure, sprinkled with spices or incense before his death. King dies, goes west—"I see King in the West, out where it's gold and all that" (*CSEW*, 268)—and is reborn, resurrected on Easter in the conception of his sons, who were born "King all over again, if you want to know it" (*CSEW*, 267).

King's dramatic disappearance has very little effect. He is no more or less than Frazer's oak consort when he meets Snowdie under the oak tree and impregnates her. Katie, however, cannot rest easy in her storytelling; the fact that Snowdie gives birth does not significantly alter the plot. King is still gone, still mysterious, still exciting: "I wish I'd seen him! I don't guess *I'd* have stopped him. I can't tell you why, but I wish I'd seen him! But nobody did" (*CSEW*, 266). Katie wants to see King because only his physical presence will allow her to weave him into the text, to make him more than an abstraction. She promises her husband that she will "quit keeping count of King's comings and goings, and it wasn't long after that he did leave the hat. I don't know whether he meant it kind or cruel. Kind, I incline to believe. Or maybe she was winning. Why do I try to figure? Maybe because Fate Rainey ain't got a surprise in him, and proud of it. So Fate said, 'Well now, let's have the women to settle down and pay attention to homefolks a while.' That was all he could say about it" (*CSEW*, 265). Katie might have seen King's act as kind because the physical presence of the hat gives her something real to use as material for her narration. Only by speculating about King, by immersing herself in the excitement of King's comings and goings, can Katie pull herself out of the predictable world of Fate Rainey and his demand that she settle down to home folks.

Fate, the notion that all of life is predetermined, does not allow for mysteries, for storytelling, or for writing. Although the battle against fate is the central thesis in the heroic myth, the fate facing the hero and the fate facing Katie Rainey are completely different. While the hero battles against his own mortality, Katie battles her husband Fate as he symbolizes the social restrictions in her life. Katie's speculation that maybe Snowdie was winning indicates that Katie has not only defined the struggle as a battle but, more importantly, has changed the terms of this battle by telling Snowdie's side of the story, by offering a different perspective, and by suggesting that the man is not always going to win. From the first pages of her story, Katie reminds us of Snowdie's hidden power: "And Snowdie as sweet and gentle as you find them. Of course gentle people aren't the ones you lead best, he had that to find out, so know-all. No, sir, she'll beat him yet, balking" (*CSEW*, 264). Taking herself out of the realm of the obedient wife, and not allowing women folks to settle down to a world without surprises in a life resigned to fate (Fate), Katie becomes, rather than suggests, an alternative to Snowdie's quiet rebellion.

The difference between Katie and Snowdie is that Snowdie will settle into her maternal role while Katie wants to rage and storm. Snowdie will "glow" (*CSEW*, 266) rather than speak. "Except none of us felt very *close* to her all the while. I'll tell you what it was, what made her different. It was the not waiting any more, except where the babies waited, and that's not but one story. We were mad at her and protecting her all at once" (*CSEW*, 267).

Katie, Lizzie Stark, and all the other women want Snowdie, their subject, to be someone else, to rage and storm, to allow for more than one story, but their female subject does not express their rage, anger, or sexual excitement. She does not give birth to a little girl, as Lizzie Stark would have hoped. She gives birth to male twins. The women hate Snowdie's complacency and yet they protect it, for she is, except for one measly hat, the only story they have. This is the source of Katie's frustration and the other women's anger. Welty does not hide this anger: "When I asked the way he looked, I couldn't get a thing out of my husband, except he lifted his feet across the kitchen floor like a horse and man in one, and I went after him with my broom" (*CSEW*, 268). Katie uses the broom, the symbol of women's economic and social enslavement as housewife and her freedom as witch, to drive away her husband who has turned from a man to a centaur, half man, half beast. At the same time, Katie is beginning to realize the power of the imagination and of art. As if in response to the realization that she could spend all of her time and creative energy worrying about King, she tries to place the responsibility for King's disappearance back upon the male governor: "Men! I said if I'd been Governor Vardaman and spied King MacLain from Morgana marching in my parade as big as I was and no call for it, I'd have had the whole thing brought to a halt and called him to accounts" (*CSEW*, 268). This is exactly the struggle that Katie goes through to tell Snowdie's story. King marches in Katie's and Snowdie's parade "and no call for it," and she brings the whole thing, her parade, her story, to a halt for a moment to take Fate and Governor Vardaman, if not King himself, to accounts.

Interestingly enough, the one person who does see and describe King is a black man, Old Plez. Old Plez sees King when there is no one else on the road to see him, when he is at his most vulnerable and thus most conspicuous. The black man is as much of an outsider in the heroic narrative as the white woman. Being on the outside, the black man can see King as a human being, not as a hero, and can record the event that would otherwise go unnoticed. The women believe and trust Old Plez because he does not threaten or silence them. He is the something from the outside that enables Katie to tell the story. She not only defends Old Plez's credibility but also spares him the criticism that she levels at her husband and all other men—that they do not look closely enough.

At this point, Katie cannot move beyond conjecture, anger, and self-conscious speculation. She remains too trapped within her day-to-day existence to be able to see the full extent of women's oppression, long before she was twelve years old, but she has salvaged the fragments: "Outdoors the leaves was rustling, different from when I'd went in. It was coming on a rain. The day had a two-way look, like a day will at change of the year—clouds dark and the gold air still in the road, and the trees lighter than the sky was. And the oak leaves scuttling and scattering, blowing against old Plez and brushing on him, the old man" (*CSEW*, 273).

The oak leaves are blowing against the old man. The seeds are dropping from the branches and scattering to the wind, to die and to be given a new life in the spring. The change warns us of the death of the old king, symbolized by the oak, the death of the old way, and the beginning of something different. Snowdie does not have a baby girl, but Katie does. As in Jewett's *The Country of the Pointed Firs* (1–10), the men in Katie's life are dying out. Her son is dead and her husband sickly. The rain will come, the tears will come, and with them an emerging woman's text. This is the background from which Cassie, Loch, and Virgie will be able to see and hear the lost face and voice of the woman artist.

Because a Fire Was in Her Head

Reading and Writing For/e Mothers in "June Recital"

The masculine presence symbolized by the omnipotent King MacLain in "Shower of Gold" appears in "June Recital" as Loch Morrison, the sick little boy, who is dependent on his sister, housekeeper, and mother—a mother who would keep "him in bed and make him take Cocoa-Quinine all summer, if she had her way" (*CSEW*, 275). Loch's mother waits for the young hero to give up and swallow, knowing that he will eventually have to breathe, take his medicine, and live, whether he likes it or not.[1] When Loch calls for Louella to get him ice cream, she bangs her pans at him. In "June Recital" the conflict between Morrigana and Cuchulain has shifted from the public domain to the private. No longer does King MacLain, the quintessential hero, define the time and place of the narration, commanding Snowdie to meet him in the woods at night. The two houses, the Morrisons' and the MacLains', are side by side.

As Anne Ross reveals in *Pagan Celtic Britain*, in the *Tain Bo Cualnge*, which contains the story of Cuchulain and Morrigana, the Loch Mor is one of the enemies of Cuchulain, a lesser hero himself (220–21). The name Loch Morri-son, while alluding to the Loch Mor, also has associations with the goddess Morrigana and reminds us that Loch is the "son" of the goddess. In her portrayal of Loch, Welty exposes the physical condition of the masculine hero who has become disconnected from earth, women, and his own body. Stripped of his mythological trappings, he is vulnerable to the bite of a tiny mosquito. Mrs. Morrison is the queen who locks her son up in a tower like a male Danaë or Rapunzel to keep him from taking over the story. At the same time, against her husband's will, she allows Cassie to sneak out on hayrides, to grow up, to become sexual.

Although his mother has protected Loch's body, his mind and eyes are free to roam. He spends the summer looking out of his window through his father's telescope, which was "hitherto brought out in the family group for eclipses of the moon; and the day the airplane flew over with a lady in it, and they all waited for it all day, wry and aching up at the sky, the telescope had been gripped in his father's hand like a big stick, some kind of protective weapon for what was to come" (*CSEW*, 277). In a lunar eclipse the earth moves between the sun and the moon. Symbolically the earth crosses the boundary between the masculine sun and the feminine moon, while the woman pilot crosses between earthbound reality and the spirituality of the sky. This double crossing is threatening to masculine dominance because it challenges a linguistic system based on separation and differentiation. Unlike Daedalus, who flies so close to the sun that his wings melt, the woman pilot survives and returns to earth.

Even though there is no real danger in the eclipse or the woman in the airplane, the father projects onto these events his fear of losing power. The telescope supports this fear by making objects appear larger than life. Mr. Morrison puts the telescope between himself and the lady in the airplane "like a big stick, some kind of protective weapon," just as the hero must put the sword between himself and the female dragon. The word *telescope* means an instrument for viewing things at a far distance, but it also means "to force together, one into another, or to force into something else in the manner of a jointed telescope" (*American College Dictio-*

nary, 1963). The telescope indicates an attempt to force things together that do not want to go together, whereas the sword symbolizes only an attempt to kill. There is some progress towards understanding in the move from the phallic sword to the phallic telescope.

With the aid of the telescope, Loch defines the house next door as vacant. He is not personally involved and reports the scene as a journalist (his father is a newspaper editor). He sees everything in the minutest detail but leaves out any personal comment, feeling, or experience. He telescopes awareness by seeing the world as "if he possessed it—from its front porch to its shed-like back and its black-shadowed summerhouse. . . . The hay riders his sister went with at night (went with against their father's will, slipped out by their mother's connivance) would ride off singing, 'Oh, It Ain't Gonna Rain No More.' Even under his shut eyelids, that light and shade stayed divided from each other, but reversed" (*CSEW*, 276). As Loch's eye catches the separation between masculine and feminine, light and shadow, father and mother, Loch and his sister, youth and age, innocence and sexuality, we see both the stagnation of his vision (the children singing "Oh, It Ain't Gonna Rain No More") and the possibility of all opposites coming together in confluence or regeneration. The feminine shade is like a boat moving, and the masculine sun is shooting. As Loch shuts his eyes, the light and the shade reverse.

The first time Loch looks next door, he thinks, "The house's side was like a person's, if a person or giant would lie sleeping there, always sleeping" (*CSEW*, 275). As he watches the house, the giant wakes up, and gradually a scene with real people replaces the fairy tale landscape of his creation. Though Loch would like to think of himself as "wild as a cowboy" (*CSEW*, 276), the quintessential American hero, the spring rain from the gutter washes away the stagnant image of cowboy or giant: "It was the leaky gutter over there that woke Loch up, back in the spring when it rained. Splashy as a waterfall in a forest, it shook him with that agony of being *made* to wake up from a sound sleep to be taken away somewhere, made to go. It made his heart beat fast" (*CSEW*, 277). This waterfall, as the mother goddess who lets her tears fall in the spring to bring the young fertility god back to life, would make Loch's "heart beat fast," shaking him "with that agony of being *made* to wake up from a sound sleep" (*CSEW*, 277).[2] As the young hero, he is waking to the presence of the silenced old woman, Miss Eckhart, which comes to him not in words but in her music and actions. Hearing Mr. Fate Rainey singing "Buttermilk? / Buttermilk. / Fresh dewberries and—/ Buttermilk" (*CSEW*, 278), Loch imagines an echo behind his song: "Was it an echo—was an echo that? Or was it, for the last time, the call of somebody seeking about in a deep cave, 'Here— here! Oh, here am I'" (*CSEW*, 278).

In this response to Fate Rainey's song, Loch alludes to the myth of Echo and Narcissus. Hera, after finding out that Echo has been distracting her while Zeus makes love to other women, punishes the young nymph by depriving her of her power of speech and decrees that Echo will only be able to repeat the last syllable of words that people speak to her. A few weeks after Hera's punishment, Echo falls deeply in love with a young boy named Narcissus. He cannot understand her declarations of love and turns instead to love his own reflection. She flees and hides her grief in caves, where her body wastes away, and all that is left of her is the echo of her voice (*New Larousse Encyclopedia of Mythology*, 152–62).

In Ovid's *Metamorphoses*, Narcissus speaks the words, "'Here we shall meet,' . . . and Echo never / Replied more eagerly— 'Here we shall meet'" (97). The repetition of the word "here" and the fact that Echo's voice comes from deep within a cave parallel Loch's dream and suggest that Welty is including fragments from Ovid's version of this myth. When Echo tries to embrace Narcissus, he runs away crying "No, you must not touch—/ Go, take your hands away, may I be dead / Before you throw your fearful chains around me" (97). Echo turns away from Narcissus "to haunt caves of the forest" (97). Narcissus spurns Echo's love, just as Cuchulain spurned Morrigana's. Like Christ turning from Mary in the garden, saying, "Touch me not for I have not yet ascended to my Father" (John 20:17), Narcissus rejects the body of the woman and her chains and connects these chains with his death. In her death Echo's voice comes from deep within a cave as Echo loses her body to become a shade. Echo's disembodied voice expresses sorrow not only over Narcissus but also for her own regenerative body, which he has rejected. When he turns to his own reflection, he finds no love, only death. "His love was cursed. Only the glancing mirror / Of reflections filled his eyes, a body / That had no being of its own, a shade" (Ovid, 97). In rejecting the feminine as dangerous, he has effectively effaced his own physical self. He has projected the image of his own death and mortality onto the feminine body that could be his source of life and continuity. By not allowing her to touch him or make love to him, he gives up that which would keep alive his communal self as well as his individual self. In his love for a bodiless mirage of himself, the reflection in the pool, Narcissus will die, but both Ovid and Welty recognize that "she's heard by all who call; her voice has life" (97). Without the female voice there is no life.

In the ancient goddess religions, Echo was Acco, "the last echo of the Voice, meaning the voice of creation . . . the words she spoke heralded the final phase of the sacred king's fatal drama" (Walker, *Woman's Encyclopedia*, 269). Her voice was the warning that the young fertility god would die, to be reborn in the spring. In the classical version of the myth, Echo, the goddess who originally controlled the hero's destiny, is stripped of her voice, separated from her body, and rendered powerless, punished for her earlier role. For Echo to call Loch is for the distant fragments of the voice of the goddess to reassert themselves into this text. The goddess reminds Loch of his mortality. Rather than waiting for the masculine to return to the feminine, Welty reverses the roles and allows the female, in this case Virgie, to take control of her own sexuality. In fact, the call of the echo that Loch hears is interrupted by Virgie and the sailor going into the vacant house, the MacLain house and thus the masculine house: "It was she that had showed the sailor the house to begin with, she that started him coming" (*CSEW*, 278). According to Merlin Stone in *Ancient Mirrors of Womanhood*, the goddess Morrigana was thought to take the form of a sea goddess and to lure unsuspecting sailors to her rough waters. Under Virgie's rule the sailor is lured into her rough waters to become her consort, a complete reversal of the control that Narcissus has over Echo. (49)

Loch easily assumes the role of omniscient narrator. He not only says that the invaders (Virgie and the sailor) are his, but "He had not shared anybody in his life even with Louella" (*CSEW*, 278). Yet the moment Loch makes these proclamations of autonomy and dominance, the insistent voice, the echo, forces him to give up this stance. For the first time Loch recognizes that "silence closed over the house next door. It closed over just as silence did in their house at this time of day; but like the noisy waterfall it kept him awake—fighting sleep" (*CSEW*, 279). Just as the waterfall wakes Loch up, the silence makes him fight for consciousness. It is the silence—the tabula rasa—that will allow him to move beyond his egotistical perspective. Only after Loch hears the echo can he experience silence, and only after he recognizes the silence can he hear the voice again, this time in a much more developed form.

In the feminine domestic sphere to which the cave has moved, the buttermilk man does not sing songs of life giving milk, but instead he beats his horse with its red rose, the traditional symbol of female sexuality in masculine literature. Although this is a scene of abuse, it is at the same time a scene of rebirth. In Loch's dream, "the horse itself, a white and beautiful one, was on its way over, approaching to ask some favor of him, a request called softly and intelligibly upward—which he was not decided yet whether to grant or deny. This call through the window had not yet happened—not quite. But someone had come. He turned away. 'Cassie!' he cried" (*CSEW*, 279).[3] In *The White Goddess*, Robert Graves relates that in ancient Ireland a king underwent "symbolic rebirth from the White Mare," crawling "naked towards her on all fours as if he were her foal" (384). Loch really has no choice as to whether he will grant or deny this voice of life and death. There is no place for him to escape from women, from his sister Cassie who brings him "miserable girls' books and fairy tales" (*CSEW*, 277). By appearing at the exact moment at which Loch hears the call, Cassie actually embodies the female voice.

When Cassie walks into Loch's room, she tells him, to "Trim up those Octagon Soap coupons and count them good if you want that jack-knife" (*CSEW*, 279). Not only does the goddess of death cut the thread of life with scissors at the end of the masculine god's term, but as Frazer points out in *The Golden Bough*, the reign of many ancient Greek kings was limited to eight years. While there is a brand of soap called Octagon, the eightsided soap might also refer to this eight-year term.[4] If Loch cuts up the Octagon soap coupons, he acts out his own scattering, and he can become the king of the new year and receive his sword, in this case a jackknife. Frazer explains that "it was a rule of the Spartan constitution that every eighth year the ephors should choose a clear and moonless night and sitting down observe the sky in silence. If during their vigil they saw a meteor or a shooting star, they inferred that the king had sinned against the deity, and they suspended him from his function until the Delphic or Olympic oracle should reinstate him" (325–26). The Greeks chose eight years because of their desire to reconcile lunar and solar time. Every eight years the sun and the moon eclipse each other. As the masculine solar religion began to replace the feminine lunar religion, this reconciliation smoothed the transition.[5]

All of Frazer's conditions are present in Welty's story: the eclipse suggests a moonless night; Loch mentions the silence, and later in this story we hear that Miss Eckhart drew symbols on her student's music sheets that looked like meteors or shooting stars. Loch does not know what Cassie is doing in her room. He has the feeling that "something was being counted" (*CSEW*, 279), but he does not fully comprehend what is happening. Sometimes counting by fives and sometimes by tens, following neither the lunar nor the solar cycle, he wants to call out, "Coming, ready or not!" (*CSEW*, 279) but he does not. In this narrative Loch is not the author of his own destiny. In his sickness Loch is going through a premature death and rebirth, but this is not a rebirth that will make him a hero or a king. It is a rebirth into a world in which masculine and feminine are equal, a world in which the women will define the narrative until that equality is established.

The voice returns again, but this time it comes in the form of a real sound, not one heard in a dream, and we hear it against the background of the ladies of Morgana. Loch observes a "lackadaisical, fluttery kind of parade, the ladies of Morgana under their parasols, all trying to keep cool. . . . Miss Perdita Mayo was talking, and they were clicking their summery heels and drowning out—drowning out something. . . . A little tune was playing on the air, and it was coming from the piano in the vacant house" (*CSEW*, 280).[6] The ladies of Morgana are walking under parasols, protecting themselves from the masculine sun, and in this fluttery kind of parade there is a languor, a lack of desire. At the same time something is changing. This is not a stagnant or dead scene. Instead of a voice with recognizable words, there comes a tune that articulates the pain of the silenced feminine voice more clearly than words. The tune depends upon interpretation, upon remembering a history and a context, neither of which Loch can supply. The voice also comes in its true state, as it is always present in the world, being drowned out by the babble of the conventional women—the lackadaisical parade. For a moment, Loch balances on the edge of understanding as the tune comes again, "like a touch from a small hand that he had unwittingly pushed away." The tune calls Loch back to a "country all its own, where no mother or father came," back to his childhood when "his sister was so sweet," and "they loved each other in a different world," before puberty separated the sexes so dramatically, but most significantly it takes him back to Loch the boy, who does not have to live the solitary guarded stance, "all eyes like Argus" (*CSEW*, 280). Before the figure of Argus intrudes, the tune brings fertile tears to Loch's eyes.

In Greek mythology Argus, the son of Arestor, is the giant with a thousand eyes, half of which stay open while the others close in sleep. Graves writes that Argus is known for having slain Echidne, mother of the Harpies; the Chimaera, sister of the Medusa; and the serpent Ladon, who guarded the apple tree in the garden of the Hesperides (Graves, *Greek Myths I*, 127; *New Larousse Encyclopedia of Mythology*, 101, 106, 123, 124). Echidne's upper body is that of a young nymph and her lower body that of a horrifying serpent (Graves, *Greek Myths I*, 127–30). Argus kills the female monster in her two forms: as the nymph and as the serpent, the dual masculine perception of the triple goddess as the fair virgin and the evil Eve. Loch observes Miss Eckhart with the power of the supervisor in Michel Foucault's panoptician who is able to watch all the inmates but who cannot himself be seen (*Discipline and Punish*, 200–201). In ancient mythology Argus was called Argus Panoptes. Loch fluctuates between the two choices: the guarded stance of the giant in the mythological realm and the boy with tears in his eyes in the social realm. He knows that Cassie in the next room is "carrying on some girls' business that, at least, smelled terrible to him" (*CSEW*, 280). He calls out to Louella who asks him "to favor her with some rest or she would give up the ghost right then" (*CSEW*, 281).

Only after he has stopped trying to hold on to the scene, only after he recognizes that there is a woman's world that smells terrible and is separate from him, where Louella can refuse him, can he see Miss Eckhart as "an old lady. No, she was an old woman, round and unsteady-looking—unsteady the way he felt himself when he got out of bed—not on her way to a party" (*CSEW*, 281). Recognizing himself in an old woman Loch crosses a boundary between self and other and begins to let down his guarded stance: "Suppose doors with locks and keys were ever locked—then nothing like this would have the chance to happen. The nearness of missing things, and the possibility of preventing them, made Loch narrow his eyes" (*CSEW*, 281).[7] Loch realizes how easily what is occurring in the house next door could go unnoticed; how locks could keep things from happening. Loch could have been and potentially is the "lock" that blocks our understanding of Miss Eckhart. As Loch watches the house he sees "three party ladies" pass by "duck-like" and observes that they "just missed sight of the old woman. . . . They would have stopped everything" (*CSEW*, 281).

When we learn of Miss Eckhart's fate, we begin to wish that someone had tried to stop everything. The sad fact is that the puffing ladies cannot see Miss Eckhart. Though they are described in metaphors that include the swan and the number three—both symbols of regeneration, divination, and the triple goddess—these ladies have lost their mythological memory. They have been reduced to ducks, powerless and unable to soar to the swanlike heights it would take to see and save Miss Eckhart. But Welty sees. By pulling together the fragments of myth and symbol, she creates meaning where there would have been silence. Welty fills the "empty air behind everybody" as "butterflies suddenly crossed and circled each other, their wings digging and flashing like duelers' swords in the vacuum" (*CSEW*, 281), with a scene of life fighting back. Butterflies symbolize resurrection. The movement in the image of "wings digging and flashing like duelers' swords" suggests both an unresolved conflict and the possibility of change—a vibration in the air. Miss Eckhart's story still goes untold, however: "Nobody saw the old woman but Loch, and he told nothing" (*CSEW*, 283).

In the passage following this vision of dueling butterflies, Loch moves the telescope to see Virgie and the sailor lying on the mattress together in the attic of the vacant house. He describes the scene in terms that do not conform to any conventional language of sexuality; he tells how they "held pickles stuck in their mouths like cigars" (*CSEW*, 282). Then he goes on to say, "Sometimes they lay just alike, their legs in an M and their hands joined between them" (*CSEW*, 281). Loch then compares the lovers to paper dolls and finally to grasshoppers: "Like a big grasshopper lighting, all their legs and arms drew in to one small body, deadlike, with protective coloring" (*CSEW*, 282). Loch moves from the phallus (the pickles) to the alphabet (the "M"), to the image of paper dolls, to the grasshopper—a truly deconstructive progression.

Pickles not only suggest the phallus but describe it as something that is preserved, not something growing and natural. When Welty includes a single letter in this collection, it often indicates a point in the narration at which there is no social language to describe a particular event. The letters return us to an elemental stage at which we can invent new forms of expression. The paper doll, when cut out of newspaper as Cassie does, transforms the serious news of patriarchal society into a plaything. Loch's last image, the grasshopper, takes us beyond social stereotypes and gender dichotomies.[8] If Welty had been confined to using social language, she would have limited our perception of the event, either judging Virgie as a nice Southern girl gone bad or silencing the whole scene. When Loch leans back after seeing this, he "clasped the cool telescope to his side, with his fingernail closed its little eye" and said, "Poor old Telescope" (*CSEW*, 282). The phallic telescope has a little eye and is poor and old because it does not have the power to perceive what Virgie and the sailor are doing. Sexual passion, lust, or lovemaking cannot be collapsed into something trite or superficial.

To see Miss Eckhart, Loch must make a similar move away from conventional language. Rather than using symbols or metaphors, Loch expands our understanding of Miss Eckhart by including many fragments, any one of which alone would be reductive. At first Loch frames Miss Eckhart with stereotypical names such as the "sailor's mother," a "school teacher" a "girl" (*CSEW*, 282–83), but as he includes all of these stereotypes, our image of Miss Eckhart expands: "She was pushing a big square of matting along on its side; she wove and bent and struggled behind it, like a spider with something bigger than he can eat, pushing it into the parlor" (*CSEW*, 283). From mother, teacher, and girl, Loch extends his vision to the more mythological image of a spider. In the Pueblo tradition spider grandmother is the spinner of tales, the one who keeps the culture from dying out. In Greek mythology the spider is associated with the second aspect of the triple goddess, as the spinner of fate, (or Clotho), and as the death aspect or third aspect because, like Echidne who was accused of eating men, the spider was condemned for eating her mate (Stone, *Ancient Mirrors of Womanhood* 289, 300). In later classical mythology she was Arachne the maiden whom Athene turned into a spider because Athene was jealous of her. As a spider Arachne continued to weave and spin, activities that, since ancient times, have symbolized women's power and the continuity of life. With this reference to the spider, Loch inadvertently transforms Miss Eckhart from a crazy old lady messing up her living room to an artist engaged in a life and death struggle.

Loch's ability to let us see Miss Eckhart is limited, because he is "pressed forward, cramped inside, checkerboarding his forehead and nose against the screen. He both wanted the plot to work and wanted it to fail. . . . This house was something the old woman intended to burn down. And Loch could think of a thousand ways she could do it better" (*CSEW*, 283–84). Loch realizes that Miss Eckhart wants to build a fire, but he does not begin to understand the fuel behind this desire. He never recognizes that she might want to kill herself. While assuming godlike, authorial power over life and death, Loch can see the factual problem—that Miss Eckhart cannot make a fire burn in an airless room—but he cannot see the "kind of near" things. Loch cannot understand Miss Eckhart's recital room and why her fire has no air; he cannot understand why she has closed the windows, why she is shutting out a draft; he does not understand that this stifling room is her life, her personal suffocation, what has been done to her, not by her. He does not understand the connection between her fire and the rest of the world. In fact he misses so much that he says: "She was not connected with anything else, with anybody. She was one old woman in a house not bent on dealing punishment" (*CSEW*, 283).

At the same time, Loch is right. Miss Eckhart's fire cannot breathe. She is alone. She is disconnected. The old woman who dedicated her life to teaching music and never had a chance to show her talent fails in this last symbolic act of burning down the house of confinement because she has had to protect herself from life—from the very air that would let her fire burn. Even though the air is freedom, it is also symbolic of the masculine mythological sphere, the autonomy of King MacLain, the world to which women in general and Miss Eckhart in particular have been denied access. Only when Loch puts down the telescope, crawls out on the tree, "holding by the knees and diving head down, then swaying in the sweet open free air and dizzy as an apple on a tree" (*CSEW*, 285), can he begin to understand. Loch, allowing himself to become an apple, the symbol of feminine fertility, instead of the serpent Ladon who protects the apples, sees power in Miss Eckhart's planning that he has not seen before. For the first time he connects the tune to the artist. For the first time he sees the metronome and thinks that it might be a bomb, and as he listens to it ticking "his hopes suddenly rose for her" (*CSEW*, 285). Interestingly enough at this very moment he hangs "still as a folded bat" (*CSEW*, 285); bats are blinded by daylight and can see only at night. Before Loch can hear the new female voice, he must experience silence. Before he can see the new female character, he must learn to see at night.

Unlike Loch, Cassie does not actually watch Miss Eckhart. As she approaches Miss Eckhart, Cassie enters a world of experience and memory. Cassie can easily name the tune as "Für Elise" because she has heard it played a hundred times. Cassie answers the call of the tune with what, we find out later in the story, are Miss Eckhart's own words, "Virgie Rainey, *danke schoen*" (*CSEW*,

285). As Cassie holds Miss Eckhart's words in her mouth, she becomes Miss Eckhart (at least for an instant), and it is this shared subjectivity that allows her to enter Miss Eckhart's life. Unlike Loch, Cassie does not put herself in a superior position to her subject. When she looks at the house, she sees just a house, with "not a soul in sight . . . but Old Man Holifield," and she remembers that his presence never kept her mother from "going right ahead and calling the MacLain house 'the vacant house'" (*CSEW*, 285). She sees without fantasy, without giants, or cowboys, or obelisks that are about to explode. She describes the place as "overgrown," "still as noon all day," an image of stagnation where "rainless" and "windless" "the town of Morgana, life itself, sunlit and moonlit, were composed and still and chinalike" (*CSEW*, 285–86). But as she watches, "there was agitation. Some life stirred through. It may have been *old* life" (*CSEW*, 286). As in Sarah Orne Jewett's *The Country of the Pointed Firs*[9] and Kate Chopin's *The Awakening*, we begin to see Welty focusing on something that she calls the rebirth of old life. This agitation in the shade—the feminine half of Loch's vision— warns us of the fact that the woman artist is beginning to stir and to occupy the men's house—the schoolhouse in *Country of the Pointed Firs* and the recital room in *The Golden Apples*. This is the house of the transmission of culture from one generation to the next—the house of the teacher, the artist, and the student. Cassie realizes that a "restless current seemed to flow dark and free around it," a "line of poetry tumbled in her ears" (*CSEW*, 286), and she remembers "Though I am old with wandering" from the Yeats's poem "The Song of Wandering Aengus" (*Selected Poems*, 22).

As Cassie thinks of this line, she is in the middle of mixing colors for a tie-dyed scarf. "In surprise, but as slowly as in regret, she stopped stirring the emerald green" (*CSEW*, 285). In stopping her mixing of the emerald green, a color that "is associated in Celtic folklore with Fairies' clothes" (Graves, *The White Goddess*, 171), Cassie leaves the child's world of make-believe.

This change brings her into direct contact not only with the line of poetry but with Miss Eckhart. Cassie and Miss Eckhart are creating sunburst designs at the same moment—Cassie a tie-dyed scarf and Miss Eckhart a maypole—and in doing so they are taking on the power of the sun as their own. The pattern of the sunburst or spiderweb in Cassie's scarf and in Miss Eckhart's maypole of newspaper strips is the same pattern that Dorothy sees in the mirror in *Middlemarch*,[10] that Eleanor draws on her blotting paper in *The Years*,[11] that Woolf draws at the top of each chapter in the manuscript of *The Pargiters*, that Miss Julia Mortimer draws on the map for Judge Moody in *Losing Battles*,[12] and the same pattern that we will find throughout *The Golden Apples*. In mirroring the sun, flowers, organic growth, and expansion, the structure of this image suggests infinite possibilities. Unlike the structured checkerboard or the closed obelisk, the sunburst with its strokes raying out is open; the strokes can move in any direction or dissolve entirely.

The map of the spiderweb on the scarf plots the narrative journey that Cassie will take through her memory. Like Katie Rainey, Cassie must begin the expansion within herself. Cassie has shut herself off from her brother and the world with a sign on her door that says "Everybody stay out!!!" and it is "signed with skull and crossbones" (*CSEW*, 286). She shuts out temporarily the masculine world, her brother's calling, in order to hear the voice of the woman artist within. When Loch calls to her, "Come here!" she reverses the Echo myth and refuses, saying "*I ain't got time!*" (*CSEW*, 287). The newly awakened feminine consciousness does not have the time to listen to masculine requests. She is attuned to the old life—the agitation in the shade. The sound of Miss Eckhart's playing "Für Elise" comes to Cassie three times, and as she listens she changes from an ordinary little girl to a mythical creature. We begin to see her in a new light. She has papers in her hair which Louella put there to make her look pretty for the hayride but which make her look like the Medusa with her snake hair. She has spilled every color of the rainbow on her smock; "she was holding a spoon up like a mean switch in her right hand, and her feet were bare" (*CSEW*, 287).[13] As Cassie changes, she appears "pathetic—homeless-looking—horrible" (*CSEW*, 287). It is at this moment, when Cassie is most outside her social self, homeless, and thus most within her mythical self, that the memories that "Für Elise" has evoked overwhelm her: "Then the wave moved up, towered, and came drowning down over her stuck-up head" (*CSEW*, 287). Cassie cannot resist the wave that will take her back to her matriarchal past. When Cassie hears the poem again, she moves further away from the center and remembers the Yeats line, "*I will find out where she has gone*" (*CSEW*, 287). As Cassie continues to listen to the music and concentrate on her spiderweb design, she asks, "Where had Miss Eckhart gone?" Whereas Yeats, under the persona of Aengus, searches for his lost muse or female love, the woman artist searches for herself, for her spiritual and artistic history, for her foremothers and teachers. Thus Cassie, unlike Loch, cannot see the vacant house as other, a thing she possesses or creates; it is within her. Her stuck-up head will be brought under. "Für Elise" appeals to Cassie's "uncritical self" (*CSEW*, 287).

One of the first things Cassie remembers about Miss Eckhart is that she graded Cassie's lesson immediately after Virgie arrives with a magnolia blossom (another point with strokes raying out), which Cassie calls "too sweet and heavy" (*CSEW*, 290). The blossom, a sexual symbol, is a physical manifestation of the relationship between Virgie and Miss Eckhart. If we tried to name this student/teacher relationship, the terms "too sweet" and "too heavy" would do better than "love" or "friendship" or any other socially defined word. As Virgie waits in the corner, Miss Eckhart, trying to play her role as teacher, "checked the questions missed, sometimes the question answered; but every question she did check got a heavy 'V' that crossed the small page like the tail of a comet. She would draw her black brows together to see Cassie forgetting, unless it was to remember some nearly forgotten thing herself" (*CSEW*, 290). What spills out of Miss

Eckhart is the symbol of the V, like a comet without a direct destination which bursts forth in a flame of glory and then falls burnt-out to the ground. The thing she has forgotten is her hidden artistic power—too secret and too full—her love not directly for Virgie but for what Virgie brings out in her, for the music that they both play. What spills out of Miss Eckhart in the symbol of the V is her "self" as passionate artist. In fact, as Miss Eckhart draws her brows together, she becomes the V.

If we remember that the comet was the portent of the end of the eight-year reign of the king, then Miss Eckhart's V is a portent of the coming of a new power. At this point Miss Eckhart's desire—can find release only in the flash of the comet. Like Echo in the cave she cannot articulate her love of, and her concern for, her students, let alone her artistic vision. The German words that Miss Eckhart calls out, the words that the children do not understand, "*Danke schoen*" and "*Mein liebes Kind*" (*CSEW*, 291) are the voice of the teacher and the mother, the identities that are buried by bitter loss. By not caring to ask—or being afraid, like the others, that asking was like "belling the cat"—(*CSEW*, 291), Virgie loses her understanding not only of Miss Eckhart but of her own self. The children have added "*danke schoen*" onto Virgie's name, recognizing, on some subconscious level, that Miss Eckhart is part of Virgie as Virgie is part of Miss Eckhart. Virgie does not care because she has not been taught to pay attention to this old woman, her artistic guide into the world of art and passion. The connection between the two is so vital, like two heads of the Medusa, that when Virgie stops taking lessons, she takes "away Miss Eckhart's luck for good," and "Virgie's hand lost its touch" (*CSEW*, 306).

These two artists cannot survive in a world where "nobody wanted Virgie Rainey to be anything in Morgana any more than they had wanted Miss Eckhart to be, and they were the two of them still linked together by people's saying that. How much might depend on people's being linked together?" (*CSEW*, 306). Welty answers her own question by recognizing the need for the connection of one woman artist to another from generation to generation. Without this cultural continuity from mother to daughter there is only forgetfulness—the greatest tragedy. This is a very different vision from that of the hero myth, which insists on the autonomy of the son from the mother. Virgie is Miss Eckhart's muse but, more importantly, Miss Eckhart is Virgie's muse. This intersubjectivity does not allow one character to ignore, to belittle, or try to kill another because his or her identity is dependent on the full awareness of all others.

In *One Writer's Beginnings*, Welty observes, "Not in Miss Eckhart as she stands solidly and almost opaquely in the surround of her story, but in the making of her character out of my most inward and most deeply feeling self, I would say I have found my voice in fiction" (101). For Welty to bring this old woman artist/teacher to life is for her to bring the buried history of women's art to life and thus literally to find her voice—a woman's voice—as an artist. Welty goes on to say, "Inasmuch as Miss Eckhart might have been said to come from me, the author, Virgie, at her moments, might have always been my subject" (102). Ironically, Miss Eckhart never acts as narrator and Virgie rarely acts as the subject of the stories. In fact, within the internal structure of *The Golden Apples*, Virgie is more often the narrator and her subject is her search to remember her mother and her teacher, Miss Eckhart. If Welty's subject is Virgie, then in turn her subject is, through Virgie, her own attempt to remember and to articulate and in doing so to discover her voice as an artist.

This degree of identification between artist and object collapses the duality of the subject/object split and allows for a much more fluid relationship between author and text. Welty's subject, in the sense of topic, is her subject in the philosophical sense. Rather than maintaining the distance of an objective omnipotent narrator or a powerful creator, Welty takes on the perspective of a subjective equal: "Of course any writer is in part all of his characters" (101). From this perspective of Kristeva's multiple subjectivity, she can hear and see a great deal more then she could as an omniscient or first-person narrator. Virgie would still seem "right outside" for Welty because Virgie is the young woman whom she, as an older woman, is trying to understand.

Welty finds her voice not in the character of Snowdie Mac-Lain, not in the character of Katie Rainey (i.e., in the lady or the mother), and not even in Virgie (the warrior), but in the witch or crone, the third aspect of the triple goddess.[14] Cassie Morrison's mother comments that Miss Eckhart's studio "was in some ways like the witch's house in *Hansel and Gretel* . . . including the witch" (*CSEW*, 288). Welty discovers the voice of the female artist in the crone because she must reclaim not only the ability to give birth but the ability to die, to undergo the inevitable destruction or dissolution that must precede regeneration. Though the evil witch in masculine literature has the strength to kill—even this is an imposed rather than actual power, projected on the female by the male—she does not have the power to die. Welty writes, "Exposing yourself to risk is a truth Miss Eckhart and I have in common . . . . the love of her art and the desire to give it until there is no more left" (*One Writer's Beginnings*, 101). Giving of oneself until there is no more is the artist's authority over death; only if one is willing to die to the art can she not be afraid of being killed by it. The heroic narrative depends on the control of the crone because only the crone lives outside the realm of masculine need; only the crone threatens the masculine hero's claim to immortality and omnipotence. She is the third aspect of the triple goddess, the one who cuts the thread of life.

For Miss Eckhart, Virgie symbolizes freedom, the soaring comet, but for Virgie, at this point in the story, Miss Eckhart symbolizes only entrapment and death. This is the exact relationship of the masculine hero to his mother or lover. By copying the masculine model, Welty rejects the idea that the hero must be male, but in order to find the voice of the woman artist she empties this model of meaning by allowing Virgie to perform it fully and in "The Wanderers" to move beyond it. As the heroine,

Virgie has an "air of abandon" (*CSEW*, 291) and does exactly what she wants to do; she is not trapped in Miss Eckhart's stifling world. At the spring picnics, "Virgie let herself go completely, as anyone would like to do" (*CSEW*, 297). Virgie assumes masculine privilege to the point that Cassie even thinks that Virgie wrote "Für Elise." Cassie remembers that everyone at Sunday School thought that Virgie would go "somewhere away off" (*CSEW*, 292). "Miss Lizzie Stark's mother, old Mrs. Sad-Talking Morgan, said Virgie would be the first lady governor of Mississippi, that was where she would go. It sounded worse than the infernal regions" (*CSEW*, 292). Virgie may go to the infernal regions but she has not yet gone. If Snowdie is the white, birth aspect of the triple goddess and the confined lady, and if Miss Eckhart is the black, "death" aspect and the old crone/witch, Virgie, in "her middy blouse . . . trimmed in a becoming red . . . [and] her red silk lacers . . . full of the airs of wildness" (*CSEW*, 291) is the red, life aspect. Unlike Cassie or Miss Eckhart, Virgie, as the goddess of love and battle, is sexually active and free. Like the goddess Morrigana, she tells the sailor what to do; she can love Cuchulain passionately and fight him just as passionately; "she swayed, she gave way to joys and tempers, her own and other people's with equal freedom—except never Miss Eckhart's, of course" (*CSEW*, 291). To surrender to Miss Eckhart's joys and tempers would be to give in to the death aspect, to become one with the tragic witch locked away from the world.

Virgie must face death and return in order to realize her own creative power, but she does not yet have this power. She will not become a famous musician, she will not become a lady governor, and she will not even leave for some place far away until she faces the Miss Eckhart within herself. There is a difference between incorporating the world of the burning witch and limiting oneself to that subjectivity. One stance is empowering; the other is debilitating. The goddess Morrigana moves freely between all three aspects of the triple goddess; she is the lover/mother, the warrior, and the witch. No one can live only as the maiden, or only as the crone.

The dance of this story is the dance of the three heads of the Gorgon monster as they find each other once again. Whereas Virgie must look to Miss Eckhart to learn how to die, Miss Eckhart must look to Virgie to learn how to live. Miss Eckhart has faced the sword of the vaunting hero in the form of his denial of her artistic self. Since she believes that men wield the sword and inflict the wounds, her life depends on shutting them out and inviting only "all female Morgana" (*CSEW*, 311) to her recitals. Virgie shows Miss Eckhart how to live by ignoring and thus expanding the boundaries of this sterile world. However, to play her role as teacher and to make a living, Miss Eckhart must keep her heart disciplined to the steady beat of the metronome, the obelisk. The beat of the metronome is like the toll of the bell.

As Cassie remembers Virgie's refusal to use the metronome, she remembers that her own mother hated metronomes. When Cassie's mother tells her that the metronome is "an infernal machine" and that she wants "a song to dip" Cassie asks her, "What do you mean, dip? Could you have played the piano, Mama?" and the mother answers, "'Child, I could have sung,' and she threw her hand from her, as though all music might as well now go jump off the bridge" (*CSEW*, 293).

We begin to see a connection between the emergence and renewal involved in a "dip" and the emergence and renewal of art. If a song does not dip—that is, die and come back to life—it does not live. Both Miss Eckhart, with her metronome trying to control time, and Virgie, in running from Miss Eckhart, try to avoid the dip of life. Mrs. Morrison cannot sing so she wants music to commit suicide. Jumping off the bridge is not a dip. By telling Miss Eckhart that she will not play with the metronome ticking, Virgie begins to open up a whole new world of possibility: "Anybody could tell that Virgie was doing something to Miss Eckhart. She was turning her from a teacher into something lesser. And if she was not a teacher, what was Miss Eckhart?" (*CSEW*, 294). When Virgie takes away Miss Eckhart's power as a teacher, she gives her something much greater; she gives her life in all its splendor and horror.

The moment Virgie takes the metronome away from Miss Eckhart, Mr. Voight violates the studio: "When he flapped his maroon-colored bathrobe, he wore no clothes at all under-neath. . . . Cassie saw that Miss Eckhart, who might once have been formidable in particular to any Mr. Voights, was helpless toward him and his antics—as helpless as Miss Snowdie Mac-Lain would have been, helpless as Miss Snowdie was, toward her own little twin sons—all since she had begun giving in to Virgie Rainey" (*CSEW*, 294–95). Miss Eckhart as the witch and Miss Snowdie as the lady, in their roles as characters in masculine myth, are helpless against a masculine intrusion into the female sphere. Virgie maintains the upper hand because she does not pretend, as Miss Eckhart would like for her to do. Unlike Loch she not only knows but she will tell. By playing on stronger and clearer, she uses her music as a weapon, a sword itself, against the intrusion and the aggression of Mr. Voight and against Miss Eckhart's threats. Even when Virgie tells, her words have no meaning because no one listens: "Virgie told on Mr. Voight too, but she had nobody to believe her, and so Miss Eckhart did not lose any pupils by that. Virgie did not know how to tell any-thing" (*CSEW*, 295). Virgie and Cassie cannot create meaning simply by uttering words in a world that does not privilege these words.

When Cassie tells her parents what Mr. Voight did, her moth-er only laughs and her father, whose head is a "solid silhouette where he sat against the day," returns to his newspaper, the *Morgana-MacLain Weekly Bugle*, saying that he does not believe her, that "Mr. Voight represented a large concern and covered seven states." He adds his own threat to Miss Eckhart's: "no picture show money" (*CSEW*, 295). Mr. Morrison can hide be-hind the words in his paper. He can define what is news and what is not, what has meaning and what does not. Cassie realizes that "for what Mr. Voight did there were no ready words—what would you call it? 'Call it spontaneous combustion,' Cassie's mother said. Some performances of people stayed partly untold

for lack of a name, Cassie believed, as well as for lack of be-
lievers" (*CSEW*, 295–96). Cassie struggles with the thinness of
language here in much the same way that Katie struggled with
trying to articulate those "kind of near" things of King's world.
However Cassie does remember her mother's words, which are
more significant than they might first appear. If we consider how
long it takes Miss Eckhart to light her fire and how poorly it
ignites, then we can realize how difficult it is for something to
combust spontaneously. Mr. Voight does not have to struggle to
obtain power; he has power bursting out of him. Only Virgie's
disinterest begins to weaken Mr. Voight's grasp on the girls and
Miss Eckhart.

As Welty attempts to describe this scene and to give masculine
intrusion into the feminine sphere a name, layers of hidden
meaning begin to unfold. Miss Eckhart, afraid of losing pupils,
attacks and threatens the girls: "Tell a soul what you have seen,
I'll beat your hands until you scream" (*CSEW*, 295). Rather than
attacking the real enemy, Miss Eckhart turns against the girls;
seeing herself as a victim, she wants the girls to become victims.
It is crucial for Virgie and Cassie and for the continuation of the
narration that they do not let her do so. If they did, the story
would mirror the narration of that hero myth in which the
wicked stepmother or witch destroys the young children. Miss
Eckhart's words do not frighten the girls; "To Cassie [Miss
Eckhart's threat] was as idle as a magic warning in a story; she
criticized the rhyme" (*CSEW*, 295). Not only does Cassie recognize the difference between a magic warning in a story and the
reality of this event, but she achieves the stance of a conscious
artist as she realizes that "seen" and "scream" do not rhyme and
do not go together. If Virgie and Cassie had screamed at Mr.
Voight, they would have been reacting in the stereotypical feminine manner. Instead they react intelligently; they tell their parents what they have seen. They know that the magic warning in
stories, the fairy-tale world of queens and princesses, the world
of emerald green, will not serve to explain this intrusive act.

Finally Cassie must reject social definitions of, and reactions to, the event and return to her own visual memory to find language to describe this "kind of near thing." The "least describable thing of all had been a look on his face; that was strange. Thinking of it now, and here in her room, Cassie found she had bared her teeth and set them, trying out the frantic look. She could not now, any more than then, really describe Mr. Voight, but without thinking she could *be* Mr. Voight, which was more frightening still" (*CSEW*, 296). In this scene Cassie does what the artist must do to create a character and what the woman character must do to become an artist; she crosses over into another character, giving of herself until there is no more to give. Only then can she see the scene for what it really is: frightening and at the same time not frightening because Mr. Voight is nothing more than "a turkey gobbler" (*CSEW*, 296). Cassie's bared teeth and frantic look are not only the look of Mr. Voight, they are the look of the Gorgon Medusa and the female monster of masculine fiction. This face is not one of fear or terror but of anger. Cassie's realization that Mr. Voight was frightening does not paralyze her but instead brings back a deeper, suppressed rage.

As Cassie changes the colors on her scarf, Welty connects us back to the narrator and then out again—a different color—and Cassie's journey continues deeper into the consciousness of Virgie and Miss Eckhart, into realms previously beyond her reach. The movement of Cassie's memory mirrors the pattern on the scarf. Welty does not narrate chronologically but instead adds texture and color, layering one design on top of another. By weakening Miss Eckhart, Virgie has opened the little locked metronome world, not only to the pain and horror of the Mr. Voights of society, but to the possibility of regeneration and renewal that openness must bring. She has started Miss Eckhart's fall, and as the teacher falls the witch gradually becomes a whole person. Welty transforms the layers of stereotype into a single entire human being, one who has emotions and can be afraid of love: "There was another man Miss Eckhart had been scared of, up until the last. (Not Mr. King MacLain. They always passed without touching, like two stars, perhaps they had some kind of eclipse-effect on each other.) She had been sweet on Mr. Hal Sissum, who clerked in the shoe department of Spights' store" (*CSEW*, 296). Unlike the fictional lady or princess, the crone as the death aspect can eclipse the hero; Circe can hold Ulysses captive. King MacLain and Miss Eckhart are neither sun nor moon, masculine nor feminine, but two stars. Like Circe, to whom Cassie later compares Miss Eckhart, she only fears the hero as a man in the social/sexual world in which she is still a victim. Cassie remembers that even though everyone thought Miss Eckhart was sweet on the shoe salesman, "She didn't know how to do about Mr. Sissum at all" (*CSEW*, 296). Welty asks the question that defines the problem: "But what could they either one have done?" (*CSEW*, 297).

In traditional masculinist literature, the witch, the grandmother, the old maid schoolteacher, and the old crone do not have active sexual lives. Describing Miss Eckhart's sexual life requires a new approach to language. The Western myth of romantic love has nothing to do with Mr. Sissum and Miss Eckhart. The male shoe salesman plays high up on the wooden platform above the earth, while the female true musician sits on the damp grass, earthbound and silent. How can these two people ever connect in the socially defined world of romantic love or even in something called "sexual union"? What could they "either one have done?" Neither of them do anything, and finally Mr. Sissum dies. Unlike King MacLain, who seems to play with death in a possible mock suicide, Mr. Sissum actually falls in the Big Black River and drowns. In this story Welty brings the male character down to earth; he is mortal and can die. At the funeral some said that if "Dr. Loomis had not caught her she would have gone headlong into the red clay hole. . . . But Cassie had the impression that Miss Eckhart simply wanted to see—to see what was being done with Mr. Sissum" (*CSEW*, 299). As Katie wants to see King MacLain, Miss Eckhart wants to see Mr. Sissum's dead body so that it does not take on the overwhelming mythic proportions of King MacLain's missing one. Cassie rescues Miss Eckhart from the role of the thwarted female lover, elevating her to the role of death crone.

Cassie remembers that unlike Mr. Sissum, who stayed high up on the platform, Virgie "put a loop of clover chain down over Miss Eckhart's head, her hat—her one hat—and all. She hung Miss Eckhart with flowers, while Mr. Sissum plucked the strings up above her. Miss Eckhart sat on, perfectly still and submissive. She gave no sign. She let the clover chain come down and lie on her breast. Virgie laughed delightedly and with her long chain in her hand ran around and around her, binding her with clovers. Miss Eckhart let her head roll back, and then Cassie felt that the teacher was filled with terror, perhaps with pain" (*CSEW*, 298). What Cassie neglects to see is the exquisite connection that Virgie's clover chain represents. Miss Eckhart is filled with terror and pain because once she lets in one emotion she must let them all in. The clover chain is not like the chain of Loch's ironclad checkerboard pattern. The clover chain, like the chains that Narcissus fears, is of the earth, not really a chain at all but the natural world holding Miss Eckhart to the earth, to Virgie Rainey, to her own pain, to her own love. It is a chain of connection and, unlike Narcissus, Miss Eckhart does not reject Virgie's advances, no matter how painful they may be, but she does give a sign. She allows the chain to lie on her breast. Virgie Rainey's name reminds us that she is a fertility goddess, a bringer of rain.

There are two June recitals in this story: one occurs after lessons one day when Cassie, Virgie, and Lizzie are stranded in Miss Eckhart's studio because of a terrible thunderstorm, and the other Miss Eckhart arranges for the girls every year. As the rain pours down outside, almost without warning, Miss Eckhart begins to play the piano.

> The piece was so hard that she made mistakes and repeated to correct them, so long and stirring that it soon seemed longer than the

day itself had been, and in playing it Miss Eckhart assumed an entirely different face. Her skin flattened and drew across her cheeks, her lips changed. The face could have belonged to someone else—not even to a woman, necessarily. It was the face a mountain could have, or what might be seen behind the veil of a waterfall. There in the rainy light it was a sightless face, one for music only— though the fingers kept slipping and making mistakes they had to correct. And if the sonata had an origin in a place on earth, it was the place where Virgie, even, had never been and was not likely ever to go. (*CSEW*, 300–301)

In this scene Miss Eckhart becomes both the voice of the woman calling to the young hero "behind the veil of a waterfall" and the young hero who is being awakened by the rainstorm in the spring. In writing this passage with all its physical reality— the face, the fingers, the mountain, the waterfall—Welty has found a way to express the passionate emerging voice of a woman artist, not as identity, not even as a woman necessarily, but as the crossing between worlds. The voice calls her from a place in which literary history and social convention have no power. Miss Eckhart makes mistakes, but these are the mistakes any artist makes; they are not the same as the absent-minded "V" marks. For Miss Eckhart this crossing over, after years of confinement, is violent. She is not an artist observing the storm and the moun- tain but the storm and the mountain themselves: "Performing, Miss Eckhart was unrelenting. Even when the worst of the piece was over, her fingers like foam on rocks pulled at the spent-out part with unstilled persistence, insolence, violence" (*CSEW*, 302). Miss Eckhart has become the storm at sea, the sea at its wildest, and as the sea she beats against the solid world that has held her. She does not let up on the music that has now become her target as well as her sword. She fights with the same per- sistence, insolence, and violence that have been meted out to her.

As Welty brings back the power of the old witch, as she ex- poses the crime of the suppression of Miss Eckhart's talent, she must turn to the hard material reality. Cassie is correct in perceiving that "it took only a summer rain to start it again; she had been pricked and the music came like the red blood under the scab of a forgotten fall" (*CSEW*, 301). Only through the language of open scabs, blood, rushing rain, the blows of Miss Eckhart's strong left hand, a Christmas firework, all feebly guarded by the "faintly winking circle of the safe in the wall," could Welty cut through the abstract systems that have kept Miss Eckhart confined. Virgie has opened Miss Eckhart's wound and the blood has started to flow. It is fertile blood, like the rushing rain, but it is full of the debris and damage of the storm. She is the artistic perspective completely without consciousness and without the letter "I." The problem with this existence is that it cannot last. Miss Eckhart has no control over her storm. She must play until she is spent, and then she will stop as quickly as the storm itself stops. In this chaotic outburst Miss Eckhart cannot retain a sense of her own artistic power. In fact when the girls ask her what she was playing: "'I couldn't say,' Miss Eckhart said rising. 'I have forgotten'" (*CSEW*, 302).

Miss Eckhart has not forgotten how to play the music or the feeling behind the music; she has forgotten how to say. She has forgotten how to create a language that will enable her to remain conscious of her artistic ability. To release herself from a confinement that is at once physical and psychological, she fights only against the tangible, beating her way out as a trapped bird beats its wings; she tries to burn down the material reality, to hit the girls, to slap her mother; she tries to become the sea, the wind, the fire, and the rain. Language depends on metaphor, the continuum between the abstract and the physical. Language is artistic distance and a bridge. It is not matter only but matter describing itself as matter. Miss Eckhart lashes out with her repressed genius just as she did with her repressed anger, but this time her hand actually strikes Jinny Love. The girls think that "something had burst out, unwanted, exciting, from the wrong person's life. This was some brilliant thing too splendid for Miss Eckhart, piercing and striking the air around her the way a

Christmas firework might almost jump out of the hand that was, each year, inexperienced anew" (*CSEW*, 301). This is a teacher, and yet genius bursts out of her. This is music, and yet it attacks and pierces. Precisely because Miss Eckhart plays the music of the forgotten fall—both the fall that the artist must experience in order to play with this passion and the actual fall of the female from power—neither the music nor Miss Eckhart is soothing or restful. While Miss Eckhart's idle threats, bound up in the socially constructed feminine fear of and thus protection of, masculine aggression, do not frighten Cassie, Miss Eckhart's piano performance terrifies her; she now sees and feels the blows that were promised on the earlier occasion.

The music draws Cassie into the depths of the past, where "things divined and endured, spectacular moments, hideous things like the black stranger jumping out of the hedge at nine o'clock, all seemed to Cassie to be by their own nature rising— and so alike—and crossing the sky and setting, the way planets did. Or they were more like whole constellations, turning at their very centers maybe, like Perseus and Orion and Cassiopeia in her Chair and the Big Bear and Little Bear, maybe often upside down, but terribly recognizable. It was not just the sun and the moon that traveled. In the deepening of the night, the rising sky lifted like a cover when Louella let it soar as she made the bed" (*CSEW*, 302). Not surprisingly, as the flood gates open Cassie's fears and prejudices, the whole racist narrative of the black rapist surfaces. By including both the stereotype of the "black stranger" and the reality of Louella in the same paragraph, Welty expands our vision from stereotype to the equality of the stars, turning our assumptions upside down, while they remain terribly recognizable. By comparing the cover that Louella lets soar to the rising sky, Welty extends her representation of Louella from the black woman servant in a southern home who is making a bed to the Egyptian goddess Nut who holds up the sky. The crossing over and confluence that Cassie experiences is not lost on the girls. Miss Eckhart's music puts the girls "on some equal footing," not just between themselves but in the world, and they are "wondering . . . about escape" (*CSEW*, 301), literally from Miss Eckhart's house but also figuratively from the house of masculine oppression: from the MacLain house.

Welty brings us back to the horror of Miss Eckhart's daily life when she asks, "Should daughters *forgive* mothers (with mothers under their heel)?" (*CSEW*, 304). In Homeric tradition the heel is the most vulnerable part of the hero's body; as the mirror of her own identity, Miss Eckhart's mother is her most vulnerable point. Old Mrs. Eckhart screams out what Miss Eckhart has tried to keep hidden. She makes fun of her teaching and interrupts the lesson, a reminder of all that Miss Eckhart has suffered, of all the pain she has tried to stifle. When she is in danger of losing pupils because of her mother's outbursts, she begins to drug her; "some people said Miss Eckhart killed her mother with opium" (*CSEW*, 307). Everyone knows her mother was in pain, but "nobody was told. What kind of pain they did not say" (*CSEW*, 307). These lines remind us that the pain that cannot be named or spoken is particularly deadly. Miss Eckhart's mother is not only her biological mother, she is her self, the woman she might become. Her mother's pain is her own pain. Her mother's stifled screams are her own stifled screams. When Miss Eckhart slaps the side of her mother's mouth during one of Cassie's lessons, striking out at the organ of articulation, she is doing to her mother exactly what society has done to her; it "seemed to Cassie that it must, after all, have been the mother that slapped the daughter" (*CSEW*, 305).

Miss Eckhart may have killed her mother, but, while this could happen so easily, so accidentally, she does not have enough mythical power to burn down the house and to kill herself. When Cassie tries to think of Miss Eckhart's pain she recalls the line in "The Song of Wandering Aengus" that reads "because a fire was in my head," and we return to the present and the fact that Miss Eckhart is trying to light a fire next door. The last lines of the Yeats poem that Cassie remembers read:

I will find out where she has gone,
And kiss her lips and take her hands,
And walk among long dappled grass,
And pluck till time and times are done,
The silver apples of the moon,
The golden apples of the sun.

(Selected Poems, 22)

It is no mistake that Welty entitled this collection *The Golden Apples*. In one of the earliest mentions of the golden apples, Mother Earth gives her daughter Hera a gift of this fruit on her wedding day (Graves, *The Greek Myths I*, 50–55). The Mother Earth of classical mythology is the ancient triple goddess and the apples are a symbol of feminine fertility. Mother Earth gives Hera, the new female goddess in patriarchal religion, a gift of female sexual power. Just as Hera's marriage to Zeus heralds the triumph of the worship of masculine gods over the ancient worship of the triple goddess, so the golden apples signify the ongoing struggle to maintain feminine control; and Hera's many fights with Zeus, which have been interpreted by modern mythologists as the anger of a jealous wife, represent the fury of a dispossessed queen/goddess (61) Hera knows that the apples must be protected as she must protect herself from Zeus's overwhelming power, and she places these apples in a secret garden called the garden of the Hesperides, which is an all-women's sphere not to be entered by any man (50–55). The three Hesperides, another classical shadow of the triple goddess, watch over the golden apples.

The story of Miss Eckhart as she plays the piano for the three girls mirrors this myth. As the storm howls outside, the old earth mother gives the three girls, the Hesperides, the gift of music, of female artistic creative power, divulging a secret that is so old she has even forgotten how to speak its name. Miss Eckhart's music, a gift from a mother to a daughter, symbolizes the regenerative and creative spirit of women. The threat of the sword, the fear of the violent entry of Heracles, Perseus, Theseus, Actaeon, or Mr.

Voight into the women's sphere creates a separation that distorts the simple act of human regeneration. In early versions of the myth, the goddess takes the hero into the world of the dead at the end of his reign, as in Britain where mythologists reveal that "each king who ruled Britain had to be chosen by the Triple Goddess, and later slain by her crone form, Morgan, lady of the blood-red pentacle and keeper of the Apple-Isle in the west."[15] In later accounts, the masculine hero actively intrudes on the female sphere to steal the symbols of fertility. The masculine and the feminine, the sperm and the egg, must connect. If the male sees the feminine as enemy—other, death—then he will have to conquer, attack, or rape this female in order to create what he now sees as his own regeneration. In one version Atlas asks Heracles to hold up the world while he goes to steal the golden apples (Graves, *The Greek Myths II* 146); whereas in another version the Hesperides themselves give away the golden apples. In the classical myth of the golden apples, Hera hires Ladon, the serpent and the brother of Echidne, to guard the golden apples, and Ladon coils himself among the trees to protect the apples. In "June Recital," Loch drops himself from the tree outside his window and looks down at the figs, which are both a Christian and pagan symbol of female sexuality. Like Ladon, Loch both protects through recording his observations and violates by peering at Miss Eckhart without her knowledge.

If we keep these myths in mind, we can imagine Miss Eckhart as an old goddess protecting the realm of women's art with her maypole, her summer solstice piano recitals, and her locked-up metronome. While Miss Eckhart is downstairs trying to burn down the house, Virgie is upstairs sleeping with the sailor. From Miss Eckhart's point of view, by sleeping with the sailor—giving away her virginity in a society that would never allow a fallen woman to amount to anything—in the same house in which she received the gift of music, the golden apples, Virgie is giving away her gift to the masculine hero, giving away that with which her teacher entrusted her, giving away the music that was "Für

Elise"—for Elizabeth, Miss Eckhart's first name. What Miss Eckhart does not understand is that Virgie is actually learning to accept her gift on a much deeper level. In sleeping with the sailor she is actually taking back her name, by defining "virgin" as a woman who takes control of her own sexuality rather than as a woman who is not sexual.

Whereas Cassie remembers Yeats's lines "the golden apples of the sun,/the silver apples of the moon," she does not try to unlock the secret fully by remembering all the associations of the golden apples. The dichotomy that the Yeats poem insists on between the golden apples of the sun and the silver apples of the moon is the exact duality that Welty seeks to overcome. The golden apples are of the sun and of the moon, of the connection between the masculine and the feminine, and of the way that this connection leads humans through the cycle of birth, life, death, and rebirth.[16]

In the second June recital, Miss Eckhart is the perfect teacher. There is no sign of the "face for music only"; now she cares about the girls' dresses and wants them to be starched and color-coordinated, the dresses in combination to make a perfect rainbow pattern (in effect replicating the rainbow design of Cassie's scarf), and she makes all of the mothers promise to sew the dresses and have them ready on time. She gives each girl a princess basket full of flowers. The whole event revolves around secrets: "The preparations went on for many hot, secret weeks—all of May. 'You're not to tell anyone what the program is to be,' Miss Eckhart warned at every lesson and rehearsal" (*CSEW*, 308–9). These are strange secrets, however, that always end with the same revelations, the same choices, and the same music; they are secrets that do not really matter to anyone. In this setting Miss Eckhart seems totally out of her element, like a "brown bear in a frill" (*CSEW*, 311).

All female Morgana attends this stifling event: "The night of the recital was always clear and hot; everyone came. The prospective audience turned out in full oppression" (*CSEW*, 311).

This recital—with its flowers, heat, and somber music—seems oddly like a funeral, and in important ways it is a funeral. The real secret is that June is the ritual time for the community in pagan societies to bid farewell to the old king, the sun god, who is moving west or dying as the days begin to shorten and the year approaches its end, and to rekindle the spirit of the new king. It is a ceremony of birth and death: "For the recital was, after all, a ceremony . . . [it] celebrated June" (*CSEW*, 311). The shadow of this ancient fertility ritual hangs over the recital. This is why everything must be done the same way every year. This is why only female Morgana must come.

Just as in the fertility ceremonies described by Frazer and Harrison, the first half of the recital is solemn, with flowers and military marches, and the second half breaks loose in celebration. Cassie plays a difficult piece called, appropriately anticipating the renewal of the sun in the spring, "The Rustle of Spring," but the real turning point occurs when Virgie plays a much more complex piece entitled "Fantasia on Beethoven's Ruins of Athens." Virgie appears wearing "a Christmas-red satin band in her hair with rosettes over the ears, held on by a new elastic across the back; she had a red sash drawn around under the arms of a starched white swiss dress. She was thirteen. She played the *Fantasia on Beethoven's Ruins of Athens*, and when she finished and got up and made her bow, the red of the sash was all over the front of her waist, she was wet and stained as if she had been stabbed in the heart, and a delirious and enviable sweat ran down from her forehead and cheeks and she licked it in with her tongue" (*CSEW*, 313). While Cassie only plays music about the changes in the earth, "The Rustle of Spring," Virgie plays music about the changes in cultural history. She plays specifically about the ruin of Athens, the place that holds the history of the triple goddess, the place in which people celebrated the Dionysian marriage of the king and the queen of the May, where male kinship was preceded by female kinship (Frazer, 179). Together Cassie and Virgie reclaim both the earthly, seasonal changes and the cultural, historical changes. As soon as Virgie finishes playing, everything breaks loose. Everyone hugs. Now when the MacLain twins run downstairs firing cap pistols, the noise of all the girls and the piano drown them out. The twins are ignored.

But there is something going on beneath this turmoil. Miss Eckhart is hiding a secret: "Her hair was as low on her forehead as Circe's, on the fourth-grade wall feeding her swine" (*CSEW*, 314). The fruit, the symbol of women's fertility throughout the story, has drowned in the women's punch cups and has brought about a change in Miss Eckhart. Miss Eckhart looks like Circe. In Welty's version of "Circe," a story in *The Bride of the Innisfallen*, Circe is not the evil witch who destroys the visiting sailors. It is the men who are cruel because they leave after living off her generosity for a year. Circe's plight in Welty's story is similar to the plight of Miss Eckhart. Miss Eckhart, who does not have the power to break through the restrictions of the outside world, gives her life to teaching these girls but, like Odysseus' men, they do not understand her. Once Circe gives her love to Odysseus, she is helpless before his demands and loses her magical powers. Once Miss Eckhart gives her love to Virgie, she is helpless before the Mr. Voights of the world and they can intrude into her space. Although it might seem strange to think of Virgie as an Odysseus, Virgie actually becomes the hero of Miss Eckhart's ritual. Virgie goes through a trial, the playing of the hardest piece, and she emerges triumphant but wounded and "bleeding."

If we remember that Virgie has just played "Fantasia on Beethoven's Ruins of Athens" we can assume that she has also been through the fall of women goddesses and has emerged renewed on the other side. However, Virgie is not actually the hero. Although Virgie's ordeal has given her a power that the other girls do not share, she has not been through a physical trial. The blood can be seen to represent the menstrual blood of the developing and maturing woman, a blood that challenges the heroic wounded blood of the hero. Hers is the blood of life, his the blood of death. His power comes in confronting death, hers in bringing forth life. Yet this rebirth, this entry into womanhood has not yet occurred. Virgie is playing a fantasia, and she looks only "as if" she had been stabbed. As with King MacLain, hers is a fantasy of death and renewal, not yet a physical regeneration. The feminine aspect in the collection will not fully eclipse the hero until Easter goes through an embodied death and resurrection in "Moon Lake."

Virgie's Christmas-red sash, connects the two events, Christmas and the summer solstice, linked together here, as they have been at least twice before—once when Loch sees that "the old woman was decorating the piano until it rayed out like a Christmas tree or a Maypole. Maypole ribbons of newspaper and tissue paper streamed and crossed each other" (*CSEW*, 283), and again when Cassie mentions that Miss Eckhart's playing, which takes place in June, is like a Christmas firework. The two times of year mark the pagan birth and death of the young fertility god and the sun. Like the Halloween celebration, the winter and summer solstices involve elaborate rituals and ceremonial fires to rekindle the power of the sun and to ward off evil spirits, particularly those of witches.

This fact makes Miss Eckhart's fire especially significant. Miss Eckhart sets up her fire as a maypole, and she wishes to burn it like a bonfire in the middle of the year at the summer solstice, thus combining both the resurrection of the female May goddess and the rekindling of the June sun god. At both the summer and winter solstices, people from many different cultures throughout Europe set large bonfires to rekindle the sun god as he made his way through the heavens. These fires were especially important during the summer solstice because the sun was beginning to wane and needed strength for the upcoming year (Frazer, 90–91). Because Miss Eckhart's recital is actually a celebration of the summer solstice, it is both a funeral and a birth. However, this recital and the fire that Miss Eckhart lights are not in celebration of the old male sun god; they are performed in honor of the new spirit of renewal and the female artists, Virgie Rainey and Miss

Eckhart herself. The spirits that Miss Eckhart wishes to burn out are not witches, but the people who have silenced her artistic passions. When Miss Eckhart plans the fire she stuffs the walls with the town paper, "The Bugle," which is edited by Cassie's father, Mr. Morrison. A bugle is also the hunter's horn used to announce the arrival of the male hero or hunter who will kill the witch, as in *Hansel and Gretel*, or who will kill an innocent animal. Loch, who plays the bugle in "Moon Lake," sees the mustached face of Mr. Drewsie Carmichael, his father's candidate for mayor in two places in the fire. Loch also thinks that Miss Eckhart would probably like his Octagon soap coupons. By burning these symbols of masculine domination, Miss Eckhart burns the old king and brings in energy for the new king or, we might say, queen.

This is at once a fertility fire and a fire of fury, anger, punishment, and retribution. When we realize that witches were burned at the stake for centuries and that Miss Eckhart is considered a witch, when we realize that Halloween fires and other fires were often burned to rid the towns of witches, then we can see the anger in Miss Eckhart's fire. Her fire smolders with the fires of Bertha in Brontë's *Jane Eyre*, of Eugenia in Virginia Woolf's *The Years*, of Sylvia in Marilyn Robinson's *Housekeeping*. Describing Miss Eckhart's fire, Loch comments, "Flames arrowed out so noiselessly. They ran down the streamers of paper, as double-quick as freshets from a loud gully-washer of rain. The room was criss-crossed with quick, dying yellow fire, there were pinwheels falling and fading from the ceiling" (*CSEW*, 317–18). In Loch's vision the fire—"flames"—and the storm—"a loud gully-washer of rain"—have come together, symbolizing both release and fertility, death and birth, movement and change that are not under his control. The pinwheels refers to the fact that, as Frazer writes, one of the main events in fertility rituals was the rolling of a burning wheel down the hill. The wheel of fortune was the wheel of life, and during the midsummer festivals, according to Frazer, the young boys would roll burning wheels down into the river to symbolize the rising and setting sun:

"Again the common practice of throwing fiery discs, sometimes expressly said to be shaped like suns, into the air at the festivals may well be a piece of imitative magic" (90–91). We know that Miss Eckhart's fire does not symbolize the sun but rather the fertility, passion, and creativity of female sexuality because she places a large magnolia blossom, the kind Virgie brought to her, in the center of her fire. Loch perceives that Miss Eckhart is like a bird jealously gathering scraps to build a nest, and like a bird she has laid her egg, this blossom, a symbol of sexuality and rebirth, in the center of her fire, her plot. This blossom is dangerous and potent and Loch believes it could blow up. By noting that Miss Eckhart has "owl eyes" (*CSEW*, 317), Loch unconsciously links Miss Eckhart to her ancient foremother, the goddess of wisdom, Athena.

At this moment the masculine world intrudes. The two men who represent the law, Old Man Moody and Fatty Bowles, wander over to the MacLain house and see smoke pouring out from it. In every aspect of their character, from their appearance to their names, they are ridiculous. They are earthbound, in fact covered with mud and grime from their fishing trip, their heels are muck-coated. They are the hunter/father in *Hansel and Gretel*, come to save the children, but there are no children to save, only a witch to attack. When they confront Miss Eckhart, whose name in German means "eck"—corner—and "hart"—pain or hard, they literally force her to back "into the blind corner" (*CSEW*, 318). Because she does not have air—that is, the strength and support of a community—she has nowhere to go. She cannot see past her own room. The two men act like slapstick stooges, leapfrogging and jumping about. Frazer writes that people once believed that if they or their livestock jumped over a fire they would increase fertility (Frazer, 746). For the first time we see men reduced to this level—needing to increase their fertility and their virility by putting out this old woman's fire. But the imbalance is so severe from the start that Miss Eckhart does not really have a chance. She has no social power to protect herself from their intrusion; her fire will not burn. These two idiot men, hardly heroes, put out the fire simply by jumping around on it.

Loch keeps imagining that the metronome is a bomb that will explode. There is definitely something that should blow up and in a way has blown up, but it is not a danger to the two men. It is Miss Eckhart's lost dreams and thwarted ambitions: "What happens to a dream deferred . . . does it dry up like a raisin in the sun .. or does it explode?" (Langston Hughes, "Harlem"). When Loch, after the turmoil is over, with the "quarter moon" "high in the sky," asks Louella, "Reckon it's going to blow up in the night?," we are not sure if he is referring to the moon or the metronome, the one representing Miss Eckhart's artistic dreams, the other her social power. In this line the two merge. When the man in the golden panama hat arrives (Loch identifies him as Mr. Voight and Miss Eckhart identifies him as King MacLain) he laughs at the two buffoons and at the fire, which he says they pretended "was bigger than it had ever been" (*CSEW*, 320). Mr. Voight/MacLain does not even see the fire, particularly the fire in Miss Eckhart's head. He kills off Miss Eckhart's artistic spirit without even a pretence of conflict. When Miss Eckhart does not speak, these men taunt "cat's got her tongue" (*CSEW*, 320). In actuality, a cat does have her tongue. The cat, the witch's medium—or her power, her spiritual essence—holds her tongue, and keeps her from being able to tell them what they are doing to her. What Miss Eckhart cannot do is move between the spiritual artistic realm—the world of the waterfall, the witches, and the cat—and the social realm, the world of the metronome and piano lessons. She is either completely divorced from social reality in the depths of an ancient power or completely immersed in the social world as teacher. She either serves punch at her military recital for all of female Morgana or plays brilliantly in the eye of the storm. She cannot use language to bridge the two worlds and so cannot speak the fury of centuries to the very enemies who have denied her the power to speak.

As the man Miss Eckhart thinks is Mr. MacLain, steps into the house and begins rummaging among the ashes, he picks up "a seashell. The old lady advanced on him and he put it back, and as he came up he took off his hat. It looked more than polite. There close to the old lady's face he cocked his head, but she looked through him, a long way through Mr. MacLain. She could have been a lady on an opposite cliff, far away, out of eye range and earshot, but about to fall" (*CSEW*, 321). The moment the masculine presence, in this case Mr. MacLain (the more powerful version of Mr. Voight), actually intrudes on Miss Eckhart, she fights back. He does not intrude by entering the studio, the house of confinement that she wants to burn down, but instead he violates her when he picks up the seashell, the ancient symbol of women's power, of Venus/Aphrodite born of the sea. For Miss Eckhart, the house of feminine artistic creation has moved outside, to the land of the mountain and the waterfall, back to the ancient sources of women's creativity before the hero myth. At this point Miss Eckhart is on the cliff and about to fall—the kind of fall that will bring renewal, the kind of fall that the heroic narrative claims for its own. She does not feel threatened until this part of her world is exposed. When the men taunt her with "cat's got her tongue," they are talking to a person who is very far off, living only in the world of the waterfall. In this sphere she has no language.

However, when they reach for the metronome, Miss Eckhart moves temporarily into the social realm as she holds "her possession to her, drawn to her big gray breast. Her eyesight returned from far to close by. Then she stood looking at the three people fixedly, as if she showed them her insides, her live heart. And then a little whir of her own voice: 'See . . . See, Mr. MacLain'" (*CSEW*, 322). In this scene the figures of King MacLain and Mr. Voight merge in Loch's mind. They are both salesmen who travel all over, who come and go as they please. They are both sexually intrusive. Mr. Voight is merely a grubbier version of MacLain, a reduced version, but MacLain is the real symbol of masculine intrusion into the female sphere for Miss Eckhart. In the social world she is not a passing planet eclipsing King. He becomes the symbol of masculine dominance, someone to whom she wants to show her material, social self, her metronome heart. For a moment Welty brings the two worlds together, Miss Eckhart's sight from far to close up. The metronome comes to symbolize more than the dictates of time and becomes the visible and thus tangible symbol of both her artistic dreams and her role as a teacher. It is her power and it is her heart. For one moment she desperately wants these men to see this solid object, the ticking that has taken over where the fire stopped: "The fire had had a hard time, but fire could manage to connect itself with an everlasting little mechanism that could pound like that, right along, right in the room" (*CSEW*, 321). Holding her life in her hands (her pain in her hands), Miss Eckhart, broken, torn from her mythic and artistic past, merely asks the hero to open his eyes and "see. . . .see." She asks him to see her life, her heart, her selfhood, her existence, and his answer is, "I never saw her in my life" (*CSEW*, 322).

At this denial of her existence, Miss Eckhart grabs the candle and tries to light the fire again but this time the fire ignites her own hair. In *The Golden Bough*, Frazer connects burnt hair directly with punishment of witches: "Here in Europe it used to be that the maleficent powers of witches and wizards resided in their hair, and that nothing could make any impression on the miscreant so long as they kept their hair on. . . . Women suspected of sorcery have to undergo the same ordeal: if found guilty the same punishment is awarded, and after being shaved, their hair is attached to a tree in some public place" (789). Walker writes, "A comet was supposed to be a tendril of the Great Mother's hair, appearing in the sky as the world was slowly overshadowed by her twilight shadow of doomsday. Most forms of the Death-goddess showed masses of hair standing out from her head, sometimes in the shape of serpents, as in the Gorgonieum of Medusa-Metis-Neith-Anath-Athene" (*Woman's*

Encyclopedia, 367–371). In a final insult the men throw an old dishcloth over "the fire in her head." Miss Eckhart is defeated and they can lead her off to a mental institution. It is a scene of resignation and despair, but at the same time Miss Eckhart's regenerative power lives on in Loch's and Cassie's narration.

Loch's desire to have the metronome blow up shows that, although he is still disconnected from the actual problem, he does (unconsciously perhaps) recognize the existence of an unnamed power. Cassie, however, when she sees Miss Eckhart's white vulnerable ankles, finally understands and lets out a cry. She watches the men carry Miss Eckhart off with "some nameless kitchen rag" on her head. The kitchen rag becomes a sackcloth forcing her into her penitent place as housewife. Cassie sees Miss Eckhart but she cannot do anything to save her. Cassie cries "'You can't take her! Miss Eckhart!' She was too late for anybody to hear her, of course. . . . She turned, with her head still swimming high in the air, and cried softly, 'Oh, Mother!'" (*CSEW*, 324). Cassie cries, for her own mother who is not there to save Miss Eckhart, for Miss Eckhart as her mother, for the lost mother of ancient mythology. When Virgie leaves the house she passes Miss Eckhart without seeing her. Virgie saves Miss Eckhart by surviving the fire and by walking on, by becoming the resurrected version of Miss Eckhart after her fall. She is the symbol of fertility; in front of the whole town, the sailor, the masculine consort, appears with his clothes half off, and the queen Virgie walks by all the women "as if her mother didn't have enough on her, just burying her son" (*CSEW*, 326). Virgie defies the world and becomes the hero in the face of her brother's death. The male dies in battle while the female moves defiantly into the world of sex and fertility. Cassie cannot save Miss Eckhart because her head is "still swimming high in the air." After the men take Miss Eckhart away, Loch tries to steal the metronome, but Cassie fights with him for it; he wins. The masculine hero still controls the social world of plots and battles. He still controls time. When

Cassie's father returns home, her mother says to him, "'Cassie says King MacLain was here and gone. That's as interesting as twenty fires'" (*CSEW*, 327). Welty writes: "Cassie shivered." Cassie shivers because King's comings and goings are still more interesting than Miss Eckhart's fire. What Cassie fears is that Miss Eckhart's final creative act and the full horror of what was done to her will go untold for lack of an audience. Miss Eckhart's pain, her story, are not as interesting as King's appearances and disappearances. The hero still holds dominion over the world of the imagination.

As Cassie lies awake at night, she thinks over the events of the day, and the characters begin to move together in her mind. She lies thinking in her "moonlit bed" and she is at one with the earth and the constellations. Her arms still smell of hay from the hayride as she thinks of Moon Lake. Cassie not only reduces the hero/sailor to a "mer-man"—half man, half fish, the species usually associated with the feminine,—but she recognizes the distance that Miss Eckhart and Virgie have traveled, a long journey that the sailor is only starting. No one can touch Miss Eckhart or Virgie because they have passed through social convention. They are deliberately terrible. That night as Cassie fell asleep, "into her head flowed the whole of the poem she had found in that book. It ran perfectly through her head, vanishing as it went, one line yielding to the next, like a torch race. All of it passed through her head, through her body. She slept, but sat up in bed once and said aloud, '*Because a fire was in my head*.' Then she fell back unresisting. She did not see except in dreams that a face looked in; that it was the grave, unappeased, and radiant face, once more and always, the face that was in the poem" (*CSEW*, 330). This time as Cassie listens to the Yeats poem, she lets it flow through her. The words of the male poet served to bring her to this level of understanding, but this poem, vanishing as it went, passes through her body and makes room for other memories that will appease the radiant, as yet unappeased face.

This is the face that was always hidden in the teacher, Miss Eckhart. It is the face of the muse in masculine poetry. It is the face of artistic creation in femin/ine/est literature. Through poetic language Cassie realizes that the fire in the house is the fire in Miss Eckhart's head, a fire that only a poet, a fellow artist, could understand.

4

And into Each Fell
a Girl

Rape and Female Resurrection in "Sir Rabbit" and "Moon Lake"

Kate Chopin's *The Awakening* upset the sensibilities of reviewers and critics so profoundly that they banned the book, calling it "vulgar" and "poisonous" (145–53). Perhaps more dangerous to the critics than the explicit adultery was the unbounded female sexuality. Edna Pontellier, who knows her lover Robert would soon "melt out of her existence," feels desire, not for the missing phallus, but for the sea, "seductive, never ceasing, whispering, clamoring, murmuring," (Chopin, 113). In the middle three stories of *The Golden Apples*, "Sir Rabbit," "Moon Lake," and "The Whole World Knows," Welty explores female sexuality within and without the constraint of masculine violence. She creates a representational universe that exposes and deflates the heroic rape narrative by setting it within the intertextual symbology of female desire. In all three stories we hear the seductive whisperings and murmurings of female erotic passion emerging in a code of metaphors and textual references.

In "The Laugh of the Medusa," Hélène Cixous claims that "except for a few rare exceptions there has not yet been any writing that inscribes femininity" (248), writing which she defines as "working (in) the in-between, . . . undoing the work of death . . . the ensemble of the one and the other, not fixed in sequences of struggle and expulsion or some other form of death but infinitely dynamized by an incessant process of exchange from one subject to another. A process of different subjects knowing one another and beginning one another anew only from the living boundaries of the other" (254). In this passage Cixous both prescribes what feminine writing could be and describes what she sees as the fixed sequences—rape, murder, incest, genocide, marriage—that have dominated phallocentric narratives. By the beginning of the twentieth century in American literature, female sexuality as feared enemy in a binary opposition has been raped, murdered, sodomized, dismembered, trivialized, made "into one" so often that the male hero with no adversary, with no horrible monster left to kill, must rape and murder the already murdered and raped female other. The act of necrophilia is a central phenomenon in Faulkner's *Light in August*, Wright's *Native Son*, and Mailer's *An American Dream*. The creation of one-dimensional women characters is a fixed sequence in Hemingway's *For Whom the Bell Tolls* and *The Sun Also Rises*. There is no process of exchange, of knowing, no encounters, no transformations between genders. Female is only a dim projection of a tired and deadly male fantasy.

Although Cixous and other feminist theoreticians reject phallocentric discourse in order to rediscover "la jouissance," to invent "l'écríture feminine," in their rejection of patriarchal discourse, they neglect the female subject. Alice Jardine notes, "Because in the past women have always written as men, Cixous hardly ever alludes to women writers" (62). The assumption that women have always written as men is the fallacy/phallusy that can be perpetuated because we have not yet created a language capable of responding to an emerging female inscription, and without this language we can too easily see or invent a patriarchal narrative where a complex narrative of gender transformation is emerging—Cixous's "beginning one another anew at the living boundaries of the other." Jardine contends that "Those writing modernity as 'a crisis-in-narrative,' and thus in legitimation, are exploring newly contoured fictional spaces, hypothetical and un-measurable, spaces freely coded as feminine. Gynesis, designat-ing the process of internalizing these feminine spaces while ac-counting for those crises, is either static or dynamic depending upon the narrative in which it is embedded" (69). The crisis in narrative, or the modernist terror at the rupture of the heroic narrative, is brought on neither by the appearance of the female as the abstraction "feminine" nor by the seemingly deterministic biological identification of her as body—both potentially dead and deadly classifications—but by the resurrection of female(s) as erotic, dynamized sexualities, living bodies, bodies that are aroused, arousing, uncontrollable. Jardine's so-called crisis is not a disaster but an emergence born out of the emergency of the erotic as endangered species. It is only a crisis to the heroic discourse that cannot invite female(s) to wander freely. In fact, as the erotic female(s) appear not dead, the author committed to the heroic discourse that depends on female subservience must find new ways to kill her. I agree with Jardine, however, that when female(s) emerge in a narrative of female becoming, they gain the dynamic quality that this birth demands. Theoretically, narra-tives of female emergence can be written by anyone, male or fe-male; however, female authors appear to write narratives of female erotic resurrection much more frequently than their male counter-parts. In fact it is a rare document in which the male writer allows the female subject to explore her sexuality and erotic energy unchecked. Of course, in making these kinds of distinctions, we are assuming that there is something we can call female erotic identity, an identity in flux but an identity nonetheless.

Jardine characterizes the difference between the French and American ways of thinking as "the conflict between woman as process and woman as sexual identity" (41). When Jardine wrote this statement American feminism was actively engaged in the task of reconstruction, of reclaiming and remembering buried female textual and subject bodies. Since that time, African

American, Jewish, Chicano, lesbian, and other theorists have called the identities "woman" and "female" the creation of white middle-class Protestant women. The recent work of Diana Fuss, Giyatri Spivack, and Judith Butler on essentialism has reminded us that there can be no eternal or original essence of woman. Fuss, however, allows for the possibility that political strategy requires a simultaneous engagement and disengagement with female as identity. She writes, "For Irigaray the solution is again double: women are engaged in the process of both constructing and deconstructing their identities, their essences, simultaneously" (70). She concludes: "Essentially speaking," we need both to theorize essentialist spaces from which to speak and, simultaneously, to deconstruct these spaces to keep them from solidifying. Such a double gesture involves once again the responsibility to historicize, to examine each deployment of essence, each appeal to experience, each claim to identity in the complicated contextual frame in which it is made" (118).

Such a political strategy is also necessary when we discuss artistic or imaginative creations. We can assume the sign "woman writer" and the character sign "female," recognizing that she/it must be contextualized, historicized, and even emptied if necessary as she is brought into being. Complexity and difference demand the dissolution of the sign woman even while political necessity demands that we encourage her incarnation. Welty engages in just such a project throughout *The Golden Apples*. In "The Wanderers," Welty defines Fuss's double gesture in more literary terms: "Virgie never saw it differently, never doubted that all the opposites on earth were close together, love close to hate, living to dying; but of them all, hope and despair were the closest blood—unrecognizable one from the other sometimes, making moments double upon themselves, and in the doubling double again, amending but never taking back" (*CSEW*, 452–53). By amending, changing, adding, but never rejecting—"taking back"—Welty enables her female characters to be in process, extending beyond sexual identity but never fully leaving the experiential body behind.

This historization precludes the French metaphorization of female into process or gynesis. In fact, Welty's project simultaneously allows the woman character free play through metaphorization and empowers her through incarnation. This is to say that both acts must occur simultaneously, a double gesture. Although American feminist critics have traditionally recovered the female subject from male aggression and demanded a place for her in history, Cixous and Irigaray teach us that when we leave this place in history, what they would call a patriarchal house, we find a living body; they speak openly of "caressing the breasts, touching the vulva, opening the lips, gently stroking the posterior wall of the vagina, lightly massaging the cervix etc" (Irigaray, "Ce sexe qui n'en est pas un," 103). The freeing of the female from history should not be confused with the freeing of the female critic from the task of recovering the female subject or from releasing the female author from her text. For it is the female subject who can leave us the fullness of this imaginative journey, the inscription of her sexuality, the history of its emergence and incarnation, and the narrative of her disengagement from this historical identity.

Addressing the London National Society for Women's Service on 21 January, 1931, Virginia Woolf stated, "Telling the truth about my own experiences as a body, I do not think I solved. I doubt that any woman has solved it yet" ("Professions for Women," 61–62). However, immediately after stating this fact, Woolf tells a narrative of the sexual-creative emergence of a woman writer who let

> her imagination sweep unchecked round every rock and cranny of the world that lies submerged in the depths of our unconscious being. . . . Her imagination had rushed away. It had sought the pools, the depths, the dark places where the largest fish slumber. And then there was a smash. There was an explosion. There was foam and confusion. The imagination had dashed itself against something hard. The girl roused from her dream. She was indeed in a state of the most acute and difficult distress. To speak without figure she had thought of something, something about the body, about the

passions which it was unfitting for her as a woman to say. Men, her reason told her, would be shocked . . . . She could write no more. The trance was over. Her imagination could work no longer. (61–62)

There is a subtext in this passage, a possible clue to understanding emerging female creativity. When the girl's imagination hits "something hard," there is a crash, an explosion, foam and confusion. Although the result is damaging—"she could write no more"—the event is dynamic, alive, a meeting on the living boundaries, a real experience that awakens her from a "dream" or "trance." In this passage women's creativity moves in and out of "consciousness" as it faces obstacles and dangers. This portrayal of the female artist directly confronts the masculinist image of the artist as a solitary bard peacefully isolated in his study or turret. Creativity for the woman writer might entail simultaneous emergence and emergency, an emergence/y.

In the anthology *Pleasure and Danger: Exploring Female Sexuality*, Carole Vance clarifies this dynamic emergence/y as the tension between the "dangers" versus the "pleasures" of sexuality.[1] She realizes that "The horrific effects of gender inequality may include not only brute violence, but the internalized control of women's impulses, poisoning desire at its very root with self-doubt and anxiety"(Pleasure and Danger," 4). This far more insidious danger is at the heart of Woolf's words—she could write no more. Without the impulse, without the passion, without what Vance calls the infantile and non-rational, without human connection and sensuality, without the felt experience, there is no writing, and ultimately there is no life. Vance also reminds us that some feminists have not seen sexuality as a political topic, that "to talk of it betrays bad manners and bad politics on the part of sexual betters toward the deprived, who reportedly are only interested in issues that are concrete, material, and life-saving, as if sexuality were not all of these. The result is that sexual pleasure in whatever form has become a great guilty secret among feminists" (7). If we replace the word sexual with artistic or creative, we realize a striking similarity between the two oppressions. The imagination, that erotic moment of becoming, has been seen by many as politically insignificant, when in reality the most dangerous act for any group is to cease imagining themselves. Gloria Anzaldua emphasizes that the spirit of the words "moving in the body is as concrete as flesh and as palpable; the hunger to create is as substantial as fingers and hands" ("Tlilli, Tlapalli," 71). This is the basis of the erotic language that Welty discovers and resuscitates in the three stories that comprise the middle section of *The Golden Apples*. In these three stories Welty, honoring the erotic movement of words through her textual body, writes into being the possibility of a new female narrative that does not accept the inevitability of rape.

According to the conventional rape narrative, the young princess or ingenue is in danger because a cruel man or beast wants to capture her and take her precious virginity. Either the would-be rapist turns into a good guy or a knight in shining armor saves the princess, and marries her. If this savior does not arrive, the princess succumbs to the assault and usually dies. The princess has no agency in this situation. Gayle Rubin's essay "The Traffic in Women" reminds us that this is merely an exchange in a masculine economy not an act of salvation for the female character; whether she is being raped or married off, she is controlled. To write a narrative in which the male character cannot gain control over the female through either rape or marriage is to destabilize, to create free play in this economic structure.

Welty confronts the rape narrative most directly in "Sir Rabbit," "Moon Lake," and "The Whole World Knows." These three stories alter, and recreate the literary representation of female eroticism so that the rape narrative is no longer deadly to emerging female sexuality/creativity. Welty actually takes the reincarnated female body that she has saved in "Shower of Gold" and leads her back into a carefully reconstituted gender battle.

In the first of the three stories, "Sir Rabbit," Welty seems to treat rape as a mythic, dreamlike, inescapable, part of the natural order, the domain of gods and rabbits, but there is a subversive subtext. By including the children's rhyme "Sir Rabbit," Welty suggests that to save Mattie from the constraints of the heroic rape narrative of Yeat's "Leda and the Swan," she must recreate her in the innocence of childhood. She must find a new language for her that will begin as myth, metaphor, and dream and become more incarnate in "Moon Lake," and "The Whole World Knows." Against the setting of this seemingly all-pervasive male sexuality, Mattie Will begins to define an emerging sense of self.

The Greek myth of Leda and the swan narrates a rape; Zeus appears to Leda in the form of a swan and rapes her. She has no power to resist him. The question Yeats asks in his version of the myth is interesting: "Did she put on his knowledge with his power / Before the indifferent beak could let her drop?" ("Leda and the Swan," *Selected Poems*, 121). Yeats asks this question because Leda might have taken on the knowledge that she will engender Greek civilization, that she will be the mother of Helen of Troy, the twins Castor and Pollux, and Clytemnestra. Both Clytemnestra and Helen, like Morrigana, are powerful women who are able to control the fate of men. Mattie, the poor-white-trash-nobody in her intertextual identity as Leda, represents the mother of Greek civilization. These connections allow us to recognize that, in her sexual encounters with the MacLain twins and with King, she is not simply a powerless victim. Although she might seem to be a child, she is potentially a queen or goddess. Her name, Mattie Will Sojourner, indicates that she has her own will and that she is a traveler, on a sojourn.

In the first sentences of "Sir Rabbit," Mattie Will remembers that, when she was a young girl, she felt as if "somewhere a little boat was going out on a lake, never to come back—to see two little meanies coming now that she'd never dreamed of, instead of the one that would have terrified her for the rest of her days" (*CSEW*, 331). The MacLain twins approach "like a pony pair that could keep time to music in the Ringling Brothers', touching shoulders until the last" (*CSEW*, 332). In the symbology of *The Golden Apples* a little boat going out on a lake is synonymous with a girl growing into womanhood, experiencing herself as a sexual being, losing her virginity. (Welty uses this image several times in "Moon Lake.") Mattie's tumbling on the wet spring ground with the MacLain twins is neither rape nor lovemaking, but both and neither simultaneously. The multiplicity of meanings allows Mattie to escape the constraints of the heroic narrative. In this way Welty amends without taking back. Rolling around on the wet spring grass, she is like a child or an animal—the wet spring grass suggests renewal, not a violation that will terrify her the rest of her days. The twins are young and like animals, (ponylike in comparison to Zeus's swan) and when they approach her, they take her off guard, tease her, make her dizzy, causing her to believe she was going to be carried off by King MacLain. They pin her to the ground, but unlike Leda, who in Yeats's poem is described as "helpless" and "staggering" (*Selected Poems*, 121), Mattie insists that "they were all in this together, all in here equally now, where it had been quiet as moonrise to her, and now while one black crow after another beat his wings across a turned-over field no distance at all beyond" (*CSEW*, 332).

Before the twins arrived it had been quiet as moonrise. In Welty's fictional universe quiet is not necessarily good. Quiet would mean the end of Mattie's newfound storytelling abilities. As in "Shower of Gold," the story arises from the crossroads, the dynamic meeting at the boundaries of the one and the other, of male and female. The all-female quiet is disturbed by the young twins who, like the young male fertility gods, represent both death and renewal, the fertility of the recently turned-over field— the old seed and the new. The crows could come and violate the field by eating the seed, keeping it from growing, but they are a distance away. There is time for the meeting of seed and earth before the crows come. The swan in Yeats's poem with its great wings beating, an overpowering symbol of masculine prowess, becomes the carrion crow, the symbol of death and weakness, a scavenger.

The crows are not on top of Mattie as Yeats's swan is on top of Leda but beyond her, a distance that indicates that the shadow of the Leda myth falls on Welty's narrative, but it is separate, amended; it does not overwhelm. In "Moon Lake," the MacLain twins, older now, become the carrion crows, the ones lurking in the woods outside the girls' camp at Moon Lake.

In "Sir Rabbit" the twins disturb Mattie into finding her voice. Her emergency is not terribly serious but it does evoke an emergence. Trying to tell this story, to think this story, to figure out "who had the least sense . . . for fifteen" makes Mattie realize that "Junior Holifield would have given her a licking for, just for making such a story up, supposing, after she married Junior, she had put anything in words. Or he would have said he'd lick her for it if she told it *again*. Poor Junior!" (*CSEW*, 333). Mattie's announcement that she would get in as much trouble for telling the story as for tumbling with the twins, merges the act and the telling, joining sexuality and voice. In order to recover the voice that she lost in her marriage, Mattie must recover her sexuality and confront the one that would have terrified her. Unlike Leda, Mattie has been approached by two ponies, not by a swan so strong that Yeats must ask the question, "How can those terrifed vague fingers push / The feathered glory from her loosening thighs?" (*Selected Poems*, 121). Mattie has not been terrified, but in order to move into the realm of verbal and linguistic fertility, to be able to speak whether Junior Holifield wants her to or not, Mattie must meet or at least imagine she has met and, like Katie Rainey, seen King MacLain—eye to eye, I to I.

As focalizer Mattie tells us that, when she and Junior Holifield are out hunting in the woods, King MacLain, looking like a combination of the sun and the swan in his "yellowy Panama hat and a white linen suit" (*CSEW*, 337), peers out from behind a tree. This is the first time in *The Golden Apples* that Welty describes a character catching a glimpse (whether in her dreams or not) of the elusive King MacLain. In this scene King has Mattie in the same way that he has had—slept with, raped, made love to, had sex with, copulated with, procreated with—so many other women, but this time, while Junior Holifield sleeps, "he clasped her to his shoulder, and her tongue tasted sweet starch for the last time. Her arms dropped back to the mossiness, and she was Mr. MacLain's Doom, or Mr. MacLain's Weakness, like the rest, and neither Mrs. Junior Holifield nor Mattie Will Sojourner; now she was something she had always heard of. She did not stir" (*CSEW*, 338). For the first time we hear the female telling the story of her "rape" at the moment it occurs, forcing us to question whether, if she is fully conscious and articulating what is happening to her, if she is the imaginative impulse behind the story, we can call this representation rape. For the representation of rape to emulate rape, it must take away the authorial and vocal power of the victim. If the focalizer is the one defining her own loss of identity, can she really have lost identity? Beyond the names "Mr. MacLain's Doom" and "Mrs. Junior Holifield" is the unnamed "something she had always heard of" (*CSEW*, 338). In Mattie Will's telling of her story, the conventional rape narrative has been disturbed. Unlike Leda, Mattie is not a helpless victim, not "mastered by the brute blood of the air"(*Selected Poems*, 121). She is both subject and object, both artist and artifice, both author and text—and thus is Cixous's "two," not identifiably either.

In this context Welty cannot, nor would she want to, write an embodied description of rape. Only the phrases "he clasped her to his shoulder" and "her arms dropped" imply embodiment, and even in these phrases we hear the mention of very few body parts, certainly nothing sexual. As the author/text Mattie portrays MacLain's life not as a romantic adventure but as doom and weakness. We only understand what King does to women on an abstract level. Because he is a myth or a legend, he gives them something that as literary representations of femininity they are all supposed to want: to be swept up by the gallant knight, to be wanted by the king. At the same time he is the evil rake who ravishes them and takes away their identity. There should be a hero lurking in the woods to save Mattie, but Welty inverts this narrative in two ways. Junior Holifield does not fit the bill of the savior, and Mattie does not seem to need or want saving. Although she says that she has become Mr. MacLain's, Mr. MacLain has also becomes hers—her terror, her dream, her wish, her nightmare, her love, her knight, her vision, her subject, her voice, her story. Mattie Will Sojourner might lose her identity, but for a moment she is conscious of the loss. Her loss of self would signal the end of the text, but it does not end. Instead she repositions herself outside the traditional roles of victim, lover, and wife in a way that Snowdie, Katie, Cassie, and Miss Eckhart never do. Her subjective voicing allows her to achieve this repositioning.

Although she has to suffer under Junior Holifield's bumbling threats and King's aggression, something happens to Mattie Will out here in the woods that could not happen to a woman confined in the subject position of wife and mother. She not only sees King, as Katie wished she could, she sees him sleeping. In Mattie's crossing over into masculine space, we watch her change from one subject position to another, quite literally as she goes down on hands and knees to contemplate him. As she watches, "her hair fell over her eyes and she steadily blew a part in it; her head went back and forth appearing to say 'No.' Of course she was not denying a thing in this world, but now had time to look at anything she pleased and study it" (*CSEW*, 339). As she blows a part in the hair that falls over her face, she divides herself vertically, while she is shaking her head horizontally. With these two actions she literally crosses herself, not in a religious sense but in the sense of crossing over, of being able to occupy all points on the axis. By altering her physical position, Mattie Will takes on the knowledge of the mythical subject position that King inhabits. Mattie has taken on his knowledge with his power. Mattie Will is not saying "no" to anything in this world, but she is saying "no" to something in another world. If King can sleep and she can contemplate him, then she can say "no" to the

MacLain twins. She can say "no" to Junior Holifield. She can even say "no" to King MacLain. She can say "no" to rape. The fact that her head goes back and forth means that, unlike the Medusa, she has a head and that this head is attached to her body and with this head she can study anything she pleases.

By taking up the spectator position, inhabiting the space of the conventionally masculine gaze, looking at and studying King MacLain in a way that Katie Rainey never could, Mattie realizes his vulnerability and consequently his potential fertility.

> With her almost motherly sway of the head and arms to help her, she gazed at the sounding-off, sleeping head, and the neck like a little porch column in town, at the one hand, the other hand, the bent leg and the straight, all those parts looking no more driven than her man's now, or of any more use than a heap of cane thrown up by the mill and left in the pit to dry. But they were, and would be. He snored as if all the frogs of spring were inside him—but to him an old song. Or to him little balls, little bells for the light air, that rose up and sank between his two hands, never to be let fall. (*CSEW*, 339–40)

Through Mattie's connection to motherhood, to the physical ability to give birth, and to the spiritual mother of the earth, Welty gives Mattie power to look at King. What Mattie Will sees is a myth, a construction, made up of parts that can be deconstructed. His neck is a little porch column—echoing back to the Hermes, the phalli of the ancient fertility rites, and to the fallen porch columns of the southern plantation—yet his neck is small, insignificant. He is diminutive, vulnerable, not a dangerous adversary. In this vulnerability lies her sexual connection to him, for he is no more or less than a heap of cane thrown up by the mill and, as cane, a potential fertility consort. This heap of cane is dead but Mattie knows he will not stay that way.

Mattie knows that, although MacLain looks as if he is of no use, he will be of use again, he will be resurrected. He is both full of frogs, a symbol of fertility and the advent of spring, and an old song, and he is juggling the little balls or bells, the golden apples, not letting them fall. He is both the fertility god and the strong Atlas holding up the world. As he sits under the tree, a whiter-than-white letter drops from his pocket. In this tabula rasa, we find the possibility latent within the sleeping body of King MacLain. The story of the hero is no more fixed than anyone else's story. He could do or become anything. Welty has taken the mythical, romanticized giant and made him human by letting Mattie see him asleep, in parts, instead of in an irrefutable, predefined whole. As a vulnerable heap of cane, a scattering of little lights, King does not take up all the mythical space. Mattie's vision, the female vision in the story, improves.

Unlike Snowdie, Mattie does not have to strain her eyes to see: "Down an arch, some old cedar lane up here, Mattie Will could look away into the big West. She could see the drift of it all, the stretched land below the little hills, and the Big Black, clear to MacLain's Courthouse, almost, the Stark place plain and the fields, and their farm, everybody's house above trees, the MacLains'—the white floating peak—and even Blackstone's granny's cabin, where there had been a murder one time. And Morgana all in rays, like a giant sunflower in the dust of Saturday" (*CSEW*, 340). As Mattie Will's vision improves, her perception opens up and she sees both the white floating peak and Blackstone's grandmother's cabin. She can see the lives of males and females, blacks and whites, young and old. She can see life and death. With her eyes free to see, she spreads before us Morgana, a point with rays stroking out. In this more expanded vision she can confine the MacLain twins to those "two gawky boys. . . . They were soft and jumpy! That day, with their brown, bright eyes popping and blinking, and their little aching Adam's apples—they were like young deer, or even remoter creatures . . . kangaroos. . . . For the first time Mattie Will thought they were mysterious and sweet—gamboling now she knew not where" (*CSEW*, 340–41). Mattie returns the twins to

the natural world as deer but more remotely as kangaroos because the Western imagination does not have as specific a symbolic or mythic association with kangaroos. Welty leaves the
reader with a riddle but no answers, with our expectations
thwarted. When Mattie thinks of King MacLain, she thinks of
the rhyme

> *In the night time,*
> *At the right time,*
>> *So I've understood,*
>>> *'Tis the habit of Sir Rabbit*
>>> *To dance in the wood—* (CSEW, 340)

King MacLain as Sir Rabbit is a far less omnipotent image
then King MacLain as Zeus or even as a king. Welty's description
of the rape in this story is still played out on the level of metaphor. In "Sir Rabbit" King MacLain is just a rabbit proliferating
the species at an alarming rate. In "Moon Lake" and "The Whole
World Knows" the male character appears more embodied, less
mythical, and therefore more ominous.

In "Moon Lake," the pivotal story in *The Golden Apples*, Welty
challenges our critical vocabularies more directly than in "Sir
Rabbit" by confronting the violence of female sexual emergence/y. In this story the orphan Easter literally falls into (rather
than metaphorically floats out on) a lake and is rescued by the
young Boy Scout Loch. Several critics have read this lifesaving as
a rape. In "The Case of the Dangling Signifier: Phallic Imagery
in Eudora Welty's 'Moon Lake,'" Patricia Yeager argues, "Rescued as Easter is from the masculine lake by the masculine 'Loch'
Welty suggests that Easter must become the patriarchy's first
victim. It is as if she has traveled too far into masculine territory
and must learn 'feminine' passivity through the violence of ritual
rape. This 'rape,' which is also a life saving, defines Easter's rite
of passage from an active, androgynous life to the stunted and
conventional life defined by masculine hierarchy" (Yeager, 438).

Although Yeager's argument is ostensibly feminist, by privi

leging a set of phallic signs to the exclusion of a set of what we could call clitoral signs, Yeager performs on Easter and on the text a clitoridectomy, or a silencing of the signs/sights that signify women's pleasure and defiance. She insists on a univocal victimization reading of a text whose metaphors and images call out for a multivocal reading—a recognition of the dance between phallic and clitoral symbols. In such a reading phallic and clitoral become acts of power and pleasure that any male or female character may perform, rather than states of being that define and circumscribe character development.

In "Golden Apples and Silver Apples," Julia L. Demmin and Daniel Curley emphasize that, when writing about *The Golden Apples* it is "much more difficult to elucidate that aspect of the book relating to female magical power, for that power is not expressed in the form of clearly developed myths but in symbols, familiar enough but still mysterious . . . it is with 'Moon Lake,' the middle story, that the power of Zeus wanes and the symbols of female power begin to come into prominence" (134–36). Although it may be difficult to elucidate the aspects of *The Golden Apples* that are related to female magical power, it is far from impossible, and it is crucial to undertake this task if we are to undertand the complex subject of women's voice in literature—an emergence/y based not on capitulation to some nebulous original structure called "patriarchal power" but on entry into the ambiguous openings in the echoing caves of phallic discourse. By imposing expectations of violent patriarchal domination on this text, Yeager misses the subtle unfolding of Welty's vision.

If we accept the dualistic Freudian reduction of sexual signs from a multitude of sites of pleasure to only the phallus and vagina and the accompanying narrative that this reduction demands—a masculine oblong shaped object (a gun, pole, key) that fits into a feminine empty space (a cave, hole, sanctuary)—we have neglected the metaphoric resonance and power of the clitoris, the organ of female stimulation and excitement that makes a joke of this simple story. The clitoris has nothing to do with the economy of masculine power or the economy of female reproduction. It is neither the dominant phallus nor the receptive vagina. It is related only to the experience of pleasure, and as such it occupies both the space of the phallus and the vagina and no space at all. It crosses boundaries and questions the duality. Robert Scholes, in "Uncoding Mama: The Female Body as Text," reminds us of the problem with this simple duality: "this part, which does not fit into the neat binary scheme, is what Freud called (in his essay on fetishism) 'the real little penis of the woman, the clitoris'" (*Semiotics and Interpretation*, 128). Although Scholes and Freud seem to have trouble naming the clitoris without reference to masculinity, the "problem" with the clitoris is not that it looks like a little penis but that it is independent of the economy of reproduction and masculine desire. It has nothing to do with them.

I do not present clitoral as a binary symbolic opposition to phallic but as the symbol that makes the binary opposition between phallic and vaginal impossible. I also do not present clitoral to essentialize female anatomy as determinant of female creativity but to awaken the sites of pleasure in all bodies, an awakening that questions phallic narratives and thereby questions essentialist thinking. By acknowledging that clitoral imagery in women's writing may be a historic response to the monolithic raping phallus, a move from one to not one as Irigaray proposes, we begin to see the waning of the masculine power to dominate. In recognizing what Judith Butler calls, in *Gender Trouble*, the performative repetitive nature of the phallic narrative, we can begin to see the vulnerability and ultimately the death of the narrative of masculine sexual dominance. Uncovering the dualistic symbolic structure on which the phallus depends, Welty creates an intertextual weaving of female and male symbology in which the metaphoric challenges and interacts with the literal, and the oral (embodied) challenges and interacts with the literary. (C)lit/oral response to texts recognizes the interplay between oral and literary, between the voice and the womb: the voicing of pleasure and the reproduction of culture. When read with an eye to the (c)lit/oral, the textured narrative of "Moon Lake" becomes an exciting and terrifying story of female empowerment, not a tale of female passivity. This reading can begin to correct the kind of textual clitoridectomy that Scholes describes and yet perpetuates.

It is not my desire to argue point by point with Yeager's essay; in fact I think her work is an important contribution to Welty studies. Instead I would like to set my interpretation beside hers to show how a detailed analysis of allusion, metaphor, and symbol allows different narratives to emerge. Yeager's article marks a historical moment in feminist literary criticism when critics recognized the threat of violence and domination in the representation of the phallus. Anger at the monolithic rape and silencing that this symbol represented may have led us to overlook the possibility of a subversive engagement with the phallus, the phallus as space to be occupied as well as thrust to be received.

The representation of the clitoris cannot be easily reduced because the very nature of clitoral eroticism is diffusion—a blurring of boundaries. However, when we see a symbol that seems to invade clear distinctions and to assume phallic as well as vaginal space, appearing to emanate from a point but radiate beyond this point, then we most likely have clitoral imagery. Perhaps the most suggestive literary representation of the clitoral symbol comes from Woolf's creation of the "point with rays stroking out"—a point that melts and diffuses beyond any distinct boundaries, like Cassie's tie-dyed scarf.

"Moon Lake," more than any of the other stories in *The Golden Apples*, relies heavily on Frazer's *The Golden Bough*, particularly those sections entitled "King of the Wood" and "The Seclusion of Girls at Puberty."[2] Frazer's text, based as it is on classical myths and oral narratives, is a lit/oral text, and echoes of it occur throughout Welty's collection of interrelated short stories that she suggestively names *The Golden Apples*. In the first pages of *The Golden Bough* Frazer sets his work in "the little woodland lake of

Nemi-'Diana's Mirror,' as it was called by the ancients. This is the sacred sanctuary of Diana Nemorensis, the ancient goddess of the moon and of the wood" (1). Just as Frazer depicts the lake at Nemi as three miles from the town of Acricia, Welty writes that Moon Lake is three miles from Morgana. The mythological and literary references open up the possibility that Moon Lake is at once the sanctuary watched over by the goddess of the moon and the site of elaborate male fertility rites, of the battle between the old year and new year, the old fertility god and the new, the old king and the new.

Frazer writes of a certain tree in the sacred grove "round which at any time of day, and probably far into the night a grim figure might be seen to prowl. In his hand he carried a drawn sword, and he kept peering warily about him as if at every instant he expected to be set upon by an enemy. He was a priest and a murderer and the man for whom he looked was sooner or later to murder him and hold the priesthood in his stead" (1). Frazer's description of the grim figure mirrors Welty's description of Loch Morrison. The grim Loch stands by a certain tree, and although he does not carry a sword, he does carry a bugle: "he stood against a tree with his arms folded. . . . Sometimes he would take aim and from his right cheek shoot an imaginary gun at something far out, where they never were" (*CSEW*, 342). Frazer tells the story of the dying of the old king, the old sun, the old man; his ritual murder by the young king; and the return or resurrection of the old king's symbolic son, the new sun, the new year. Through this ritual drama, originally dedicated to Diana or to the ruling queen, the male consort eventually takes over permanently, reigning as king over the female queen. It is important that Loch is a teenager, not a boy, in this story because the emergence of woman's regenerative sexual power would have no meaning if the only male in the story were too young to be sexual. In order for the story to progress, the girls must not be threatened by a masculine sexuality of exploitation and rape. Instead they can experience masculine sexuality in a potent, but not deadly, form. The big boys with their phallic guns, like the crows in "Sir Rabbit," stay on the edge of the woods and wait for the camp to end; for the moment, the girls can develop. They do not need to be protected or hidden. With the male voice muted but still present, the female power can come into its own. Both the male and the females in this story are virgins.

But "Moon Lake" is not a story about female oppression or even victimization. It is a story about transformation, and Loch is as affected by the girls as they are by him. He does not want to be at this camp, but "he had been roped into this by his mother" (*CSEW*, 342). The seven-day ordeal was her idea. By insisting that Loch go off to this girls' camp, Mrs. Morrison is attempting to undo God's creation of an omnipotent Adam and to remake the world into one in which Adam and Eve, neither more powerful than the other, can listen to each other. The story is about the creation of something new, something that takes seven days and seven nights, something that is a mother's idea. As we are introduced to Loch we are also introduced to symbols of an emerging female fertility and sexuality. He blows his horn into a scene that includes trees "weighted with dew" and "smelling like big wet flowers" and minnows "trembling and running wizardlike," not yet turned into frogs, waiting to mature much like the girls (*CSEW*, 343). But they are also wizardlike, implying suppressed magical power. The trees are weighted with dew, and smell like big wet flowers, a clitoral image that evokes a pervasive surfacing female sexuality against which Loch's horn seems small and insignificant but potentially fertile.

In this story the hero's sword/phallus, which had turned first into a telescope in "June Recital," now turns into a bugle in "Moon Lake." The bugle is at once a weapon and an artistic instrument. Although at reveille Loch harangues the woods, when the sun is going down, "he played taps for them, invisibly then, and so beautifully they wept together, whole tentfuls some nights" (*CSEW*, 343). The newly awakened woman character can embrace a boy's trumpet much more readily than a man's sword.

Although the male hunters will inhabit the lake after the girls leave, the Boy Scout lives in an all female world. There is time for change and the possibility of connection. In the shadow of the moon, of the goddess Diana, in this place where girls are reaching maturity, change can occur, subtly at first, but growing in symbolic significance to the point at which Easter's experience answers the Miss Eckharts of women's history, the unappeased face in Cassie's vision.

Welty joins Frazer in his project of revealing the pagan roots of Christianity, but she goes further by replacing the male god-king with a female goddess or queen. Initially Loch has the power to save lives, and the girls can barely swim, but by the end of the story the girls have resurrected their power. The concept of the male as "Life Saver" (*CSEW*, 343) parallels the Christian belief in Christ as the savior of mankind. Using the story of Christ's resurrection as proof, Christianity claims for the male the power not only over the physical reality of birth but over the language that can describe this reality. The biblical narratives that depict Christ's birth and resurrection are based on the assumption that a man can be born without a sexual mother and reborn from God the Father. This is a fragile artifice, but it has provided a powerful symbol of autonomous artistic resurrection for the male artist. On some level every artist must die to the vision of her work, as Welty writes in *One Writer's Beginnings*. To give the female character the power to die and return, the power of the artist, Welty rewrites the biblical story of Christ's resurrection with a female savior. Welty begins "Moon Lake" with the sentence, "From the beginning his martyred presence seriously affected them" (*CSEW*, 342). If we read "from the beginning" as "from the beginning of time" and "his" as the symbolic male lifesaver or Christ figure, then we can understand how his presence has seriously affected them, meaning all the girls at Moon Lake as they move into womanhood. His martyred presence, Loch's and Christ's, circumscribes who the female can be and what she can achieve.

Easter, like all of the other orphans, has been sent to Moon Lake by the men's Bible class. The men's Bible class could be seen to represent the soul of Christ, the male priest. Although the men think they are keeping Easter out of trouble, they are actually sending her into battle. From the beginning Easter fights for her position as the next in line for fertile power. If Loch is looking for his murderer, the one who will take over his role, he will find this person in the female world; the only person powerful enough to meet Loch is Easter. "Mr. Nesbitt, from the Bible Class, took Easter by the wrist and turned her around to him and looked just as hard at her front. She had started her breasts. What Easter did was to bite his right hand, his collection hand. It was wonderful to have with them someone dangerous but not, so far, or provenly, bad" (*CSEW*, 347).

Not only do we begin to see a return of female power in this scene, but, unlike Mattie in "Sir Rabbit," the power is not metaphorical but incarnate. Easter's breasts have started to develop, and she quite literally bites Mr. Nesbitt's hand. This is a direct body to body confrontation, not a mythic or symbolic encounter. For the other girls, it is wonderful to have Easter, someone dangerous, because she will refuse to be victimized or controlled by the lascivious male gaze. By biting Mr. Nesbitt's hand Easter lets him and all the girls know that she owns her body; by connecting the female body to the word through physical action, she takes away from the male gaze the power to define what becoming a woman, growing breasts, will mean. Mr. Nesbitt might want to collect from her, but what she will give him is a direct corporeal rejection of his authority.

For the moment, however, the girls, not yet reborn into their adult sexuality, are still constrained by symbols of masculinity. When they go in the lake they sing a song to Mr. Dip, which is, as Yeager points out, masculine and, I might add, ominous. The girls are afraid of creepy crawling things, water snakes and alligators, the unknown, the invisible, the unexpected, and the danger of getting sucked under; most of all they are afraid of dying. As long as they are afraid to die, as long as the natural world is an invisible enemy, then the girls will remain protected from life in the superficial feminine sphere of bathing caps, bathing slippers, and scheduled dips, the protected world of Prenshaw's mothers. They will never be artists.

On one of the very few occasions that Easter talks before her fall, she tells Nina and Jinny: "I haven't got no father. I never had, he ran away. I've got a mother. When I could walk, then my mother took me by the hand and turned me in, and I remember it. I'm going to be a singer" (*CSEW*, 358). With these words Easter answers Mrs. Morrison from "June Recital" directly. She does not speak in the past tense as a victim—"I could have sung"—but instead states very clearly, "I'm going to be a singer." Being a singer means expressing oneself in the oldest form of poetic language, combining sound, movement, and meaning. The bard of any community sings the history and stories of that community. Easter is going to be a singer specifically because she remembers her mother. She has the power and dominance derived from having no father, from not thinking of herself as determined and ruled by the patriarchal past in the way that Cassie, Virgie, or even, as we find out later, Nina does. The first step toward remembering, reclaiming a spiritual artistic past for women, is to rebel against the father. The second most important step is to remember one's mother.

In the beginning of "Moon Lake" the girls are afraid of the water and the sun, both ancient symbols of male sexuality. In "The Seclusion of Girls at Puberty," Frazer is amazed that the two "rules—not to touch the ground and not to see the sun—are observed either separately or conjointly by girls at puberty in many parts of the world" (690). He uses as an example, interestingly enough, "The old Greek story of Danaë, who was confined by her father in a subterranean chamber or a brazen tower, but impregnated by Zeus, who reached her in the shape of a shower of gold."[3] The girls at Moon Lake wear sandals when they wade in the river, and they are not allowed to swim in the noonday sun. The Boy Scout/lifesaver Loch Morrison can swim anytime. Not only are the campers reliving ancient restrictions on girls entering womanhood, they are also returning to Nemi, the site of their lost power. As Easter refuses the male interpretation and co-optation of her womanhood, she returns to a sacred female space to discover a new set of signs, and Nina takes on the role of the female reader who can describe these new signs.

Easter leads the girls to a spring that resembles the spring of Egeria, the goddess of childbirth in the grove of Diana. Here she can drink water directly from the spring with no cup. Easter, who unlike the other orphans, has hair not the yellow of corn silk but "a withstanding gold," who has around the back of her neck "a dark band on her skin like the mark a gold bracelet leaves on the arm"(*CSEW*, 347) begins to sound like a goddess or a queen. The gold ring signifies both the collar of captivity and the gold neck brace of a queen. The fact that this ring is pure dirt implies that the queen can move beyond captivity to fertility. The girls recognize her power and "liked to walk behind her and see her back, which seemed spectacular from crested gold head to hard, tough heel" (*CSEW*, 347). The Achilles heel is vulnerable to the deadly stroke of the enemy, but this warrior going into battle has a hard, tough heel. Nina goes on to speculate that "Easter's eyes could have come from Greece or Rome that day. Jinny Love stopped short of apprehending this, and only took care to watch herself when Easter pitched the knife. The color in Easter's eyes could have been found somewhere, away—away, under lost leaves—strange as the painted color of the ants. Instead of round black holes in the center of her eyes, there might have been women's heads, ancient" (*CSEW*, 347–48).

By comparing what Jinny sees and what Nina sees, Welty warns us not to miss the ancient female signs. Like Jinny, we might only see the phallic; we might only watch the potentially dangerous knife and miss the message buried in Easter's eyes. Easter's vision and perception come not only from the moment but from Greece or Rome, from the time of Diana and Venus.

Nina sees in Easter's eyes the old signs, a color that has been lost, something buried under leaves, ancient women's heads, like heads on coins, symbols of dead women, of spiritual women from the past. In this moment of recovery, Nina collects the coins or currency that Easter withholds from Mr. Nesbitt. Nina, through apprehending, makes the exchange a female to female sexual exchange. If we remember the association of the eye with the clitoris in interpretations of the Medusa myth, the nature of this exchange becomes even more apparent. Nina can recover these riches, this treasure, because she can read Easter's eyes. She can perceive something emerging that has no specific name. Nina, as the reader, must trust in speculation. Easter's eyes "could have been" or "might have been;" there are no prefabricated songs to Mr. Dip in this realm. She has no script to read, only eyes.

When the girls walk down to the spring, Welty fills the scene with icons that directly connect them to Frazer's girls secluded at puberty. Easter has a knife with which she plays a boy's game called mumblety-peg. Frazer mentions that at puberty a Hindu maiden "is armed against evil spirits by a knife, which is placed on the mat or carried on her person" (697). Nina has a special drinking cup of her own. Frazer writes that the Guayquiries of the Orinoco believe that a girl at puberty "drinks only out of a special vessel, because any person who should afterwards drink out of the same vessel would infallibly pine away and die" (701). As the girls huddle in the sand to play mumblety-peg, the "vivid, hurrying ants were everywhere. To the squinted eye they looked like angry, orange ponies as they rode the pine needles" (*CSEW*, 347). Frazer writes, "Other Indians of Guiana, after keeping the girl in her hammock at the top of the hut for a month, expose her to certain large ants whose bite is very painful" (697). All of the material objects that Frazer mentions are present in this scene— the knife, the cup, and even the ants. The fact that Nina will not let anyone else use her cup suggests that the girls know that these objects are powerful as relics of their captivity and as the key to their freedom. The fact that between them they possess both the traditionally feminine cup and the traditionally masculine knife indicates that they must have both the phallus and the clitoris in order to become women, in order to develop into sexually power-ful women.

During the noonday nap Easter lies "shell-like" and gives a "belated, dreaming sound," a sound of "wholehearted and fateful concurrence with the thing dreamed . . . . Easter's sighs and her prolonged or half-uttered words now filled the tent, just as the heat filled it. Her words fell in threes, Nina observed, like the mourning-dove's call in the woods" (*CSEW*, 350). Aphro-dite/Venus was born from a shell[4] and her totem or sacred bird was the dove, the bird of sexual passion.[5] The words falling in threes echo the triple goddess of birth, life, and death. The heat that fills the tent as the girls take their noon nap, like Easter's sighs, is full of sexual excitement. Jinny Love and Nina lay in each other's arms and make faces at Easter's "unintelligible words" (*CSEW*, 350). In this noonday space the girls experience a shift in perspective. They stare through the "tent opening as down a long telescope turned on an incandescent star," and they see "the spiral of Elberta's hat return" and "Exum jump over a stick and on the other side do a little dance in a puff of dust" (*CSEW*, 350). In the telescope the white girls see the brilliant white of the sun and the black people together in one sphere. Unlike Loch, who owns the telescope as he owns perception and language, the girls are inside the telescope, part of this phallic power, able to see through it.

This change in perception is evident as the girls meta-phorically and literally wake up from their naps. For the first time they begin to rebel against the restrictions placed on them. First Easter and then Jinny and Nina refuse to take the dip and instead go on a walk through the swamp. In contrast to the sterile song and ritual to Mr. Dip, Easter, Nina, and Jinny's journey takes them through a symbolically fertile landscape. Here, where everything is alive, moving, and visible, the girls are not

afraid as they are in the lake. They are surrounded by a proliferation of imagery, a confluence of symbols:

> Sweet bay and cypress and sweetgum and live oak and swamp
> maple closing tight made the wall dense, and yet there was some-
> where still for the other wall of vine; it gathered itself on the ground
> and stacked and tilted itself in the trees; and like a table in the tree
> the mistletoe hung up there black in the zenith. Buzzards floated
> from one side of the swamp to the other, as if choice existed for
> them—raggedly crossing the sky and shadowing the track, and
> shouldering one another on the solitary limb of a moon-white syc-
> amore. Closer to the ear than lips could begin words came the
> swamp sounds—closer to the ear and nearer to the dreaming mind.
> (*CSEW*, 352)

The mistletoe, which turns golden in the fall, is Frazer's gold-
en bough, the weapon that fells the hero god Balder. The mistletoe represents the bolt of the thundergod, and it topples the
old king, the oak itself. The Norse god Balder is slain by a
branch of mistletoe and burned in a great fire. In Welty's description the mistletoe is black and the buzzards circle, like the crows
in "Sir Rabbit." The old pagan and Christian stories of male
regeneration, murder, and resurrection are dead and a new story
is being born. Out of the swamp come sounds "closer to the ear
than lips could begin words," still unarticulated sounds, sounds
that follow the death of the one mythology, the one story, and
signal the regeneration out of this mythic landscape of other
stories born on the moon-white sycamore, not the oak of Frazer's
fertility god. Following the three girls—the number three signifying both the magical three and the triple goddess—is the cat,
the medium of the witch. The cat is alive, stalking and leading
Easter along the black edge of the ditch. By looking at the cat,
the girls break another one of the rules for the seclusion of girls at
puberty: "Woe betide her if she catches sight of a crow or a cat!"
(Frazer, 697). In this reference, we see that Mattie's observance of
the crows was subversive. She was breaking away from the rules

that had constrained her. As she walks through the swamp, Nina notices that Easter's dress is stained green, indicating that Easter, in direct opposition to the rules for girls at puberty, has touched a tree or plant (Frazer, 697). This green is no longer Cassie's fairy green but the organic green of rebirth. Easter also eats blackberries, the picking of which is forbidden to girls at puberty. Her lips stained with blackberry juice and her dress stained green, she becomes part of the woods, a blooming tree herself. In *The Golden Bough* the blooming tree is a pregnant woman.[6] Nina and Jinny put their arms around Easter's waist, and to Nina, Easter (like Snowdie) seems "like a sleeping baby" (*CSEW*, 353). In her defiance of the old patriarchal rules, Easter is pregnant with both a new female self and a baby, a new female character. "The swamp was now all-enveloping, dark and at the same time vivid, alarming—it was like being inside the chest of something that breathed and might turn over" (*CSEW*, 354). The "something" in this passage is both a mother's womb, the terrifying netherland that the male hero has tried to escape for so long, now represented as the source of life, and a chest, the origin of breath, voice, and singing. The girls enter the womb and the lungs to give birth to their voice. The chest will turn over as it awakens.

In a clearing in the swamp, Easter and Nina see snakes and, most mysterious of all, an old gray boat. Easter, who cannot swim, gets in the boat immediately and lies back in it like a queen or a young hero sailing down the river. In Greek, Roman, Celtic, and Egyptian mythology, boats carry the soul of the young hero/god across the river of the dead. The hero takes a journey across the river of death; in fact he escapes death in the boat. By sitting in the boat, Easter claims herself worthy of the same treatment as the hero, but this boat, unlike other boats in this collection, is chained to the shore; it is not ready to float across the lake, as the girls are not ready to enter puberty. As Nina surveys the scene she flutters her eyelids like Easter and almost becomes Easter, while "the world looked struck by moonlight" (*CSEW*, 354). In this clearing in the sand the moon appears stronger than the sun.

In the battle of symbols the male and female are still dichot-
omized; however, Nina looks at the tabula rasa of the sand and
sees it "full of minute shells, some shaped exactly like bugles"
(*CSEW*, 354). This is the first time in the story that we find shells
(the source of power for the goddess Aphrodite or Venus, the
love goddess and the only goddess born from the sea) (Graves,
The Greek Myths I, 50) linked with bugles, which until this point
in the story have been associated only with the masculine. For a
moment the two images—the masculine bugle and the feminine
shell—combine in this diminutive vision, suggesting the possibility of an equality and even a union between the two spheres.
Jinny Love, who gets stuck trying to get to this place of union,
does not understand the significance of the sanctuary. Although
she says she sees an owl, sacred to the goddess Athena, she
thinks the place smells like peepee and old erasers; she does not
see its spiritual significance. In some ways she is right; this is a
place of peepee and old erasers. While it is the scene of women's
deepest mysteries, it is also the scene of rape, defilement, and
silence—old "erasures." Yet it is in this sanctuary of women's
mystery, women's love, Diana's sacred Nemi, that the girls will
learn to know themselves and their own sexuality.

While Jinny Love builds a sand castle, Nina writes her own
name over and over again in the sand. "Her own hand was writing in the sand. Nina, Nina, Nina. Writing, she could dream
that her self might get away from her—that here in this faraway
place she could tell her self, by name, to go or to stay" (*CSEW*,
355). As if making the connection between writing and sexual
freedom, Nina suddenly demands, "Why aren't we out in the
boat?" When she looks at the boat "a picture in her mind . . .
showed the boat floating where she pointed, far out in Moon
Lake with three girls sitting in the three spaces" (*CSEW*, 355).
The girls inhabit their bodies again by opening themselves to the
old lost, forgotten earth, the old muddy boat that Nina straddles
before it takes them on their journey. Nina no longer wears shoes
to protect her feet and she sees the mud only as some awful kiss,
not something deadly. The sun has burned Easter's legs but not

killed or raped her—the symbolic sun of the Danaë myth has become the actual sun, the manifest sun. She is moving beyond the stage of the dip, beyond wearing sandals in the water for fear of what she might find. The awakening woman character is not trying to escape the earth but to become one with it, to make love to it, to walk inside the breathing space. Nina lets the water and mud lace her feet. The body of the earth and the bodies of the girls together define the abstraction we know as sexuality rather than the abstraction defining the body. The girls are able to live in the symbolically patriarchal landscape of suns and lakes rather than being secluded from it, and their habitation transforms its engendered significance.

As Nina tries to free the boat, "again she thought of a pear . . . with snow-white flesh so juicy and tender that to eat one baptized the whole face, and so delicate that while you urgently ate the first half, the second half was already beginning to turn brown. . . . She even went through the rhyme, 'Pear tree by the garden gate, How much longer must I wait?'—thinking it was the pears that asked it, not the picker" (*CSEW*, 355–56). The woman as creator feels herself baptized, not by the blood of Christ, the abstraction of the male body, but by the fruit of the earth and by a fruit whose description symbolizes the wet fertility of a woman's clitoris. One of the ways in which Christ proves his power to his disciples is by making a fig tree wither.[7] He reveals that he has control over the forces of life and death by killing the pregnant fruit. In Nina's vision she is the fruit itself, as she is also the one who longs for the fruit. This is clearly a vision of female sexuality, written by a woman for another woman, told by a woman, Nina, while thinking about herself and Easter. Through this celebration, this deeply passionate and urgent erotic evocation, Nina reclaims the voice of the silenced other. The pears themselves will ask the tree, their own mother, their own lover, their own source: "How much longer must we wait?"

Nina looks at Easter and thinks that her head looks like a pear.

Seeing in another girl the fertile possibility of the ripe pear and the source of her love, Nina confirms her own sexuality, experiencing her confluence with the earth and the other woman simultaneously, and also confirming her own erotic connection to women. When Nina writes "Nina" and then "Easter" in the sand, Easter's hand wipes out both Nina's and Easter's names; she takes the stick as did Lavinia in Shakespeare's *Titus Andronicus* (Act 4, Sc.1, ll. 77–80), and rather than writing the names of those who raped and tortured her as Lavinia does, she writes the word "Esther" in the sand. Nina says:

> "Why, I call that 'Esther.'"
> "Call it 'Esther' if you want to, I call it 'Easter.'"
> "Well, sit down. . . ."
> "And I named myself."
> "How could you? Who let you?"
> "I let myself name myself."
> "Easter, I believe you," said Nina.
> "But I just want you to spell it right, Look —E-A-S—"
> "I should worry, I should cry." (*CSEW*, 357)

At Easter, Christ is resurrected and returns to God the Father, leaving Mary, the Mother, on earth. Easter names herself after this resurrection but she is of woman born, remembers her mother and does not know her father. Easter is the lost female child whom the Christian myth omitted. She knows that her name is not written, not included in the story of Christ's resurrection. In the written record Easter's closest spiritual ancestor, the woman whose power she embodies, the woman whose name she can write because it is part of the written record, is Queen Esther in the Old Testament, the strong woman who had no mother and no father, the woman who saved the Jewish people from destruction by tricking the king, her husband, as Easter tricked Mr. Nesbitt.[8] Easter/Esther's spelling reveals the woman's story, a story not in the New Testament.

Nina has justified Easter's strange name in her mind by assuming that Easter was left at the orphanage on Easter. She never imagined that Easter could have named herself. When Nina hears the real story—that Easter has no father, that she spells her name Esther, that she remembers being turned in, that she wants to be a singer—Nina bangs Jinny "on the head with her fist. How good and hot her hair was! Like hot glass. She broke the castle from her tender foot. She wondered if Jinny Love's head would break. Not at all. You couldn't learn anything through the head" (*CSEW*, 358). When Nina actually hits Jinny physically, when she looks at Easter and sees her as beautiful, she feels temptation and she says, "Even after all this is over, Easter, I'll always remember you" (*CSEW*, 358). Never will the woman's love for another woman, never will Esther, the fatherless queen, be forgotten. Nina has become the artist and has let Easter into her imaginative universe. By speaking and contradicting Nina's story, Easter has created a physical remembering in Nina that will last longer and make Easter more real than spelling her name correctly in the sand ever could. No one can learn by demanding to know; no one can learn anything through the head, through correct spelling. Nina learns through her body and her heart. She must protect Easter's name with her own body.

Because of their new awareness of themselves, because they are able to name each other and their sexuality, these three girls can return to camp and put Loch Morrison in his place. All three girls can hear in Loch's trumpeting "a fairy sound" and they can also hear the equally powerful silence—not a cry of anguish but a silence: "Nina could see the boy in the distance, too, and the golden horn tilted up. A few minutes back her gaze had fled the present and this scene; now she put the horn blower into his visionary place" (*CSEW*, 358). Jinny can tell him to shut up as they turn to the cat that, having caught something in its mouth, "didn't look especially triumphant; just through with it" (*CSEW*, 359). Nina, Easter, and Jinny as representatives of the old female power of the triple goddess, of the three in one, are not especially triumphant—they have not yet floated out onto the lake—but they are through with Loch's vaunting. Having caught their own power in their mouths, having named themselves, they are ready to tell him to be quiet and let the fairy sound live.

After this journey through the swamp, the girls have more power. At one of the camp fires by the spring, they sing a song called "Little Sir Echo," reversing the roles of Narcissus and Echo so that the woman speaks while the male turns into the diminutive echo. As they return through the woods at night, "nobody needed light. The night sky was pale as a green grape, transparent like grape flesh over each tree. Every girl saw moths—the beautiful ones like ladies, with long legs that were wings—and the little ones, mere bits of bark" (*CSEW*, 359). Every girl, not just Nina or Jinny Love, becomes an artist, seeing, in place of the dueling butterflies and mosquitoes, moths that look like ladies with wings. In the night Sister Spights sees a spider. The symbols of female fertility—the grape—and of female creativity—the spider—merge and out of them come clouds of fireflies that have no symbolic connection to either masculine or feminine. The girls enter a mysterious, magical realm between symbol and incarnation for which they do not yet have words. In the free, fluttering shape of the moth in search of the light, they reclaim the voice of the poet.

After experiencing this vision, Nina thinks again of the boat, giving it more symbolic significance. When Nina can understand that the helper's boats (which was "niggers" in the first edition) might be full of silver fish, she begins to experience the magic. In the first edition, by placing the black people out on the boat in this spiritual and powerful position, Welty reveals that she sees black people as poets. Old Plez recognizes what Snowdie and Katie do not recognize. Twosie perceives what Jinny, Nina, and Easter do not perceive. Nina knows that, since each poet will see a different part of the constellation, it is only in seeing through all eyes that we can encompass the whole. In this scene Nina recognizes confluence, movement, the turning of the world, the boat drifting, the water, and the sky and the moon turning so that the conventional world, the world of oppression and constraints, of prejudice that evokes words like "nigger," drifts forgotten. Nina brings the "niggers" into the world of the poet. They become dreamers like any poet. All people are poets, catching silver fish, as the "dreamed-about changed places with the dreamer" (*CSEW*, 360). Ironically by changing the word to "helpers" Welty weakens her political commentary.

As the girls go to bed, Miss Moody's candle lighting evokes a religious ritual. Even in the false act of putting on mosquito repellent we find an anointing like Christ's anointing. The girls are going through an initiation into a new world, the beautiful moon-filled world of the lake, magical and strong, but also the world of the black mistletoe, the real drama of life—birth and death and rebirth. The false world of Miss Moody's rouge and eyebrow tweezers, of mosquito repellent, represents the fiction of the feminine and lies side by side with a bottle of a compound made of "true and false unicorn" and "the life root plant" (*CSEW*, 360) just as the owl and the old erasers lie side by side in Jinny's mind. Nothing can be excluded in this alchemical mixing.

As the girls go to sleep, Jinny Love cries "into her pillow for her mother, or perhaps for the figs" (*CSEW*, 361). The link that we have suspected between figs, pears, grapes—any fruit for that matter—and the fertility of women appears again and brings back into focus the connection between Christ's destruction of the fig tree and the New Testament's devaluation of motherhood. In this passage Jinny Love cries "for" her mother; the preposition indicates that she cries not just because she misses her mother. She is crying for mothers, for the figs, for what has happened to them, for their fall, for those who want to pick them, for their vulnerability. She is crying because she understands for once what her mother's life has not been. The fact that Miss Moody sings the song "Forgive Me" which has the last line *"Do anything but don't say goodbye!"* (*CSEW*, 360), reminds us of Miss Eckhart's question, "Can daughters forgive mothers?" Miss Moody sings this song while rubbing sweet dreams on the little girls' backs. If the daughters wake up to a sense of their own power, they must say goodbye to their mothers; they might forgive them, but they will not have sweet dreams. They will wake up. The fireflies light the way. If the daughters move beyond the world of their mothers, they will leave the old ways of doing things, the protection of their mothers' mosquito repellent and salve. Protection means unconsciousness, taking the moon for granted. "Just outside their tent, Citronella burned in a saucer in the weeds—Citronella, like a girl's name" (*CSEW*, 361). Citronella, a fragrant grass, sounds like Cinderella. The myth of Cinderella is dying, burning in the weeds, while Miss Eckhart's fire, the fire in her head, the fire of artistic inspiration, has taken flight in the symbol of the fireflies.

In this moment between waking and sleeping, Nina realizes, "There were secret ways. She thought, Time's really short, I've been only thinking like the others. It's only interesting, only worthy, to try for the fiercest secrets. To slip into them all—to change. To change for a moment into Gertrude, into Mrs. Gruenwald, into Twosie—into a boy. To *have been* an orphan" (*CSEW*, 361). Having reached this epiphany, Nina becomes the artist as relational self—the woman artist—rather than the self-conscious "I" of the hero. This is the stance that Cassie takes when she becomes Mr. Voight. Nina realizes that she could be a boy. She could be an orphan. She could be anybody, and if she could be anybody then no one can overpower or victimize her. As Nina lies in her tent she sees that the "pondering night stood rude at the tent door, the opening fold would let it stoop in—it, him—he had risen up inside. Long-armed, or long-winged, he stood in the center there where the pole went up. Nina lay back, drawn quietly from him. But the night knew about Easter. All about her" (*CSEW*, 361). Easter's body lies, hand outstretched asleep, opening itself to the night, which is "it," no, male "he." Even though male, the night is not threatening but a giant, a dark thing, able to be graceful and obedient, not to attack Danaë as

Zeus does, or Snowdie as King does, or Miss Eckhart as Mr. Voight does, or Leda as Zeus does, or Mattie as King does. The night kneels at Easter's side. He appears, like an angel, a cherub, or a god, longed armed/ or long winged, like Hermes or Cupid, but less personified, less embodied. He is the pole, the phallus in the middle of the tent, and everywhere. As they were in the telescope, in the chest of the creature, Nina and Easter are in the night. In this reversal the masculine sun becomes the traditionally feminine night. Nina knows that the night is partial. Easter, whose hand sleeps, receives, but Nina, whose hand lies awake, does not. The two girls, the conscious and unconscious, mirror each other, learning to accept a difficult secret, a secret that Nina's watchful eye can see and articulate, but that Easter's unconscious hand can receive. Seeing the night in all its vastness, Nina gets a good look at life, the kind of look that Katie got without the danger, without the label of male sexual aggression; there is no fear in Nina's experience. Nina offers her open palm to the loving night, which in this image creates "a single ecstasy, a single longing" (*CSEW*, 362). The pole—unlike a sword, gun, telescope, knife, or pocketknife—is both a phallus and a point with rays stroking out, mirroring Nina's hand. Welty realizes through Nina that, if the woman/character/artist/subject expects to face Cuchulain, Narcissus, MacLain, Voight, and Loch, she must not only reduce the mythic power of the male hero but temporarily become the male hero; she must not only find him (as Katie Rainey does), or ask him to see her (as Miss Eckhart does), or look at him in his sleep (as Mattie Will does), she must face him in his full power, meet him in the dark. She must try to know the fiercest secrets, actually go through the process of death and rebirth, of falling, becoming completely immersed in the lake and emerging, like the moths and butterflies, renewed.

In part five of *Moon Lake*, Welty rewrites the Christian Easter resurrection so that Easter, a woman, dies and comes back to life. Welty spells Easter's name correctly, not by simply writing it in the sand but by incarnating her name in the experience of Easter.

Easter's rebirth is not a dip, not a silly song honoring the spirit of renewal, but a complete fall, total immersion, and return. When the girls are out taking their dip, Easter sits on the diving board "high above the others" (*CSEW*, 362–63), while Exum, the black boy "was apart too, boy and colored to boot" (*CSEW*, 362). Welty first describes him as monkeylike, but expands this stereotypical description by filling out the picture. Exum, who is wearing a man's straw hat that is "brilliant as a snowflake," is like "a fisherman's cork," "persistent as a little bug," who can catch anything, who will offer Loch an electric eel as a gift, who is "too everything-he-was to count as anything" (*CSEW*, 362).

In *The Golden Bough*, Frazer comments, "Within the sanctuary at Nemi grew a certain tree of which no branch might be broken. Only a runaway slave was allowed to break off, if he could, one of its boughs. Success in the attempt entitled him to fight the priest in single combat, and if he slew him he reigned in his stead with the title of king of the wood" (3). Frazer also mentions that in parts of eastern Europe there was a festival in which the village drowned or dipped a puppet or an actor in a lake or stream to ensure fertility and to help women give birth.[9] As the tree of health and renewal, the willow tree was intricately connected to these ceremonies. Perhaps more significantly, it is also, as Robert Graves points out in *The White Goddess*, a tree associated with poetic inspiration: "A famous Greek picture by Polygnotus at Delphi represented Orpheus as receiving the gift of mystic eloquence by touching willow trees in a grove of Persephone; compare the injunction in the song of the forest trees: 'Burn not the willow, a tree sacred to poets.' The willow is the tree of enchantment and is the fifth tree of the year; five (V) was the number sacred to the Roman Moon-Goddess Minerva" (174). Exum touches Easter with the willow branch in the fifth section of this story, which Welty introduces with the symbol V, doubling back to Miss Eckhart's V. As a black child Exum has a history of slavery. He does to Easter exactly what the slave challenging the priest, the black slave challenging the master, would do and at the same time he touches her with the branch that will give her mystic eloquence. The two acts are synonymous. Women will regain the voice of the muse only by reclaiming the heroic power to enter the world of the dead and return. We have already seen Easter as a kind of priest or hero of the girls; her name and her carriage give her the stature of the reigning king. In the magical sphere of Moon Lake Exum would be the next in line to follow Easter as king. The move toward the fringe of power in southern society, toward women and blacks, means that the battle is no longer a battle between the son and the father, the old king and the new, but a movement of outsiders toward the center or a complete inversion of margins and centers.

In Easter's fall we find a new telling of this ancient tale. Easter's fall is at once metaphorical and not metaphorical at all. Welty purposely describes the fall in all its physical detail; it is an embodied fall, not a fall from grace. The female body, an entity of its own, like Easter's and Nina's hands, is, for one moment at least, released from the restriction of material being, and in this release of body to blue air we see a birth. The body is handed down through women's hands like the pear falling from the tree. The body is not gendered but becomes "it," released from the weight of definition and naming. When Exum touches Easter's heel she becomes associated with the sacred kings whose heel is their most vulnerable point, with Achilles in particular but perhaps more significantly for this story, with the god Balder who was "pierced by the mistletoe flung by the god Holder at the instigation of the king."[10] When Easter drops into the water "like one hit in the head by a stone from a sling" (*CSEW*, 363), she also becomes identified with the mighty giant Goliath [11] who was felled by a boy with a slingshot. Associated with both Achilles and Goliath, Easter exists at once as victim and hero as is Jesus in the Christian myth of resurrection. She is also poised on a high wooden scaffolding that suggests a cross.

After Easter has fallen, Exum lets out "a girlish howl and [clings] to the ladder [12] as though a fire had been lighted under it"

(*CSEW*, 363). Balder, the fertility god or symbol of fertility, was tied to a tree and burned after being ritually murdered. Burning at the stake was also the punishment for witches in the sixteenth century. When Exum cries out, he becomes both the old year, the fertility god about to die, and the old witch—giving the girlish howl. Exum clings to the ladder because the ladder symbolizes his escape to heaven, as the dead king's soul ascends to heaven on a ladder. Easter falls positively. This is no quick dive, splash, spit, and repeat performance like Loch's. In fact Easter's fall forces Loch to immerse himself in the water. As he pulls up weeds and mud, he is indeed completely entrenched in the earth and matter. This time he does not dive alone; he dives to recover the female body while the girls watch him. Half submerged in the water, the girls stand in the same formation that Miss Eckhart draws on Cassie's music, as the number V that the willow branch symbolizes, as the number of this section of the story. While Miss Eckhart draws the V, the girls become the V.

Welty may have had many things in mind when she used the letter V; not only does Virgie's name begin with V, so does that of Virbius the King of the Wood in the story of Nemi and the name of the goddess Venus, to whom Virgie refers at the end of "The Wanderers." V is an ancient symbol of women's sexuality. In *The White Goddess*, Graves connects the V formation to the swans of Nemesis, who "were sacred to the goddess (Nemesis or Leda) because of their white plumage, also because the V formation of their flight was a female symbol and because at midsummer, they flew north supposedly taking the dead king's soul with them" (126). Welty develops the image of the swan and of birds in general throughout *The Golden Apples*. Snowdie's lack of coloring is directly connected to the swan. In "June Recital," Mrs. Morrison talks about the little swan ice creams at the party she attends, and Loch compares Miss Eckhart's preparations to building a nest. The swan in "June Recital" is still made of a cream puff—not fully developed—, whereas Welty's description of the girls at Moon Lake moves the feminine fully into the epic world of Graves. In the beginning of "Moon Lake," Welty writes that, as the girls took off their dresses to go swimming, they were "like a whole flock of ferocious little birds with pale topknots building themselves a nest" (*CSEW*, 344). The girls go to a woman's sphere, Moon Lake, in the middle of the summer, taking with them the soul of the dead king—many of the girls are orphans and are sent by the men's Bible class. Finally they stand in a V formation in defiance of the lifesaver, and this V formation suggests that they are going to gain power to fly from this place.[13] In *Heathen Gods and Heroes*, William King writes: "The Swans were called the birds of the Muses, who are described as very beautiful young Virgins, with Crowns adorned with Feathers, Flowers and Leaves, especially of the Palm Tree" (161). The camp at Moon Lake can be seen as a nest in which the girls grow until they come to sexual maturity and actually give birth to themselves. The swans of Nemesis fly to the land of the dead or the sunset.

We are again reminded that the struggle for power between Loch and the girls, between Loch and Easter, is the struggle for participation in the forces of birth and death. Loch, the hunter, Boy Scout, lifesaver, must fight with Easter for her life and thus for power over life and death; the girls see Loch "snatch the hair of Easter's head, the way a boy will snatch anything he wants, as if he won't have invisible opponents snatching first" (*CSEW*, 364). The moment Easter does not respond to Loch's efforts, Loch's belief in male pride, his belief that a boy or a man can have whatever he wants, without struggle, has been challenged. Face to face with death, Loch cannot command. He is not in charge of leniency here. The girls are beginning to recognize this pride for what it is and to realize how it intrudes upon and belittles them, just as the false femininity of Miss Moody—which hides her passion for Ran MacLain—and the rough assumed masculinity of Mrs. Gruenwald—which hides the red of her loosened red corset—keeps them from their own adult sexuality.

Fortunately, however, Loch is not like King MacLain. We can see his physical person in all its vulnerability: "He shook himself in the sun like a dog, blew his nose, spat, and shook his ears, all in a kind of leisurely trance that kept Mrs. Gruenwald off—as though he had no notion that he was interrupting things at all" (*CSEW*, 364). Loch interrupts, not only because he disturbs the complacency of the asexual world of the protected, isolated girls, not even because on a more mythological level he endangers the feminine space of Moon Lake, intruding like Actaeon, but because he interrupts the natural process of death and renewal of which he is an integral part. There is no time for vaunting in this real drama. In the same scene, after Loch yells at them, the girls stand in the water "until they felt the weight of the currentless water pulling anyhow" (*CSEW*, 364). In the face of Loch's superiority the girls feel the weight of their restriction for the first time. They experience their oppression physically. As they watch him spread Easter out, "the sun like a weight fell on them" (*CSEW*, 364–65).

As the Boy Scout takes Easter out of the water, the women pick up the fallen body. Miss Moody takes Easter's legs and Jinny Love scoops up her arms, literally carrying the weight of a newly fallen sun. They put Easter down "in the only shade on earth, after all, the table under the tree. It was where they ate. The table was itself still mostly tree, as the ladder and diving board were half tree too; a camp table had to be round and barky on the underside, and odorous of having been chopped down" (*CSEW*, 365). Welty gives us this detailed description of the table because she wants to connect Easter to the ancient fertility gods, to Christ on the wooden cross, to Christ at the last supper, to the tree gods in the wood at Nemi, to Diana as goddess of the wood, to the wood nymphs, to the felled oak tree that symbolizes the death of the old king. In this connection between Easter, Loch's ritual, and the annual ritual of the King of the Wood, the table, the cross, the ladder, and the diving board are all part of the live tree that has been felled just as the old king has been felled. The

Easter that Loch dumps on the ground is a completely transformed Easter. She is solidly, positively physical. She herself has
become the body as tabula rasa:

> She was arm to arm and leg to leg in a long fold, wrong-colored
> and pressed together as unopen leaves are. Her breasts, too, faced
> together. Out of the water Easter's hair was darkened, and lay over
> her face in long fern shapes. Miss Moody laid it back. . . .
> Easter's nostrils were pinched-looking like an old country wom-
> an's. Her side fell slack as a dead rabbit's in the woods, with the
> flowers of her orphan dress all running together in some antic of their
> own, some belated mix-up of the event. (*CSEW*, 365)

The image of Easter's body could be read as terrible, as a
defeated body, but it also can be read more positively as a chrysalis, a butterfly before its wings have opened, wet and not yet
formed; a leaf bud not yet opened; a baby still wet, not yet taking
a gasp of air. It is a "mix-up," or reversal of the event because
Christ, or at least a male priest, is supposed to die, not an orphan
girl.

As Easter lies in this void between waking and sleeping, death
and life, Nina sees, "her eyes were neither open nor altogether
shut but as if her ears heard a great noise, back from the time she
fell; the whites showed under the lids pale and slick as watermelon seeds. Her lips were parted to the same degree; her teeth
could be seen smeared with black mud" (*CSEW*, 366). Loch holds
Easter's head exactly as Perseus holds Medusa's head in Cellini's
bronze sculpture, but when Loch turns the head to the girls they
do not turn to stone. To the girls, Easter's eyes are like seeds, her
ears hear a great noise, and her lips are smeared with organic
black mud; she is not the dead stone or bronze of the artist. The
seeds are planted in rich soil and will grow large like a baby
(watermelons are compared to pregnant women in several scenes
in this story and in *The Losing Battles*). As Loch and Easter struggle for the breath in Easter's body, Loch takes the mud from
Easter's mouth to let her breathe. Amazingly enough, he is help-

ing her breathe rather than yelling at her to "shut up." He is clearing out her mouth rather than cutting out her tongue, or silencing her.

At the same time he gouges his hands into Easter's ribs and rides up and down on her, actions that Yeager interprets as rape. Loch's motions represent rape but they are not a rape. If we read Easter's body as the worst form of passivity—the woman's careless body, absolutely dependent on the male to be revived—as Yeager does, then she is being raped, but Easter is not a passive victim or even a struggling victim in this event. She is careless in the sense that she does not care about the actions of the boy scout. Instead she is in her own world, communicating to the girls in another language, the language of the body and of ancient women's symbols. From this other side, she actively "let a thin stream of water out of her mouth" (*CSEW*, 366). Easter is fighting back with the source of life, blood and water; she is also actively withholding. She forces the Boy Scout to work and groan, to try again and again: "Easter's body lay up on the table to receive anything that was done to it. If *he* was brutal, her self, her body, the withheld life, was brutal too. While the Boy Scout as if he rode a runaway horse clung momently to her and arched himself off her back, dug his knees and fists into her and was flung back careening by his own tactics, she lay there. Let him try and try!" (*CSEW*, 366).

The white mare has escaped. Fate Rainey is no longer beating his horse. The image is no longer a static image of victim and master but a fluid image of the Boy Scout trying to cling to the horse as she runs with him on her back. This is not a rape. In "Shower of Gold," Katie Rainey says that when we try to describe those kinds of near things you must "hold your horses." Easter's experience of death is the most profound of those near things. The line "Let him try and try" reminds us that the battle is still raging. Morrigana is still angry.

Although we could read this passage as a horrible scene of female victimization, we can also read it as an image of female resistance and strength. Unlike Danaë or Snowdie, who simply falls to the shower of gold, Easter actively participates. She is embodied. Welty even reminds us that the Boy Scout and Easter are both brutal, and she uses the words "her self, her body" to stress that we are not supposed to read this only as a rape. The word "if" complicates our initial interpretation even further. We do not even know if Loch's actions are brutal. On one level he is simply a bumbling Boy Scout, not to be taken seriously in this moment of life and death; the injunction "Let him try and try" reminds us that this is a struggle and that no one has yet won. No interpretation has won out over any other. The fact that Welty slows this moment of emergence/y down to a snail's pace indicates that she wants us to pay close attention, that she wants us to see this moment in all its newness and complexity, not read as we are accustomed to reading.

Although the older women, including the camp mother Lizzie Stark, have no power in the face of Loch's efforts, they actively belittle him with words. On the one hand, Miss Lizzie Stark tries to protect the girls from the reality of sex and their natural growing up, and on the other hand, she guards them and herself from the brutality of male impudence. Miss Lizzie stands on the sidelines making such comments as "But what's *he* doing to her? Stop that" (*CSEW*, 366), "He ought to be put out of business," and "You little rascal, I bet you run down and pollute the spring, don't you?" (*CSEW*, 367). Miss Lizzie's commentary is ineffectual, ridiculous, and accurate. On some level Loch, as representative of all males, has indeed polluted the female spring at some point in his mythic history. It is Miss Lizzie in "Shower of Gold" who "hates all men, and is real important" (*CSEW*, 267). The girls like Miss Lizzie Stark, from whom they have learned something about pride because "under her gaze the Boy Scout's actions seemed to lose a good deal of significance. He was reduced almost to a nuisance—a mosquito, with a mosquito's proboscis" (*CSEW*, 367). But Miss Lizzie's comments are like Miss Moody's butterfly cap. They have nothing to do with this very real moment, this indescribable connection between the male and the female, the reunion, the brutal cruel fact of it. It is no time to hate men or love men. It is simply a time to watch, as the girls instinctively know. Jinny Love will not leave when her Momma tells her to. Nothing Miss Stark does changes the situation. In fact as they all watch they believe that Easter has died. Changes take place in her body even if we do not hear anything from her. "No longer were her lips faintly parted—her mouth was open. It gaped. So did his" (*CSEW*, 368).

Nina's observation of Easter's ordeal is almost as vital as the experience itself. As Easter's body seems closer to death, Gertrude tried to call out "Easter's dead!" and "she was slapped rowdily across the mouth to cut off the word, by Miss Lizzie's hand" (*CSEW*, 368). We remember that in "June Recital" when Mrs. Eckhart cries out, Miss Eckhart slaps her mouth. In at least two of the stories we see girls watching older women cutting off the words of other women and girls, silencing the call of death, silencing the truth. Nina does not cut out the truth. Her hand does not try to attack but to hold out to the night in love. "It's I that's thinking. Easter's not thinking at all. And while not thinking, she is not dead, but unconscious, which is even harder to be" (*CSEW*, 368). Nina knows that you cannot learn anything through the head, and since Easter is not thinking, is unconscious, she is learning through some other source more powerful and more difficult to reach than the head. Nina realizes that being unconscious is harder than being dead because being unconscious in Nina's mind means not reacting in any of the ways one is supposed to react, not responding in any of the traditional ways, not using social language, not living in the socially defined world. It is the state that Nina tried to reach in the tent and could not. The words that interrupt Nina's thoughts—"Don't touch her"—echo the words of Christ to Mary Magdalene. When Mary Magdalene tries to touch Christ, he pulls away from her and cries "touch me not; for I am not yet ascended to my Father"

(John 20:17). Mary Magdalene's touch is dangerous to Christ because it will return him to the world of women, of sexuality, of earth and materiality, and will destroy his godlike power. Easter's resurrection is different. Easter gains power through Nina's touch. When Nina faints she does touch Easter; in fact, she becomes Easter. Although she is not able to go to the other side as easily as Easter, she lies beside her and is a companion on her journey. Unfortunately Nina cannot sustain this power and longs for home. She eventually hides under the protection of Miss Lizzie's skirt. If anyone moves from power to conventionality it is Nina, not Easter. Nina will not risk unconsciousness and death, in order to return reborn.

Nina's touch occurs immediately after Ran MacLain appears on the scene with his dogs and guns. Like Frazer's grim figure, Ran stands under the tree with his gun. In "The Golden Apples and Silver Apples," Demmin and Curley argue that it is Ran who brings the source of "life and fertility" (134). But they also argue that once his work is done he is no longer needed, that "male power passes into eclipse" (134). Instead we can read Ran's presence to mean that Easter's victory is a real victory only in the face of a grown sexual man with King's lineage. Ran stands under the tree and passes on his fertility to Easter, who wakes up soon after he appears. The male power is eclipsed. In "The Whole World Knows," Ran cannot keep his wife Jinny Love from having an affair with his neighbor Woody Spights. He cannot control women's sexuality.

To the girls, Easter represents the sexual words they are not allowed to speak, the world they are not allowed to enter; she is the underworld that the hero travels through but that Gertrude Bowles cannot even mention. Except for Innana in the Sumerian text of this name, there are very few records of a woman entering the underworld. There are women who were sent to the underworld—Persephone/Demeter—there are women left in the underworld—Eurydice—but few women travel there and return. The girls' greatest fear and greatest excitement is the "danger that Easter, turned in on herself, might call out to them after all, from the other, worse, side of it? Her secret voice, if soundless then possibly visible, might work out of her terrible mouth like a vine, preening and sprung with flowers. Or a snake would come out" (*CSEW*, 369–70). Easter's secret voice has the power to make the soundless visible and to create out of silence something growing, the power to speak in both traditionally masculine (the snake) and traditionally feminine (the flower) symbols. Once Easter passes over to the other side, she has crossed the greatest barrier; there can be no binary oppositions, no dualities created by linguistic abstractions. When the Boy Scout crushes Easter's body, blood comes out of her mouth and "for them all, it was like being spoken to" (*CSEW*, 370). The blood that girls at puberty must see to know that they are women, that they can give birth to children, speaks to them of their own power as women to create; similarly the blood pouring from Easter's mouth speaks to them of the bleeding wound of the silenced voice, of suffering, of the silencing of the women's mouth, of the mud-caked mouth, of the act of creating, of giving birth through language that has been drowned, of Mrs. Morrison's singing, of Miss Eckhart's piano playing, of the lost, the stolen, the beaten, the killed. The blood speaks to the girls both of the bleeding wound of the silenced voice, and of the menstrual blood of female creation; of giving birth through language, and of women's regenerative power.

After the appearance of this blood, the Boy Scout begins to move into eclipse: "By now the Boy Scout seemed forever part of Easter and she part of him, he in motion on the up-and-down and she stretched across. He was dripping, while her skirt dried on the table; so in a manner they had changed places too" (*CSEW*, 370). Easter's "face was set now, and ugly with that rainy color of seedling petunias, the kind nobody wants. Her mouth surely by now had been open long enough, as long as any gape, bite, cry, hunger, satisfaction lasts, any one person's grief, or even protest" (*CSEW*, 370). Easter's mouth is not just gaping but open to express all that women have been denied—the hunger, the grief, the protest, and the satisfaction. Easter's mouth has been open longer than any one person's because hers is not the cry of one person but the cry of a whole sex for centuries. The watermelon seeds have become petunia seedlings, the ant-colored eyes milky and the face rainy. Seedlings, milk, and rain are all images not of defeat but of renewal and growth. It is after seeing Easter's gaping mouth that Nina "spotted three little shells in the sand she wanted to pick up when she could" (*CSEW*, 370). As symbols of women's sexuality and spiritual inheritance, of Venus born from the sea, these three little shells are "one of those moments out of the future" (*CSEW*, 370). Aphrodite/Venus was the only goddess not raped by a male god, the only goddess who defined her own sexuality and actually came to embody female sexuality. By having Nina pick up the shells, Welty suggests that one day Nina will reclaim her future and name her own sexuality.

As Easter finally comes back to life, "Her belly arched and drew up from the board under her. She fell, but she kicked the Boy Scout. Ridiculously, he tumbled backwards off the table. He fell almost into Miss Lizzie's skirt; she halved herself on the instant, and sat on the ground with her lap spread out before her like some magnificent hat that has just got crushed. Ran Mac-Lain hurried politely over to pick her up, but she fought him off" (*CSEW*, 371). Easter, like a woman giving birth, arches and knocks down both the woman who cannot understand the passionate new female power and the male who cannot revive her. She halves Miss Lizzie, making her less important but also returning her to the earlier chrysalis position. As Easter sits up, straightens her dress, and looks at the girls, the sun was setting. The male power symbolized by the sun is following its natural course while the new fertility goddess takes over. Nina recognizes that "at least what had happened to Easter was out in the world, like the table itself. There it remained—mystery, if only for being hard and cruel and, by something Nina felt inside her body, murderous" (*CSEW*, 372). Easter as the victorious new queen, the new priest, has symbolically murdered the old king, the old priest. At the same time this murder has been a life saving—forcing the male back into his role as fertility god.

Before her fall, Easter has the phallic power to bite the hand of Mr. Nesbitt, to carry a knife, to engage in tomboy activities, but in all of these actions she is simply playing with the toys of patriarchy. Easter has no real power until she reverses the misogynist escape from the mother coded in the death and resurrection of Christ and replaces it with the regenerative death and embodied resurrection of the female. With this act she inscribes the name Easter on her body, spelling it correctly to make it real as Nina has asked her to do. Yeager reads a return to passivity in Easter's clodlike arm and her desire to be carried by the girls. More likely, her arm falls like a clod because it is part of the earth, and Easter asks the girls to carry her like a queen or a general wounded in battle, not as one given over to passivity. In fact, it is at the moment when Easter lies asleep, that the most powerful clitoral image appears: "The sky's rising clouds lighted all over, like one spread-out blooming mimosa tree that could be seen from where the trunk itself should rise" (*CSEW*, 373). The symbol of female sexuality and regeneration has moved from the earth to the sky, and in the sky it mirrors the earth. There is no binary opposition, no separation between sky and earth, between trunk and bloom, between male and female.

While Easter sleeps, Nina and Jinny Love, "arms entwined," walk past the Boy Scout's tent; an owl hoots "in a tree, closer by. The wind stirred" (*CSEW*, 373). As they pass the tent they see not only that is Loch undressing in front of everybody "for the whole world to see"—a far cry from King MacLain's invisible omnipotence—but that "he stood there studying and touching his case of sunburn in a Kress mirror like theirs. He was naked and there was his little tickling thing hung on him like the last drop on the pitcher's lip" (*CSEW*, 373). The girls see that he can be burned by the sun, that his mirror is like theirs, that he has no more reflective power than they have, and that his penis, his phallus, is simply a "little tickling thing." It is then that Nina says "We can call like an owl" (*CSEW*, 374) and Jinny Love adds "You and I will always be old maids" (*CSEW*, 374). At this point they go to join the other girls who are singing. The girls refer to the owl, the symbol of female wisdom and the totem of the goddess Athena. They then assert independence from men— they will be old maids—and finally they begin to sing. Of course they have not realized the sexuality that Easter has realized, but they are still able to sing. Through their connection to their spiritual heritage and the symbols of that spiritual heritage, the girls gain a voice. This is the first time in the collection that the women and girls sing aloud.

When we read the female signs in "Moon Lake," referred to here as clitoral signs, we find not what Yeager calls a "patriarchal subtext" or "counterplot" but a revolutionary undermining of the monolithic, heroic narrative that denies the penis the power to be fertile and denies the clitoris and womb their erotic and regenerative power. Instead of accepting a biological, psychological, cultural, or even political determinism, Welty, by inviting into her artistic vision all that must constitute female as body, finds the symbols and metaphors to transform the female from rape victim to conscious artist, from the decapitated Medusa of male fiction to a sea-born Venus who defines her own sexuality. Welty invents a new language, not by excluding the words of the fathers in some impossible surgery, but by writing the feminine with all the words that have constituted this representation. This kind of engagement creates a much more lasting and radical change because it allows the feminist author the power to resurrect herself from the waters that might otherwise have drowned her.

5

Was It Better than This?

Violence and Regeneration in "The Whole World Knows"

If the "rapes" in "Sir Rabbit" and "Moon Lake" are metaphorical, or dreamlike, the rape in "The Whole World Knows" seems literal. We know that Ran drives Maideen to Vicksburg, makes her drink rum and coke against her will, takes her to a motel and has "her so quick" (*CSEW*, 392). We know that Maideen cries into her pillow while lying beside him and that soon after this she commits suicide. Critics have generally defined "The Whole World Knows" as one of Welty's most depressing and unregenerative short stories. Peter Schmidt reads the ending as a rape and Michael Kreyling comments in *Author and Agent*: "It is intriguing that the darkest point in *The Golden Apples* came first. The story fraught with images of disintegration, of descent, of forlorn human hopes precedes the overarching integrative force of the work as a whole" (119).

However, this narrative can only be read as a literal rape if we ignore the symbolic and metaphoric double entendres that appear throughout the text. When read with an eye to interpenetrating narratives, the dominant reading, that Maideen is a tragic victim and Ran a spoiled, depleted, and violent hero, unravels. When we read with an eye to intertextual weaving, we find not a forlorn story, but a story of female defiance, and regeneration.

As Kreyling points out, "The Whole World Knows," was the first story Welty wrote in the collection that later became *The Golden Apples*. In this text she creates a mixing of the real and the imagined, which informs the rest of the collection. Although Diarmuid Russell objected to this mixture, Welty persisted and trusted her own sense of the direction that this story and the collection as a whole would follow. Without the "meshing of two types of 'reality'" as Kreyling calls it (*Author and Agent*, 118), Welty would not have been able to free herself and her characters, particularly Ran and Jinny, from their conventional small-town narratives.

Because of the extensive intertextuality on which this text depends, "The Whole World Knows" is not actually mixing two types of reality but combining multiple textual meanings. While the characters appear to be engaged in the age-old battle between the quest for personal freedom and the needs of the community, as the story develops personal/imaginative vision and communal/spiritual expression become interdependent. Beyond the regressive conventionalities of form and social order, what the community needs most is the vital inseminating power of the male and the vital gestating power of the female. In "The Whole World Knows" the characters find this place of communal connection by taking paths towards personal liberation and fulfilment. Ran must reconnect with the earth and his own sexuality, and Jinny must rediscover her independence and identity beyond the restricting codes of southern white womanhood. These personal journeys can only occur with the enlivening textual support of ancient fertility and initiation rituals, as described by Frazer, thus firmly rooting the personal in the communal.

This blurring of the lines between personal and communal becomes equally apparent in Welty's authorial position. Welty's voice and plot depend directly on a close intertextuality with *The Golden Bough*, the Ulster cycle, and *The Sound and the Fury*. Her vision of a vital interdependent community is supported by the ritualistic and mythological sources and set against the isolationist perspective of Faulkner's *The Sound and the Fury*. In *The Sound and the Fury* the characters cannot escape the limiting roles in which southern middle-class society confines them, so they destroy themselves and each other. In "The Whole World Knows," Welty finds a regenerative, if not peaceful, place of intersection between communal and individual desires.

It is highly appropriate for Welty to begin her deconstruction of patriarchal discourse with William Faulkner, considering how often she is compared to this great male giant of southern literature. While there are direct allusions to Faulkner's *The Sound and the Fury* in "The Whole World Knows" and in other texts by Eudora Welty, in *Conversations with Eudora Welty* she never admits to being conscious of these connections.[1] Many interviewers have suggested to Welty that William Faulkner must have been either a difficult act to follow or a tremendous influence on her work. Welty rejects the notion of influence for very good reasons. The need to legitimate Welty by making Faulkner her literary forefather is not only demeaning, it misses the point. Welty's vision is completely different from, perhaps even diametrically opposed to Faulkner's. She shares the same textual universe with Faulkner, but her engagement with him is more active, and transformative than the word "influence" allows. Faulkner's silencing and belittlement of women's experience, could not go unanswered by his only female peer. As a close comparison between "The Whole World Knows" and portions of *The Sound and the Fury* reveals, Welty's answer is subtle, respectful, and yet empowering.[2]

When Quentin thinks about his father's words, Faulkner writes, "Father said." In the first five paragraphs he repeats this construction many times. It is almost a chant.[3] In the first two pages of "The Whole World Knows" Ran MacLain says "Mother said" and Welty repeats this construction throughout the story. In fact the first lines of the story read: "Father, I wish I could talk to you, wherever you are right now. Mother said, *Where have you been son?*—Nowhere, Mother.—*I wish you wouldn't sound so un-*

happy, son. You could come back to MacLain and live with me now.—I can't do that, Mother. You know I have to stay in Morgana" (*CSEW*, 375). Whenever Ran quotes his mother the section is in italics. *The Sound and the Fury* depends on italics to signal time changes. Only in one other story in *The Golden Apples* does Welty use italics.

Ran's mother asks "Where have you been?" almost as if Welty is asking where the human connection between mother and son has been. There is no human connection between mother and son in Faulkner's work. In fact, the white mother in Faulkner's work is barely alive. She is a chronically ill hypochondriac who voices clichés and platitudes in response to her children. The connection between Quentin and his father is one of abstractions and pessimistic philosophical advice. In the exchange between father and son, the real thrust of Faulkner's vision comes forward; Quentin despairs and must kill himself because he cannot control his sister's sexuality and he is ashamed of his own virginity. When Quentin's sister Caddie runs off with Dalton Ames, Quentin wants to kill him. He meets him in the woods and tells him, almost comically, that he has to be out of town by sunset. Quentin has no power to control Caddie's sexuality any more than Ran has power to control Jinny's; however, there is a big difference. Although it is none of Quentin's business when and with whom Caddie chooses to lose her virginity, he makes it his business—it becomes the deadly serious reason for his suicide. Ran has no power over Jinny's sexuality and he also takes it seriously, but it is his business. In fact, whereas he has much more reason to be upset than Quentin, all of the ladies in town tell Ran not to take it so seriously, to forgive. As Miss Perdita Mayo says, "Thing of the flesh, I told my Circle, won't last" (*CSEW*, 380).

They wish, like his mother, that he was not so unhappy. They do not take his desire to kill Woodrow seriously and they certainly do not take Woodrow seriously. They realize that this is all part of Ran's dream world. Miss Perdita Mayo reminds Ran,

"That's no way to do, bear grudges. Your mother never bore your father a single grudge in her life, and he made her life right hard. I tell you, how do you suppose he made her life? She don't bear him a grudge. We're all human on earth" (*CSEW*, 376). She lets him know that it is no big deal that Jinny had an affair. It is no big deal that Caddie had sex with Dalton Ames. The boys all take themselves too seriously in Faulkner's work. In fact, Quentin takes himself so seriously that he kills himself. Miss Perdita Mayo reminds Ran that men have done what Jinny did for years and the women always forgave. Now, it is time for the men to realize they cannot control female sexuality—to wake up and realize that they invented the concept of virginity and that their seriousness about it causes murder and suicide. Welty returns the boys to their human dimensions and human responsibilities. "Mother said, *Son, you're walking around in a dream*" (*CSEW*, 380).

Even Snowdie MacLain does not recognize the dimensions of the lesson Ran needs to learn. She tells Ran that he could come back to MacLain and live with her now. Ran knows he cannot, that he must remain in Morgana, Mississippi. Whether we think of Morgana as alluding to Morgan Le Fay, the Celtic Goddess Morrigana, or the Fata Morgana, the name has definite feminine origins. MacLain, however, means son of Lain and is masculine. Ran must remain in the feminine Morgana and learn what all the women—Miss Perdita Mayo, Lizzie Stark, Jinny Love, his mother, Maideen, even the old dog Bella—have to teach him. He cannot escape the female by disappearing or going out west like his father and brother or by committing suicide like Quentin. In the new narrative that Welty constructs, Ran MacLain must face his fear of female sexual independence.[4]

At the end of the story Maideen tries to convince Ran not to use his gun against her, against himself, or against Woodrow Spights:

> Then while she spoke to me I could hear all the noises of the place we were in—the frogs and nightbirds of Sunset Oaks, and the little

idiot nigger running up and down the fence, up and down, as far as it
went and back, sounding the palings with his stick.

   "Don't, Ran. Don't do that, Ran. Don't do it, please don't do it."
She came closer, but when she spoke I wasn't hearing what she said.
I was reading her lips, the conscientious way people do through train
windows. Outside, I thought the little nigger at the gate would keep
that up for ever, no matter what I did, or what anyone did—running
a stick along the fence, up and then down, to the end and back again.
(*CSEW*, 392)

In the image of the "idiot nigger" Welty conflates Benjy running up and down the fence bellowing for Caddie, and all the
young black boys who had to take care of him. She also alludes
directly to Quentin's childhood memory in *The Sound and the
Fury*: "He came along the fence every morning with a basket
towards the kitchen dragging a stick along the fence every morning I dragged myself to the window cast and all and laid for him
with a piece of coal" (69). The young black boy running along the
fence has little to do with the plot of "The Whole World Knows."
He is part of the landscape of Welty's literary and by extension
Ran's personal memory or more specifically, as Ran says, part of
the place. The place is the island on the river near the battleground at Vicksburg, Mississippi. The place is Mississippi, land
from which both Welty and Faulkner write. It is the place of
Welty's literary imagination, and it is populated with Ran and
Maideen, with frogs and nightbirds, and with the literary ghosts
of Faulkner's world.

   The most significant Faulknerian ghost in Welty's story can be
found in the murderous and suicidal young male figure represented in Welty's text by Ran. Like Quentin with Dalton Ames,
Ran imagines killing Woodrow Spights. Unlike Quentin he
imagines but does not succeed in killing himself. These young
violent men could have taken over Welty's story and silenced her
vision, but Welty consciously mediates their power. They could
keep Ran from hearing Maideen, the female voice that tells him
to stop, but it is night and the sun has set in Sunset Oaks—the

sun and oaks both mythic symbols of male virility. Ran thinks the sound of the stick on the fence palings will keep up forever no matter what he does, what anyone does. The sound and the fury of the sound is not only Faulkner's words taking over or challenging the women's narrative, Maideen's voice, it is also the response of those who are left out of fiction—the "idiot nigger" demanding attention, beating on the fence that keeps him out. If Ran listens to the sound of the stick on the fence, he does not hear Maideen's voice, still feeble, repetitive and unimaginative. If Welty had listened to this sound she would have neglected her development of Maideen's strength, and Ran's violent phallic vision would have overwhelmed the narrative. But the sound does not keep on forever; it stops, Ran puts the gun to his mouth and clicks the trigger and the gun does not go off. His suicide attempt fails. "And *she* said, 'Now you see. It didn't go off. Give me that. Give that old thing to me, I'll take care of it.' She took it from me. Dainty as she always was, she carried it over to the chair; and prissy as she was, like she knew some long-tried way to deal with a gun, she folded it in her dress" (*CSEW*, 392).

The female vision—prissy and dainty, unable to articulate protest—wins over the male desire for murder/suicide; Maideen wraps the phallic symbol in the material of this new text/ile. Ran is literally being sewn into the newly designed fabric of this feminist intertextuality. Earlier in the story, when Jinny Love is sewing a button on Ran's sleeve, he comments, that he breathed out his fury. He experiences that the "air wasn't darkness but faint light and floating sound. It was the breath of all the people in the world" (*CSEW*, 391). This story expresses the meaning of the movement from fury to a sound and breath that signifies everything, particularly the passionate desire for human integration and connection.

For a woman of Welty's generation, a Mississippi writer, to freely admit that she had something to teach William Faulkner, the great master, would have been blasphemous. It would be hard even today for her to approach this subject. Eudora Welty has expressed her great respect for Faulkner's genius and his ability to write, but she does not share his vision of an unregenerative world in which individuals self-destruct as the community disintegrates around them.

In Welty's vision the two types of reality, the individualist/imaginative and the communal/spiritual, create conflicting narratives, but it is the friction and tension of this conflict that fertilizes and cross-pollinates Welty's voice, allowing her to create a regenerative answer to the disconnected and barren heroic myth. Ran's name itself embodies the whole history and tension of this conflict; his name suggests "rain," the communal need for fertility, "ran" the desire for escape, and "randy" the community's and Ran's need for sex. In the story it is hot and dry, Ran has run away from his marriage, and he is not having sexual relations with Jinny. We also know that Ran and Jinny are married, but that she is not yet pregnant. Ran is running from the spiritual call to become the consort of the queen, the same call that wakes Loch up in "June Recital." When Ran walks out of the bank, the symbol of the modern, abstract, disconnected world (as his brother Eugene walks out of the jewellery store in "Music from Spain"), the cotton field wakes him up "like a light turned on in my face" (*CSEW*, 375). When a light is turned on in one's face, one is either being caught doing something in the dark, being cross-examined for some crime, or being awakened. Ran is experiencing all three. He is on trial for not recognizing his fertile connection to the community, he is caught not performing his role, and he is being awakened to the need for his inseminating power.

In this same paragraph Ran realizes that Woody has left already to go to Jinny's. Woodrow's name suggests the wood king of Frazer's *The Golden Bough*,—wood row, i.e. a row of trees. The earth and the community depend on the fertile connection between king and queen. If Jinny cannot find fertility with one consort, she will turn to another. Miss Lizzie Stark reminds Ran that her bridge partner, Mamie Charmichael, "plays her own hand with no more regard for her partner than you have" (*CSEW*, 384), that life depends on paying attention to your partner's needs, the community's needs, the whole world's needs.

If we follow this reading then Maideen is not some lost innocent country girl but the maiden, the first aspect of the triple goddess, the one who will awaken the consort's vital sexual potency. Maideen works at the seed and feed store. During her reign as clerk, she has washed the windows, exposed the sleeping Mr. Moody, and generally revitalized the whole store. She is eighteen years old, not fourteen or some other tender young age and she aggressively goes after the boys. She stands on the drugstore step "waving a little green handkerchief" (*CSEW*, 375) which is indicative of a green light, a go-ahead, and a symbol of verdancy and fertility. When she is not riding with Ran she rides with Red Ferguson in the Coca Cola truck. Coca Cola implies modernity, a new world with a new set of rules for young girls. Red's name connotes sexuality. Fergus or Ferghus was one of the heroes associated with Chuchulain in the *Tain Bo Cualnge*. In the Ulster cycle of prose tales, "He was the first mate of the notoriously promiscuous Medb of Connacht. . . . Ferghus was known to have an insatiable sexual appetite" (Green, *Dictionary of Celtic Myth and Legend*, 96). He was in fact a giant of enormous proportions who needed seven women to keep him satisfied when he was not with Queen Medb. He is far from innocent and the fact that Maideen rides with him is highly suspicious.

In fact, throughout the text, it is Maideen who actively pursues Ran, pushes her white gloves at him, drives up and down the street with him, and waves to everyone she sees. In the first two pages of this story Welty uses the words "up and down" three times evoking both the heterosexual act of copulation and a kind of cross-pollination. It is almost as if Ran and Maideen are in a tractor that is seeding and fertilizing new rows of earth as they pass. "The Whole World Knows" is set in August in the heat of the summer, at the time when the young fertility consort is supposed to sacrifice himself to be harvested, so that his seed will fall to the earth and he will be reborn as new grain in the spring. It is harvest time in Morgana, but all of the men are either too old, dead, or have fallen asleep. The regenerative hopes of the community lie only with Ran or Woody and Woody is too young. When Snowdie Maclain, Ran's mother, tries to get him to return to MacLain, he says, "I can't do that mother. You know I have to stay in Morgana" (*CSEW*, 375). Ran has to stay in Morgana so that he can learn how to fullfill his role as consort; he must learn the lessons of this all-female realm. As the unredeemed king of the wood, a grain king who cannot find his father—thus cannot kill his father, thus cannot assert his rightful place as the next in line for the throne, and thus imagines killing, but cannot actually kill someone else—Ran is trapped, like Loch, in an all-woman's sphere. The town gossips know that, in order for fertility to return to their community, the most virile men and women must reproduce. Woody is not Jinny's equal. Miss Perdita Mayo wants the fertility king and queen to stay together in order to enhance the vitality of the community. She does not want the little boy Woody to usurp Ran's rightful place, but something is wrong with Ran. He is unable or unwilling to perform his role.

The women try everything to send him back to Jinny. They talk to him, admonish him, scold him, feed him, and threaten him, but in their desperation they also trap him with their small-town, small-minded conventionality, making it impossible for him to assert his own individual needs, explore his imaginative wanderings, let alone feel sexual passion. His mother keeps calling him, and Miss Perdita Mayo hollers at him through the cage of his bank window and tells him to go back to Jinny. Every woman in the text has advice for Ran. Referring to Jinny's relationship with Woody, Miss Perdita Mayo cries, "It's a thing of the flesh not the spirit, it'll pass" (*CSEW*, 376). What Miss Perdita might not understand is that it is a thing of the flesh and the spirit. Unfortunately it will take a form of violence and distortion to transform this stifling circle of orthodoxy into a circle of regeneration.

From the beginning of the story, Welty reveals that Ran is failing physically. After playing cards at Jinny's, he goes out into the backyard at the teachers' house to be sick so that no they will not notice. When Ran and Maideen are driving along, Maideen wonders what is wrong with Ran, why he does not see her at first. He says his eyes have gone bad, but Ran's illness is symptomatic of the whole culture; the society has lost its virility. The young people are drinking rum and coke rather than anything nourishing, playing bridge and croquet rather than engaging in games of strength and endurance, riding around in cars and gossiping rather than engaging in imaginative mental dialogue.

In *The Golden Bough* weakness or illness of any kind cannot be tolerated in the fertility king. He must be replaced as soon as there is any sign that he is weak. Frazer comments that since the vitality of the community was thought to depend on the vitality of the divine king, the moment that the young king was thought to be ailing in any way the community felt endangered. "The people of the Congo believed, as we have seen, that if their pontiff the Chitome were to die a natural death, the world would perish, and the earth, which he alone sustained by his power and merit, would immediately be annihilated. Accordingly when he fell ill and seemed likely to die, the man who was destined to be his successor entered the pontiff's house with a rope or a club and strangled or clubbed him to death" (Frazer, 310). If the king became ill he was killed and a new divine king was brought in to replace him. The king or priest might also select a new king. He could be killed for symptoms as minor as losing a tooth. It would be better for the vitality of the community for Ran to kill himself and die a violent death than to waste away like his brother Eugene. Because there are no other young men except Woodrow to take Ran's place, they are pitted against each other.

In a fit of anger Miss Lizzie tells Ran that he ailed first, that Jinny only answered him. We do not know the nature of Ran's ailment but we can assume that it is serious enough for Jinny to think that she needs to find a new sexual partner, that Ran has to be replaced by a younger, more vital fertility consort, but Ran does not let himself be killed or replaced. Instead he returns to Jinny's house, to the most heavily sensuous and coded female scene, passing "under the heavy heads of those crape myrtles, the too bright blooms that hang down like fruits that might drop" (*CSEW*, 377). As Ran enters their home, Miss Lizzie taps on the window with her crochet hook, symbolically crocheting him into the textile of this fertile scene. Ran suddenly realizes that he feels light hearted. When the fertility god was about to be sacrificed, he became very light, and was thought to ascend much like Christ. Welty writes, "Lilies must have been in bloom, somewhere near, and I took a full breath of their ether smell: consciousness could go or not" (*CSEW*, 378). Lilies are symbolic of Christ's resurrection, and like Christ Ran is rising, but these lilies are also symbolic of women's sexuality, the all-women's sphere, in which Jinny is residing. Like Eugene in "Music From Spain" and Easter in "Moon Lake," Ran must let go of consciousness, breathe in this ether substance, let go of superficial social forms, and return to the life force of nature in order to once again become a virile presence in the community.

When Ran returns to visit Jinny with Maideen, Jinny is cutting her hair. Frazer mentions that in "New Zealand the most sacred day of the year was that appointed for hair-cutting" (271) and that "in Tyrol witches are supposed to use cut or combed hair to make hailstones or thunder-storms" (273). In Sparta when the girls were about to enter marriage or become pregnant they cut off their hair.

> For their marriages the women were carried off by force, not when they were small and unfit for wedlock, but when they were in full bloom and wholly ripe. After the woman was thus carried off, the bride's maid, so called, took her in charge, cut her hair off close to the head, put a man's cloak and sandals on her, and laid her down on a pallet, on the floor, alone, in the dark. Then the bridegroom, not flown with wine nor enfeebled by excesses, but composed and sober, after supping at his public mess table as usual, slipped steathily into

the room where the bride lay, loosed her virgin's zone, and bore her in his arms to the marriage bed. (*Plutarch's Lives*, 250–251)

Jinny is cutting her hair in preparation for sexual union with Ran; she is wearing sandals and men's clothes just like the Spartan girls, and she turns to Ran, the groom, who will "tell her when to stop"(378) cutting her hair. The combined experiences of Maideen and Jinny follow the script of this Spartan narrative quite closely. The only problem is that Ran does not perform his role as well as he might. He is drunk when he takes Maideen and he takes the wrong girl, not the ripe Jinny but the underage Maideen. If we have any doubt that Jinny's action is directly linked to fertility we need only realize that she is using stork-shaped scissors to cut her hair. Jinny becomes both Perseus and the Medusa as, wearing sandals and looking into a mirror like Perseus, she cuts off her own locks. Before she comes down the stairs, Miss Lizzie changes her shoes to ones "that came down stairs like a march"(*CSEW*, 378). This is not a scene of peace and gentleness but a Spartan scene of preparation for battle; the mother is the commanding general.

As Tellie counts the people who want drinks, Ran realizes that "lightness came right back. Just to step on the matting, that billows a little anyway, and with Jinny's hair scattered like feathers on it, I could have floated, risen and floated " (*CSEW*, 378). Again Ran is rising and floating like Christ, but this time Jinny's hair becomes a nest, and Ran is brought literally into the nest of their marriage. In a reversal of the Leda myth, Ran is the one taken by the swanlike Jinny. Ran later comments that Jinny has ruined her hair. In polite southern society, a girl is ruined when she has sex out of marriage. By cutting her hair and taking on the power of masculinity, Jinny has figuratively harvested or impregnated herself. She is, by asserting her sexual power, enflaming Ran and introducing sexual passion into their marriage.

As Ran sits with the three women, Maideen the maiden, Jinny Love the fertile married woman, and the older Miss Lizzie, we see the representation of the triple goddess in her three aspects. Ran even comments that Maideen is the copy of Jinny, the child copy. By seeing their similarities he is recognizing the cycle of fertility from mother to daughter to granddaughter. As he sits with the three women, Ran listens, not to the gossip about Jinny and himself, which he imagines or actually hears, but to the ferns that "were hushing on their stands, they had just been watered. I could listen to women and hear pieces of the story, of what happened to us, of course—but I listened to the ferns" (*CSEW*, 378).

In *The Golden Bough* Frazer asserts that fern seed was thought to hold magical powers.

> But while the fern-seed is described as golden, it is equally de-scribed as glowing and fiery. Hence, when we consider that two great days for gathering the fabulous seed are Midsummer Eve and Christmas—that is, the two solstices. . . . we are led to regard the fiery aspect of the fern-seed as primary, and its golden aspect as secondary and derivative. Fern-seed, in fact, would seem to be an emanation of the sun's fire at the two turning points of its course, the summer and winter solstices . . . Thus it may be taken as certain that fern-seed is golden, because it is believed to be an emanation of the sun's golden fire.(817)

Frazer then goes on to connect fern-seed with mistletoe, sug-gesting that they are both emanations of the sun's light and fire and that as such they play a crucial role in the rituals that cele-brated the fertilizing power of the sun. By listening to the ferns Ran is returning to the source of his potency. If he has become impotent in this modern world, it is this listening that will re-store him to health.

What is interesting, however, is that immediately after saying he is listening to the ferns, Ran tells the gossipy story of Jinny's and his separation. This may be because the decoded version of Maideen's story is similar to the fern's story. When the women in the town say that Ran might kill Woody, that there is no one in the town for Jinny but Ran and Woody, they are reciting the story of the king of the wood, the necessity of communal regeneration: "How could you get away from it, right in Morgana? You can't get away in Morgana. Away from anything at all, you know that" (*CSEW*, 379).

As Ran returns to Jinny's a second time, this time without Maideen, he plays croquet with several of the young men and a small girl.[5] When the girl calls out "You're dead on Woody," (*CSEW*, 382), he hits his ball at Woody and then imagines killing Woody with his mallet. As we have seen in *The Golden Bough*, if the divine king or fertility consort were ailing, then the next in line would kill him to insure that the community did not lose its vitality. Ran reverses this process when he imagines killing the younger and more virile Woody. "I may have answered with a joke. I felt light-headed, not serious at all, really doing it for a child when I lifted my mallet—the one with the red band that had always been mine. But I brought Woody Spights down with it. He toppled and shook the ground. I felt the air rush up. Then I beat on him. I went over his whole length, and cracked his head apart with that soft girl's hair and all the ideas, beat on him without stopping till every bone, all the way down to the numerous little bones in the foot, was cracked in two" (*CSEW*, 382).

In this passage Welty is describing the cutting down of the wood spirit or king of the wood by the rival king, and the final striking of the scythe in a harvest ritual. In Ran's vision Woody topples and shakes the ground, like a tree not a human body, but before Ran imagines killing Woody, he hears the voice of Miss Lizzie—"Like the hum of the gin, it was there, but the evening was still quiet, still very hot and quiet" (*CSEW*, 382). The hum of the gin is the hum of the cotton gin harvesting the cotton. Ran not only imagines chopping down Woody as the oak king, but he is also imagining harvesting Woody, allowing Woody's fertile seed to replenish the earth. The word "cracked" suggests a grain of wheat or corn that has been opened in order to give up its seed—the act of threshing. Ran is not describing one man's kill-

ing another but a harvester's killing the last standing stalk of corn
or wheat. In connecting Woody to his natural and spiritual origins, Ran also returns the male body to its mortality and bodily
vulnerability. All of the abstractions, ideas, must be beaten out
of Woody.

At the moment when Ran's vision is most violent, most passionate, Woody gives the little William's girl a spank, and Ran
cannot bear the fact that his revelation has been violated, belittled, and reduced so blatantly. Ran, as one of Welty's passionate
artists, like King Maclain and Virgie Rainey, realizes: "And I
should have called out *then*—All is disgrace! Human beings' cries
could swell if locusts' could, in the last of evening like this, and
cross the grass in a backyard, if only they enough of them cried.
At our feet the shadows faded out light into no shadows left and
the locusts sang in long waves, O-E, O-E, and the gin ran on"
(*CSEW*, 382).

What Ran is describing here is the ancient harvest custom of
crying the neck, the calling out in celebration and passion as the
last sheaf (called the neck) is cut during harvest. What he longs
for is the moment after the harvest when all of the men and
women stand around the last sheaf and sing loud, long cries into
the night air (Frazer, 515). Ran is harvesting here not only
Woody and masculine virility but the potency of the natural
human voice. The sounds the locusts sing in Ran's vision are the
vowel sounds O and E which represent the smallest phonemes,
the building blocks of human language. His next sentence is a
wonderful poetic formation of the moment: "Our grass in August is like the floor of the sea, and we walk on it slowly playing,
and the sky turns green before dark, Father, as you know. The
sweat ran over my back and down my arms and legs, branching,
like an upside-down tree" (*CSEW*, 382). Ran experiences himself
as the tree, as the roots, not disconnected in some modernist
dilemma but organically whole, if only for a moment. Even as
the locusts sing, the gin, the technological replacement of the
human harvester, runs on humming.

As Ran returns to the three schoolteachers, the three fates, he runs through the porch and hall "like a man through a burning building" (*CSEW*, 383). There is a reason for Ran to run. As the harvest himself, as the ailing wood king, he is in danger of being sacrificed by the three Gorgons. He could be felled and burned just as he has imagined killing Woody. The three schoolteachers, as the symbols of regeneration and continuity, know this better than any one. For protection against the violence surrounding him, Ran carries a gun that Snowdie reminds him his father would never have used. King would not have needed a gun because he was an indisputably vital king.

When Ran returns the third time to Jinny's, he goes past the Spanish daggers, the spiderwebs, and walks under trees the entire way to the house, returning through the old gate by the summerhouse. The fertility imagery has intensified. Ran is surrounded by nature and flanked on all sides by women. The end for Ran in his present form is near. He has lost a button and he wants Jinny to sew it on, just as his mother and Katie Rainey used to baste things on him when he was a child. He is willingly letting himself become part of the tapestry, the textile of this new female version of the fertility myth. To get to Jinny he must go past the statue of the dancing girl, the goddess statue. Inside the gate Ran smells "a whiff of the sour pears" (*CSEW*, 383). The fruit that Loch longs for, which Nina in "Moon Lake" imagines as finally ripe and ready to be eaten, is presented in this story as overripe—Jinny, the married woman without child. Ran has not come to carry his wife to the marriage bed, however, he comes instead as a child unable to sew on his buttons and as an adolescent armed with his pistol phallus. Jinny makes it blatantly clear that she is ripe by carrying the "old broken wicker basket full of speckled pears" and not returning to shut the gate. (*CSEW*, 384). She is opening herself to Ran but he does not respond. As they go in the door they pass the dripping sprinkler, Tellie's patch of mint, the hot door handle, and Miss Lizzie's "busy cuttings in water" and during the walk "a thousand bees had droned and burrowed in the pears that lay on the ground" (*CSEW*, 384). This is a scene of bacchanalia, but through it all, Ran does not respond. Ran claims in his imaginary dialogue with his father that he does not know what ails him, but even as he asks his father this question, he stands holding a basket full of rotting pears. He is impotent. He sets the basket full of ripe pears on the ground.

Tellie, Lizzie, and Jinny are all frustrated with Ran's lack of understanding. Tellie calls him a mess. Jinny is yelling at Tellie. The stork scissors fall out of her workbasket when she goes to get a needle and thread, and Jinny stands in Mr. Comus's "little back study, 'Mama's office,' with the landscape wallpaper and Mr. Comus's old desk full-up with U.D.C. correspondence and plat maps that cracked like thunder when the fan blew them" (*CSEW*, 385). Lizzie Stark has taken over the masculine desk and filled it with maps of burial plots for the United Daughters of the Confederacy. This scene shows us exactly what tapestry Ran is being sewn into and why it might not be to his liking. If he is to join this community, he not only joins the fertility of the natural world, he also joins the troubled history of the matrilineal line of southern womanhood. By standing in this study Jinny also joins this history. In fact, it is while standing in this study that she treats Tellie, the African-American maid, most like a servant or a slave. This is the moment of confluence when the different forces vying for Jinny and Ran's virility come together. They are cornered. Jinny has been forced into the landscape of her mother's designing, and even when she trys to escape Lizzie Stark, she still ends up in her office. The thunder of the plat maps is loud and powerful, a source of creation and destruction.

At this moment Ran imagines firing his pistol at Jinny:

> I fired point-blank at Jinny—more than once. It was close range—there was barely room between us suddenly for the pistol to come up. And she only stood frowning at the needle I had forgotten the reason for. Her hand never deviated, never shook from the noise. The dim clock on the mantle was striking—the pistol hadn't drowned that out. I was watching Jinny and I saw her pouting

childish breasts, excuses for breasts, sprung full of bright holes where my bullets had gone. But Jinny didn't feel it. She threaded her needle. She made her little face of success. Her thread always went straight in the eye.

"Will you hold still." (*CSEW*, 385).

These are the words Snowdie and Katie speak to Ran and Eugene in "Shower of Gold," the words of a mother to a child, not a husband to a wife.

In this battle, and it is a battle between the masculine symbolic world of guns and phalluses and the feminine symbolic world of needles, threads, eyes, and vulvas, Jinny must concentrate, and in concentrating she begins to win. Ran's phallic energy, which is not directed towards fertility but used to destroy the source of life, Jinny's breasts, fails, and Jinny threads Ran into the life cycle. Jinny is doing the work of the second of the three fates. Clotho spins the thread, Lachesis weaves the thread (in this case threads and sews), and Atropos cuts it. Here Jinny is performing mainly the role of Lachesis but also the role of Atropos. Ran can only imagine a violent scene, the destruction of the woman's body. Instead of filling Jinny full of his sperm, the seed of life, he imagines shooting her breasts full of holes, breasts that he can only see as childish, not motherly or womanly, not capable of nourishing a child. Yet he is the one who is childish, wanting Mommy to sew on his button for him. His passion is directed toward violent misogynist imagining and fury.

After Jinny bites the thread "magnificently," Ran nearly falls and calls her "the cheat" (*CSEW*, 385). This scene can be read as a sexual act, a mythical moment, a military victory, or the ending of a child's game. Ran is turned on by Jinny's action. He breathes out his fury and breaths in disappointment like a man coming. He comments that she bites the thread magnificently, like a lover. He is counting his breaths to make sure he himself is alive and he is disappointed that she is not dead. He calls her a cheat, not just for cheating on him with Woody, but because she did not play the game fairly or, more accurately, she did not play the right game. He was duelling, she was threading needles. She was supposed to die and she is not dead. She was supposed to acknowledge sorrow and pain like a real woman, but instead she hums a little tune and turns him on. She is cheating by playing a role in a story that is different from the one he has been trained to understand; she is changing the rules of the game between men and women. She is cheating. After she has sewn on the button she tells him he is ready for croquet. Croquet involves putting balls through hoops, or we could say sperm into vaginas. Ran comments, "Maideen was out in the swing, sitting. I told her to come on down to the croquet yard, where we all played Jinny's game, without Jinny" (*CSEW*, 386). Maideen is part of Jinny's game. She will heal Ran for Jinny. She will be the sexual consort who will bring the king back ready to perform.

When Ran returns to his room he sees "Miss Billy Texas Spights outdoors in her wrapper, whipping the flowers to make them bloom" (*CSEW*, 386) Ran says to his father, "Father! Dear God wipe it clean. Wipe it clean, wipe it out. Don't let it be" (*CSEW*, 386). Miss Billy Spights has to whip the flowers because the bees are not doing their job. If the male bee were pollinating the flowers, there would be no need for the violence of whipping. Ran wants his father to wipe out the memory not only of what Maideen does to herself but of his own impotence, of his inability to fertilize this community.

At this point in the story the schoolteachers ask Ran to shoot Bella their dog to put her out of her misery. Bella—the female dog—is sick, symbolizing on one narrative plane that the social construction of female beauty is sick and dying, that the whole relationship between male and female which is based on beauty is ailing and needs to be revitalized. When Ran talks to the dog he calls her "lady," the concept of the southern lady who is ailing," but there is more going on in this passage than meets the eye. "To kill the dog" in *The Golden Bough* is a synonym for harvesting the grain. Frazer writes about how in France, Germany, and many Slavonic countries, the Wolf or dog spirit was thought to reside in the corn. "In Verdun the regular expression for finishing the reaping is, 'They are going to kill the Dog' . . . in Tyrol the man who gives the last stroke at threshing is said to 'strike down the Dog' (Frazer, 520). It is August in Welty's story. It is time for the harvest. Ran is missing his cues. Or is he? Ran says at one point that he cut the grass to make it cooler for Bella. Cutting the grass is the act of harvesting.

Cuchulain, the hero whom we have associated with the name MacLain, is also directly connected with dogs.

> His name Cu Chulainn, "the hound of Culann," was given him at the age of seven after he had been forced to kill the watch-dog of Culann, the smith. In recompense Cu Chulainn undertook to guard the king of Ulster and thus became the champion of his people . . . violence to gain his objective is typical of the hero . . . Later on he was similarly reguired to win his bride by force after undergoing violent and dangerous ordeals in foreign lands. . . . The Celtic warrior was no uncouth soldier but was able to converse on equal terms with poets and druids. . . . Before the actual battle Cu Chulainn was thus overtaken by his geasa [a ritual admonition to avoid certain actions in some situations and to perform others in the appropriate circumstances]. Three of the sorceresses of Medb were roasting a dog at the hearth as he passed. It was one of his geasa not to pass a hearth without tasting the food being prepared but it was also another geis for him not to eat dog. By taking the dog's shoulder offered to him his powers were diminished. Another series of demands were made on him by a poet who threatened to satirise him if he refused. This succeeded in disarming and mortally wounding him. Washing himself in a lake he killed an otter which came to drink the blood-stained water. He realised that his end was near as it had been foretold that his first and last exploits would be the killing of a dog—the first was the Hound of Culann and the last a water-dog, the otter. (*New Larousse Encyclopedia of Mythology*, 233)

There are many parallels between this description of Chuchulain and Ran. Ran must go through violent visions to win his bride back from Woody; he can converse with poets and druids as well as ordinary people; the three sorceresses resemble the three teachers; and when Miss Francine asks Ran to kill Bella, she is about to have a friend over for dinner.

Ran is caught. His mother is calling him back to Maclain. At work Miss Jefferson Moody talks to him in his cage in the bank, and Maideen keeps waiting on him: "I felt cornered when she told me, still as kind as ever, about the Seed and Feed" (*CSEW*, 386). By now the women should not be as kind as ever. They should and in many ways are satirizing him; after all of these warnings, he still does not understand. Maideen talks about how you can see cotton blossoms across the window and that soon "it would be sugarcane, and she told me she was thinking already about the Christmas tree" (*CSEW*, 386), Maideen is crying out that the harvest season is almost over, that it is getting late, that Ran better act fast, but she is also telling him another story.

By mentioning Christmas, Maideen connects herself directly to her role as the corn maiden. As Easter becomes the female Christ, so Maideen becomes the female grain god. When Ran is about to take Maideen to meet Jinny, she hangs her head and he sees the "extra-white part in her hair" (*CSEW*, 377). She has the white tassel of the corn maiden. Midsummer Night's eve and Christmas are the two occasions on which the community celebrates and rejuvenates the spirit of renewal.

> In the neighborhood of Balquhidder, Pertshire, the last handful of corn is cut by the youngest girl on the field, and is made into the rude form of a female doll, clad in a paper dress, and decked with ribbons. It is called the Maiden, and is kept in the farmhouse, generally above the chimney, for a good while, sometimes till the Maiden of the next year is brought in. . . . In the North of Scotland the Maiden is kept till Christmas morning, and then divided among the cattle "to make them thrive all the year round." In Aberdeenshire also the last sheaf (called the clyack sheaf) was formerly cut, as it is still cut at Balquhidder, by the youngest girl on the field; then it was dressed in women's clothes, carried home in triumph, and kept till Christmas or New Year's morning, when it was given to a mare in foal or failing such, to the oldest cow. (Frazer, 473)

Woody and the Williams girl in pigtails cast their shadows on the narrative as next years bride and groom, but this year's harvest must be completed first. Maideen as the maiden of the harvest talks to Ran about Christmas and what she will hang on Mr. Moody's tree precisely because she will quite literally hang herself on Mr. Moody's tree. Her name is Sumrall or summerall. She will only live in the summer. Once the grain king has been revitalized and she has played her role, she will die off as a sacrifice to the continuity of the community. On a narrative level the schoolteachers actually write this plot. When Miss Perdita Mayo tells Ran to go back to Jinny, she tells him, "Don't you ruin a *country* girl in the bargain. Make what you will of that" (*CSEW*, 381). Whether this idea was in Ran's head or not, Miss Mayo certainly reinforces it, and even challenges him to do so. While Maideen has her human, individual side, the side that wants Ran to meet her mother, that is embarrassed when Ran takes her to Jinny's house, that cries into her pillow after Ran has her so quickly, she is primarily the sacrifice, the doll, the last corn sheaf presented in effigy to the cattle or the cow to increase fertility. She is the gift of the community to Ran so that Ran and Jinny will be able to bear a child.

In "The Wanderers," Virgie realizes that Ran, who has been elected mayor, was elected for what he did to Maideen. Virgie recognizes that people voted for him for his story. If Ran had followed either conventional script—the one his mother wanted, that he return to her, or the one Miss Lizzie and the U.D.C. wanted, that he settle down and marry Jinny without ever experiencing anything else—he would have no narrative, and he would in no way fertilize the plot of this collection or story. He would be impotent as a character and as a husband. Instead, because he takes Maideen and has her so quickly and because she kills herself, Ran becomes a story, a narrator, a thread in the text/textile. He becomes linguistically as well as physically fertile. He will be elected mayor, the new fertility king.

Only when Ran leaves the bridge game, the marriage, the ladies advice, his cage in the bank, and returns to the Big Black, the rejuvenating river, can he regain his vitality and escape the murderous plots of the three old schoolteachers. In this fertile land "suddenly all sensation returned," and Morgana had become "a pencil mark on the sky," both a word that has lost its meaning, and a setting sun (*CSEW*, 387). In Vicksburg, however, Ran is able to see the dazzling light, to become once more the virile sun god.

Ran takes Maideen to Vicksburg on Sunday, confirming our sense that this is a religious ritual experience, not simply a sordid affair. Maideen does not play bridge. She comes from the country, she works in a store, and she is descended from common stock. She is what would be called poor white trash. She is not part of the old social hierarchy. As Ran leaves town he misses his bridge, not only the game but his bridge back over the river. Maideen is leading him, has led him, to the other side, to Hades, to the disintegration that is the necessary source of renewal. The circle of seasons cannot continue unless the world makes the passage from the fullness of the summer harvest to the death and decay of winter. The superficial desire to maintain order, to record the United Daughters of the Confederacy, stifles and kills virility.

Maideen and Ran are experiencing the necessary dip and fall before the resurrection. Maideen sits in silence reading a woman's magazine, not protesting, not frightened. They are both losing their vital power. Like the sun that is setting as he and Maideen descend, Ran's vital energy is waning. Maideen is also beginning to fall asleep. Her reign as corn maiden is almost over. When they would come home from the bridge game, Maideen would be falling asleep while the little Williams girl, the next in line, "would be chatting away in the back seat, there as far as her house wide awake as an owl" (*CSEW*, 387).

The barge and the silent black bargeman take Ran and Maideen across the river and beyond social convention, where black people who have been forced to work close to the earth have been excluded from polite society (Ran repeatedly uses the word polite, and we begin to recognize it as a psuedonym for passionless), where these people know the rules and hold the secrets of vitality. As Ran and Maideen sit in the barge bar, Ran orders rum cokes that Maideen does not want to drink. The Spartan rules for conception require that the man be sober. Maideen knows this. Ran has not grown up, nor has he learned his lesson. Even here, he holds on to the dissolute modern world. Maideen, however, is ripe fruit; the wasps skim over her hair just as they have buried themselves in Jinny's pears. The wasps are the source of fertility that Miss Billy Spights needs to make her flowers bloom; Maideen wishes that Ran would become the fertile wasp rather than drinking the stupefying and deadening rum cokes. Everything around them expresses decay. There is a smell of fish, roots float everywhere, and "a load of Negroes came over on the water taxi and stepped out sulphur-yellow all over, coated with cottonseed meal" (*CSEW*, 388) These black men, not the United Daughters of the Confederacy, personify the cotton king, the fertility of the South. They, not the gin, are of the earth, condemmed to the earth, the real harvesters of cotton.

Soon after this Ran asks Maideen if she is Catholic. She answers, "We're all Baptists. Why, are you Catholic? Is that what you are?" (*CSEW*, 389), meaning is that what ails you?, is that why it has taken so long for you to do anything? Maideen has been baptized in the waters that will heal Ran. She does not want to drink because she does not need alcohol to loosen up. She is ready, has been for a long time. Maideen observes to Ran "You don't ever dance do you" (*CSEW*, 389). She would enjoy dancing, like the cowboy and his girl dancing close together to the nickelodeon, but Ran does not dance. Ran does not touch Maideen except by accident. Now that Maideen is drunk she cannot shut the car door. In fact, she does not want to shut her door. Ran on the other hand is determined that she will and leans against it to shut it. Maideen says, as if coming on to Ran "I'll fall out. I'll fall in your arms. If I fall, catch me" (*CSEW*, 389). Like a falling star, Maideen becomes part of the natural order. She is a country girl, aware of what is happening to her.

Ran is trying to control his body even as he is rushing down

into the center, the fertile core of this land, the point of disintegration and integration, the rooting before the harvest. He does
not willingly meet the feminine. Maideen is leaning on him and
he asks her not to.

> We circled down. The sound of the river tossing and teasing its
> great load, its load of trash, I could hear through the dark now. It
> made the noise of a moving wall, and up it fishes and reptiles and
> uprooted trees and man's throw-aways played and climbed all alike in
> a splashing like innocence. A great wave of smell beat at my face.
> The track had come down here deep as a tunnel. We were on the
> floor of the world. The trees met and their branches matted over-
> head, the cedars came together, and through them the stars of Mor-
> gana looked sifted and fine as seed, so high, so far. Away off, there
> was the sound of a shot. (*CSEW*, 389–90).

The shot that he hears is his own death shot. Ran knows that
far away someone is burning something, that far away the old
fertility god and corn maiden are burning, and that the seed has
turned into stars in the sky of Morgana. Ran then goes on to
drive his car backwards up a steep incline. "At last we backed
back over the brink, like a bee pulling out of a flower cup, and
skidded a little" (*CSEW*, 390).

Ran has become the bee drinking in the pollen from the flower, but before he can connect with Maideen, give her what she is
longing for, he must heal the real wound that ails all southern
men, the wound of the Civil War. By driving to Vicksburg, Ran
and Maideen are returning to one of the most important battle-
fields of the old South, a reminder of the possibility of victory
and of the eventual pain of defeat. By driving through the Civil
War park, Ran relives and passes beyond the emasculation that
defines the construction of white southern masculinity. "We
drove a long way then. All through the dark Park; the same old
statues and stances, the stone rifles at point again and again on
the hills, lost and the same. The towers they've condemned, the
lookout towers, lost and the same. "Maybe I didn't have my

bearings, but I looked for the moon, due to be in the last quarter. There she was" (*CSEW*, 390–91).

The fact that Ran's vision passes from the stone statues to the moon that was due to be in the last quarter, a full and pregnant moon reveals that he is healing from the constricting demands of white southern masculinity: "There she was. The air wasn't darkness but faint light and floating sound. It was the breath of all the people in the world who were breathing out into the late night looking at the moon, knowing her quarter. And all along I knew I rode in the open world and took bearings by the stars. We rode in wilderness under the lifting moon. Maideen was awake because I heard her sighing faintly, as if she longed for something for her self" (*CSEW*, 391). Only after Ran breaths in the spirit of the female moon and sees the vision of Morgana fine as seed can he recognize, for the first time, that Maideen may want something for her self, may even have a self. When they move out of the natural world and onto the road by the cabins, Maideen appears to be asleep. Maideen is active, longing, wanting, desiring, not a passive victim. She falls asleep only when she is confronted with the social form of the mythic vision. The word "cabins" and the little black boy running along the fence evokes the image of slave cabins and casts the shadow of slavery across this page.

In these cabins, in the dead of night, Ran and Maideen fall asleep. After a while Maideen takes off her dress and returns to the bed, but Ran says, "Don't come close to me" (*CSEW*, 391). We have heard these words before. These are the words of Cuchulain to Morrigana, of Christ to Mary Magdalene, "Touch me not; for I am not yet ascended to my Father" (John 20:17). At this moment, Ran forgets the moon, the power of the whole world, the necessity of the pollinating bee, and reverts to his socially constructed role as dominator and resorts to violent phallic power. Maideen becomes a double image as Ran points his gun at her; she is both the image of defiled southern maidenhead, and much more, all of the visions he has experienced in the moonlit night. She is both the stereotype of the fallen, disguised woman and something else not bloody, not disgraceful. Because he cannot get her in his sights, cannot fix one interpretation on her, he sees double and cannot focus. He says again, "Don't come close to me." As Ran holds this gun, the place itself, with its fertile images of frogs and nightbirds, of sunset oaks, invades Ran's consciousness, opening up a space for Maideen to protest, to tell him not to do what he is doing. She asks him over and over in a steady voice not to point the gun at her. She is not hysterical or even frightened. Ran then turns the gun to his own mouth as if he is about to commit suicide. As he does this he performs another one of the possible roles for himself as a wounded, disillusioned young white male southerner. In this scene Welty exaggerates the action, making it appear almost melodramatic and comical:

> I drew back the pistol, and turned it. I put the pistol's mouth to my own. My instinct is always quick and ardent and hungry and doesn't lose any time. There was Maideen still, coming, coming in her petticoat.
> "Don't do it, Ran. Please don't do it." Just the same.
> I made it—made the awful sound.
> And *she* said. "Now you see. It didn't go off. Give me that. Give that old thing to me, I'll take care of it." (*CSEW*, 392)

Ran is unable to kill Maideen or himself. He is impotent in his prescribed role as disillusioned hero. Maideen on the other hand is able to get him to give her the gun, and she wraps it in her dress, literally weaving it into the textile of the narrative. This is the first time that Ran has allowed Maideen to speak in his entire narrative. Her words are repetitive but they serve their purpose. Only when the gun is out of Ran's hands can he possibly engage in fertile sexual connection with Maideen, but even then he only knows how to have sex like an inexperienced teenager or a rapist. He has no knowledge of how to love a woman.

> And I had her so quick.
> I could have been asleep then. I was lying there.

"You're so stuck up," she said.

I lay there and after a while I heard her again. She lay there by the side of me, weeping for herself. The kind of soft, patient, meditative sobs a child will venture long after punishment.

So I slept.

How was I to know she would go and hurt herself? She cheated, she cheated too.

Father, Eugene! What you went and found, was it better than this?

And where's Jinny? (*CSEW*, 392)

Maideen may be crying because she has been raped or punished as Ran calls it, but this is Ran's interpretation. He assumes she is weeping for herself. She might also be crying because as the fertility queen she must now shed fertile tears, raindrops over the male seed as fertilizer for the following year. She might be crying because he had her so quickly that she could not enjoy or feel anything. She may actually be shedding tears for her self, her life, which she must now sacrifice to the community. What we do know is that Maideen was successful. If we read the line "You're so stuck up" literally, then we know that Ran has literally got it up. When he asks his father and Eugene if what they found was better than this, he might be saying that what he is experiencing is so bad that something must be better, or he may be wondering if, after going all the way out to California, they really found anything better than what he has right here in Morgana, where the stars are fine as seed. His last question seems to support the second reading. He asks, "And where's Jinny?" We know from "The Wanderers" that he returns to Jinny, to Morgana, is elected mayor, and fathers many children. The tragedy is that the modern world has become so distorted that it takes all the power of all the females to transform the masculine energy from autonmous suicidal violence to regenerative communal connection.

It is especially important in our assessment of Welty's place in the literary canon that Welty not be positioned on the margin as one of a small group of lesser women writers next to the voice of Faulkner, but as an equal who finds her vision in a place that includes the Mississippi, the battle of Vicksburg, the Celtic goddess Morrigana, Shakespeare, Ovid, frogs, nightbirds, and William Faulkner.

6

Open the Door, James Joyce

Homoerotic Textualities in "Music from Spain"

As Michael Kreyling points out in *Author and Agent*, Eudora Welty was not sure that "Music from Spain" belonged in *The Golden Apples*, but she felt its inclusion alleviated the claustrophobic atmosphere of Morgana, Mississippi. When we examine the intertextual patterns in "Music from Spain," we can see that the geographical and textual extensions do more than alleviate claustrophobia. The literary and mythic allusions, and there are many—including the myth of Perseus and the Medusa, the myth of Atalanta and the golden apples, Grimm's story of "The Fisherman and His Wife," Virginia Woolf's *To the Light House*, T. S. Eliot's *The Waste Land*, and above all James Joyce's *Ulysses*—set the modernist tradition against the backdrop of myth, folklore, and oral history. This intertextuality occurs most strikingly in Welty's rewriting of Joyce's *Ulysses*.

Several critics, beginning with Harry C. Morris in 1955, have noticed a similarity between *Ulysses* and Welty's "Music from Spain." Morris writes:

> In *The Golden Apples*, Miss Welty has used the Danae and Perseus myths, parts from the lengthy exploits of Zeus and Aphrodite, and

the Homeric wanderings of Odysseus to order the confused and chaotic existence of the people in Morgana, Mississippi. Working in the method of Joyce, she has increased the number of myths in the framework. By following Homer's *Odyssey*, Joyce had the unity of his novel partly worked out for him. But Miss Welty had to fuse previously separate myths into an artistic whole. It is perhaps at this point that her work breaks down most seriously. ("Eudora Welty's Use of Mythology," 35)

Because Morris cannot see either the revisionary fabric that Welty's intertextual process weaves or the fact that Joyce worked out the unity for her, he finds chaos where there is lively new literary form. Thomas L. McHaney, following Morris's reference, makes a convincing argument for the correlation between Eugene and Perseus (612–18). Although I would support his reading, it seems too singular; Eugene is Perseus and Odysseus, but he is also Leopold and Stephen and Eugene himself. He is a composite. Albert Devlin mentions a more direct connection between *Ulysses* and "Music from Spain,"[1] and Louise Hutchings Westling comments on similarities between the plots of the two texts.[2] Westling's analysis suggests that Eugene is defeated by Emma's self-sufficiency. Even though the question of female superiority is at work in this text, a closer reading reveals a more complex relationship between the masculine and feminine characters, a relationship that questions the boundaries of sexuality, gender, and heterosexual romance.

As Devlin indicates, the plot similarities alone would lead us to draw a parallel between the two texts, but the direct correspondence between the structure of "Music from Spain" and both Joyce's "Plan for Ulysses" and the final text makes such a connection more convincing and at the same time more puzzling. One can hardly imagine Welty sitting with a copy of *Ulysses* and a copy of Joyce's plan and taking notes, or adding or subtracting from her manuscript in order to heighten her response to Joyce. In fact, my extreme skepticism of such a conscious dialogue made the discovery of hundreds of similarities in symbol, charac-

ter trait, image, and even word choice, surprising. The similarities are so great and so direct that one begins to suspect either
an incredible mental recall, a conscious effort, or both. Yet everything Welty says about personal literary influences would argue
against such a reading. Welty told Charles Bunting that, "Writing is an internal process. . . . Another person's form doesn't
really help. . . . You're not thinking, 'How did Joyce do this?'
That's fatal" (Prenshaw, *Conversations with Eudora Welty*, 44–45).
Welty's genius is unique and ironically what makes it unique is
its extensive intertextuality. Welty's imaginative universe is as
inhabited by what she has read as it is by her own experience.

To suggest that Eudora Welty's "Music from Spain" is an
answer to James Joyce's *Ulysses* is not only to risk what Welty calls
"making things up," it is to enter a world of literary allusion and
illusion, to walk down a hall of reflecting mirrors.[3] In *Allusions in
Ulysses*, Weldon Thorton devotes five hundred pages exclusively
to tracking down and explicating the literary allusions in Joyce's
text. This is precisely the modernist dilemma. How does one
approach the vast quantity of words already taking up space in
the literary imagination? Many modernist writers—Gertrude
Stein, Virginia Woolf, T. S. Eliot, James Joyce, and Eudora
Welty—found this problem at the center of their artistic challenge. Eliot felt the weight of the past so strongly that he wrote
"Tradition and the Individual Talent." Stein disrupts this past
with new literary forms. In *Ulysses*, Joyce laughs at, minimalizes,
transforms, and reinterprets this tradition. Why then, one must
ask, would Welty want to deconstruct Joyce's deconstruction? If
Joyce had already toppled the edifice, what was left for Welty to
do?

Although Welty gives little or no indication in her letters and
interviews that she is answering Joyce, she does let us hear some
dissatisfaction with his vision. In an interview with Martha van
Noppen, Welty responds to a question about whether the bread-
board scene in *The Optimist's Daughter* is an epiphany by saying,
"Well, I don't use such terms to myself much. I mean, it's a

Joycean term. It's much more dramatic in the sense Joyce uses it and has more reverberations. I suppose you could call it that. But I don't like pretentious words" (Prenshaw, *Conversations with Eudora Welty*, 236–37). Welty's letter to her friend John Robinson in Berkeley, whom she was visiting in San Francisco at the time she was writing "Music from Spain," provides more clues.

> Yes, Joyce seems curiously heavy-handed and non-Celtic with it all, doesn't he—the interminable thoroughness of a German, and a German's wit, the exhausting of the subject with full train of all its puns. I think all the beauty he has is almost in spite of that, the Irish song persisting through a slow, hard maze. Yet his task, his intention, courage—the actual making of a new language—if only he had been content a little sooner along the way, is a feeling I have. Some of this—but not all. The instinct I have is that a real singer like Yeats can do a chapter's worth in a single line, a word—give you that feeling of newness the way it should come, as a light breath, inspiration—.[4]

The title of the story, "Music from Spain," suggests that Welty is answering Joyce as she believed Yeats could, in a song, as a real singer. "Music from Spain" is a woman's song, the song Joyce's Molly might have sung—Molly was, after all, a singer from Gibraltar. If an indignant Joyce scholar were to ask, "What does Welty think she can possibly do to improve this monumental work?" I would have to answer that she does not desire to improve it. She simply hopes to answer Joyce, to respond, and in fact makes this work much less monumental, less pretentious. Ironically, under the guise of tearing down, Joyce reinforces the canonical literary structure. The extensive critical response to his work indicates that scholars eventually accepted him as the rightful heir to the masculine literary throne, the son of the fathers. He refers so often and so comprehensively to *Hamlet*, the *Odyssey*, and the Bible that, like a son rebelling against his father, he honors his father's power with the fury of his protest. One could argue that Welty's work also depends on this type of rebellion, but Welty does not rebuild the same edifice. In fact, in its brevity "Music from Spain" makes fun of the strongest cement of that edifice, abstract language—"the exhausting of the subject with full train of all its puns." Welty's "Music from Spain" is between thirty and fifty pages long, depending on the edition, and *Ulysses* is six hundred and some pages long, depending on the edition. Unlike Leopold or Stephen, Eugene cannot depend on language; the Spaniard cannot or does not choose to speak English.

"Music from Spain" begins when Eugene MacLain, after eating breakfast and reading the newspaper, slaps his wife in the face in response to her comment that he has a crumb on his chin. He leaves the apartment to go to his job as a watch repairman but cannot make himself go to work. The fact of having slapped Emma makes him feel that his life has changed completely. While he is walking the streets of San Francisco, he sees a large foreigner who almost gets hit by an automobile. He saves the foreigner from this fate, and they spend the rest of the day together wandering the streets of San Francisco. All day Eugene tries to make sense of the fact that he has slapped Emma. He assumes that he knows what Emma is doing, thinking, and feeling but cannot make sense of his own actions.

In *Ulysses* there are really two beginnings, Stephen's and Leopold's, but in both the men are eating breakfast. Leopold makes breakfast in the morning, brings his wife Molly her breakfast in bed, leaves the house to buy himself some kidneys, returns, fries them over a flame, leaves the house again, goes to a friend's funeral, and walks around the city for the day and most of the night pondering whether Molly is indeed having an affair while he himself follows his own sexual cravings. During his journey he meets up with Stephen Daedalus, the derelict, poetic, intellectual son of a wasted father and a dead mother. Leopold is searching for a son and Stephen for a father. Stephen is effete, abstract, full of words, and half dead—DEADalus. Leopold is alive—"Bloom"—eats heartily, abstains from too much drink, and has a sexual appetite. In some ways they are the antithesis of one another, but Leopold is really no more alive, no more resurrected from the malaise of modern culture than Stephen. Leopold spills his words in verbosity and his seed in masturbation. He has lost his only son and sent his daughter away. Stephen spills his seed in drunken orgies, and neither man fulfills his powers of creation in the intellectual, imaginative, or physical sense.

Joyce ostensibly makes fun of the heroic narrative throughout his work, but *Ulysses* mirrors the *Odyssey* in its attention to paternal and heroic narratives. In the narrative structure of the two texts, a son searches for a father and a father for a son. Both works follow de Lauretis's analysis of the heroic narrative. There is a journey away from a wife or mother, adventures, dangerous encounters with female others, a scene of male bonding, and a return to a female world. The primary difference between *Ulysses* and the *Odyssey* is that in *Ulysses* the characters encounter no physical dangers, engage in no physical battles or sacrifices, and experience no material losses. However, *Ulysses*'s antiheroic stance does not deconstruct the heroic myth; it is the defeated version of the same story. In both texts the economy of the work turns around male sexual prowess. At first glance it seems that in this context the two works diverge. The fidelity or infidelity of Penelope is central to the *Odyssey* and Odysseus's wealth depends on his wife's faithfulness, but in *Ulysses*, Leopold returns not knowing whether his wife has been faithful to him and he never really finds out. His stature in the community and his economic status do not depend on Molly's fidelity. Like Odysseus he wants to test her, but in this case such a test would be completely inappropriate.

In both works the man's infidelity is not in question. Odysseus sleeps with Circe, Calypso, and many others on his journeys and no one loses wealth or sleep over his activities; they simply prove the sexual prowess of the hero. Likewise, Molly takes Leopold's sexual adultery for granted, but in *Ulysses* the sexual energy, Leopold's and Molly's, is not what keeps the novel going. No reader can be that interested in either character's fidelity. There is too much talk of sexual activity among the characters for us to believe in fidelity. One could then claim that the motivating force behind *Ulysses* and that which separates it from the heroic literary tradition is the dissipation of male fertility. Leopold masturbates and spills his seed, wets himself. His one son has died and he has no son to whom he can pass on his knowledge and expertise. As in Eliot's *The Waste Land* the dilemma of the lost fertility god plagues the text, but this is still not what keeps *Ulysses* going for six hundred pages. Dissolution cannot sustain itself for that long. What supplies the energy to keep Joyce and the reader engaged for that many pages is the fact that Joyce replaces physical fertility and virility with linguistic fertility and virility.

In fact Joyce reinforces the heroic myth of male dominance by replacing Odysseus's physical sexual dominance with Leopold's linguistic sexual dominance. Leopold lets us know that he cannot have the same kind of conversation with Molly that he can with Stephen. Molly must ask Leopold what words mean. Leopold must supply Molly with books, and these books generally are erotic romances. She thinks he is Lord Byron or some other great romantic poet. The masculine seed is scattered like an alphabet, engendering literary allusion, wordplay, punning, metaphoric fireworks/firewords, and complex symbolic intertextualities. All of the male characters engage in this volleying of puns, jokes, and gossip. The mental acrobatics of Leopold, Stephen, Buck Mulligan, and the men they meet in the pub, the library, the street, and the beach are not only metaphorically masturbatory but actually have masturbation as their texts; more often than not the subject of the wordplay is foreplay. The repeated references to Leopold's need to come and to his mistress, the whole chapter devoted to his voyeuristic rape of Gerty, the orgy in which he and Stephen either actually or symbolically engage reinforce the erotic power of the text. Would readers keep reading if they were not turned on by the characters' sexual force poured into the linguistic gymnastics?

The tantalizing deferred gratification is then not really a deconstruction of the *Odyssey* but a modern version. The *Odyssey* gains power and momentum from the deferred gratification of the return home, the repeated challenges to Odysseus's physical prowess, the return to paternal love and filial affection. *Ulysses* gains power from the deferred gratification of the antihero's sexual cravings, the repeated challenges to Leopold's linguistic prowess. The question becomes, Can Leopold and Stephen keep it up? Can they keep up the punning, literary allusion, speculations, theories, banter, and jokes that keep the text alive? Molly's section has the same sexual tantalization that is present in the other sections but does not have the linguistic complexity. Molly can only keep this narrative up, so to speak, if she talks about all the men she has had or wants and what Leopold would think about her actions. Her linguistic masturbation is masculinist linguistic masturbation, and it is masturbation not intercourse precisely because nothing is brought to seed, engendered, or created out of the act. Her menstrual blood pours out, indicating fertility but not pregnancy. Those who argue that Molly's narrative is really feminist and liberating fail to notice that, as soon as Joyce allows the female to speak, the narrative must end. For only while Leopold sleeps can there be the necessary lack of engagement and dialogue that keeps the text teetering on the edge of annihilation. True dialogue between Molly and Leopold would take the plot out of the wasteland of literary allusion. Fertile physical connection between any two characters, Leopold and Stephen or Leopold and Molly, would end the nonregenerative, nonphysical play of male text with male text.

In "Music from Spain," Emma and Eugene are also in a passionless marriage, but in this case Eugene does not question Emma's fidelity. In fact sex, explicitly absent but implicitly coded in description and metaphor, indicates that Welty is indeed creating something quite different. Sexual activity is not at the center of the text, it is obliquely on the margins. Without the socially constructed male crutch of heterosexual exploration/

exploitation to fall back on (although he does try this for one moment in the restaurant when he hopes the Spaniard will take him to a whorehouse), Eugene's quest must be more an internal discovery than an external gratification. His journey brings him in closer contact with a father figure, who reminds him for a moment of his father King MacLain. This encounter is homoerotic, and in this meeting Eugene discovers for a moment his more animal, fertile body. He does not escape from his body in linguistic gymnastics, as do Leopold and Stephen, but instead embraces, quite literally, the lost father/son, brother/brother, male lover in himself, if only for a moment. "Music from Spain" is much less neurotic and much more erotic than *Ulysses*, primarily because Welty allows the homoerotic subtext to emerge. Welty diminishes obsessive culturally constructed issues—fidelity, faithfulness, sexual obsession—and replaces them with self-discovery, journeying, meeting an/other, and the passion that emerges from this meeting. The simple physical interaction between two human beings, made even more direct by the fact that they do not speak each other's language, forms the epiphany of this text.

If there is anything obvious about *Ulysses*, it is that Bloom can spin the wheels of cultural allusion, or rather Joyce through Leopold can spin them from here to infinity; he never really reaches the moment of human physical connection with Stephen because there are so many words dividing them. In fact Leopold cannot feel himself, really experience himself, until he shuts up or, more accurately, his mind shuts up. The only moments in which he is able to still the clamoring abstractions of his mind occur during the orgy and masturbation scenes when, in the throes of sexual excitement, his body demands his attention. During the orgy scene in the brothel and in Chapter 13 when he is masturbating while watching Gerty, his ability to rationalize, justify, judge, and explain dissipates—but not for long. He prides himself on being able to think, to rationalize, to remember even at these moments. Welty's "Music from Spain" returns the male protagonist to his body by depriving him of the crutch of words. With words the male protagonist can go on forever; in fact he is built of words, constructed of words. He has been defined and refined in cultural texts over thousands of years so that like Joyce he can keep spinning the web of linguistic creation forever; he is a word thing.

Aside from plot similarities the most convincing evidence of the correlation between the two texts comes from the direct section by section correspondence between "Music from Spain" and Joyce's plan for *Ulysses*. Welty's short story has two types of divisions. It is divided into seven sections denoted by roman numerals and into nineteen subsections indicated by line spaces. The sections separated by line spaces correlate quite closely with both Joyce's original plan for *Ulysses* and the final text. Welty probably did not see this plan when it was first circulated because she would have been too young, but she could have found it in Stuart Gilbert's *James Joyce's Ulysses* published in 1930. Joyce's plan calls for eighteen chapters that correspond to, but do not follow the exact order of, Homer's *Odyssey*. Welty's divisions in theme and symbol follow Joyce's chapters, not Homer's, making it impossible to argue, as Morris does in another article, that Welty was only writing her own revision of the *Odyssey* ("Zeus and the Golden Apples: Eudora Welty," 196–99). Although Morris brings out some interesting connections between "Music from Spain" and the *Odyssey*, he neglects to see the more complex intertextuality created by the Joyce connection. Welty demonstrates direct knowledge of the *Odyssey* but follows the plan of *Ulysses*. In his plan Joyce divides the book into chapters labeled 1. Telemachus 2. Nestor 3. Proteus 4. Calypso 5. Lotus-Eaters 6. Hades 7. Aeolus 8. Lestrygonians 9. Scylla and Charybdis 10. Wandering Rocks 11. Sirens 12. Cyclops 13. Nausicaa 14. Oxen of the Sun 15. Circe 16. Eumaeus 17. Ithaca 18. Penelope. Each chapter has a corresponding scene, time, organ, art, color, symbol, and technic. Hugh Kenner argues that Joyce referred to this plan but did not always follow it exactly. Each of Welty's divisions corresponds to at least one of Joyce's chapters, and the allusions can be charted directly from those divisions, but there are also allusions throughout the story to Chapter 18, the Molly chapter, labeled "Penelope" in the plan, and to Chapter 4, the first Leopold chapter, labeled "Calypso" in the plan. The Aeoleus references are blown throughout the rest of the text. There is not a direct equivalency throughout because there are nineteen Welty sections and eighteen *Ulysses* chapters, but the correspondence is quite close in most of the sections.

Chapter 1 of *Ulysses* in the plan is called the Telemachus section. It is set in the tower at 8:00 A.M. The color is white-gold and the technic is narrative (young). The Telemachus section of the *Odyssey* explores Telemachus's desire to protect his mother from the suitor's advances and to find his lost father. In the Telemachus section of *Ulysses*, Stephen is remembering his dead mother, whom he did not save. In "Music from Spain," Eugene rejects the mother's touch, Emma's "motherly finger" (*CSEW*, 395), and unconsciously begins his search for his lost father, King MacLain, who, like Odysseus, went west and left him long ago. There are many similarities between the first section of "Music from Spain" and the Telemachus chapter of *Ulysses*: both men are beginning the day; Stephen is eating fish and bread, Eugene is eating toast; Stephen is thinking about the death of his mother, Eugene is thinking about the death of his daughter. In "Music," Eugene sees his face pass the mirror with a smile on it, an image Eudora Welty added to the final manuscript.[5] In *Ulysses*, Stephen and Buck Mulligan have a long discussion about Stephen's face in the mirror: "He swept the mirror a half circle in the air to flash the tidings abroad in sunlight now radiant on the sea. His curling shaven lips laughed and the edges of his white glittering teeth" (*UL*, 6). Welty takes Joyce's full-blown laugh, makes a smile out of it, and reduces the amount of time spent on this narcissistic impulse.[6]

To reveal the extent of the intertextuality, we must see that there are also connections between the first section of "Music from Spain" and the second beginning of *Ulysses*, Chapter 4 or the first Leopold chapter. Like Leopold, Eugene is fixing and eating breakfast. Like Leopold he is cooking his breakfast over a flame, and Welty even adds the line "the second pan of toast was under the flame" (*CSEW*, 393). Like Leopold, Eugene is holding on to a paper while the oven roars. Like Leopold, Eugene has lost a child: Leopold loses little Rudy and Eugene loses Fan. Like Leopold, Eugene leaves the house and his wife with his paper under his arm. Leopold is middle-aged; Eugene is middle-aged. In Chapter 4, Joyce mentions that Molly is from Gibraltar, that she is a singer, and that she had "forgotten any little Spanish she knew" (*UL*, 46), thus introducing the idea of Spain and music.

If Welty were following the heroic narrative structure, then Eugene, like Stephen, would be rebelling against his mother, rejecting the female world in order to enter the male world. Thus Eugene would be slapping Emma because her motherly finger brushed a crumb from his chin. However, Eugene's slap, instead of perpetuating this myth, interrupts the usual progression of events. He waits for Emma to say "Eugene?" and his response "Yes dear?" and all the other socially expected, trite things that husband and wife would say, but Emma does not recite her script, and Eugene is left to interpret her look on his own. The only language he finds to describe her reinforces his stereotypes: "'Get-out-of-my-kitchen' and 'Come-here-do-you-realize-what-you've-done,' all her stiffening and wifely glaze running sweet and finespun as sugar threads over her" (*CSEW*, 393). By using the terms sweet and wifely, Eugene pours his clichéd description like a stiffening glaze over Emma's physical being; all Eugene actually experiences is her wounded cry. Eugene expects her to call him back but she does not. Left to discover the motivations for his actions without Emma's help, Eugene "let his breath out, and there it was: he could see it. The air, the street, a sea gull, all the same soft gray, were in the same degree visible and seemed to him suddenly as pure" (*CSEW*, 394). Eugene's release of breath is an embodiment, making him conscious of the air, the street, and the sea gull. His breath, the breath that forms words, is quite simply part of the day, not tainted with clichés but pure—a blank slate.

This exhalation begins the second break in the text of "Music from Spain," which echoes Chapter 2 or the Nestor section of *Ulysses*. In the plan and in the text, Joyce sets this section in school at 10:00 A.M. The art is history, the color is brown, the symbol is horse, and the technic is catechism (personal). Joyce follows the catechismic technic and the location of school in the plan by making Stephen a teacher who asks his students questions. In "Music from Spain," Eugene asks questions of himself and thinks about the questions[7] Mr. Bertsinger will ask him as if he were a pupil in school.[8] Although not directly connected to the plan in *Ulysses*, Deasy is trying to get his article into print. In "Music from Spain," Eugene takes the figures in his mind and imagines them on the printed page, revealing the process of abstraction from body to figure to photograph. Eugene's imagining his and Emma's photographs in the papers echoes Molly's thought in Chapter 18, "he'll write about me lover and mistress publicly too with our 2 photographs in all the papers" (*UL*, 638).[9] When Eugene considers what he might say to Bertsinger, he imagines Emma's body. He wonders if he has hurt her and thinks, "There couldn't be a mark on her" (*CSEW*, 394). Welty realizes that his slap has not altered her body, because it has not touched her actual physical body, only a social construction called "wife."

At this point Eugene thinks about the fact that Emma is bigger and heavier than he. While the literary hero has been fed on words of praise, the female, denied entry into the gates of culture, has become an expert in the material sphere. Symbolically her body is stronger, larger, more developed than his. By saying "crumb on your chin," Emma has challenged Eugene to turn his eyes from the newspaper to his body, to the food he is eating, and his chin. She has brought him out of the abstract domain of newspapers and power and into the domestic realm. In this domain Eugene only knows how to act in the most stereotypical way: he hits Emma. What Eugene realizes that Molly and Leopold do not is that beyond all of this abstract knowledge, "Emma knew he hadn't hurt her; better than he knew, Emma knew" (*CSEW*, 394). Emma does not have to prove anything to Mr. Bertsinger or the world because she already knows about her body.

One of Eugene's strongest statements about Emma is that she would insist that he eat. In Chapter 18 of *Ulysses*, Molly makes a reference to Leopold's refusal to eat.[10] In Joyce's text Molly uses food to discover Leopold's potential infidelity. In Welty's text Emma uses food to control Eugene but in a much more subtle and more powerful way. Eugene does not dare reject her food. Even if he were going to kill her, he would eat first. Food is life. Emma's command, "Sit down and tell me what you see," is Emma's way of bringing the man into her domain, the world of sight, touch, smell, and taste where, as Eugene says, "she was *sensitive*" (*CSEW*, 395). This line can be read not only that she is emotionally sensitive or fragile, but that she is aware of her senses. Eugene realizes that a quarrel could not even grow between Emma and himself; instead of using words she would cry. He goes on to comment that Emma has "a waterfall of tears back there" (*CSEW*, 395). With this description, Emma becomes the goddess who approaches Loch in the spring and calls him back to life. Emma's tears will renew the fertility consort. In this animal and mythical world, this world of the physical, the sun, traditionally symbolic of the male, is smaller than the moon, traditionally symbolic of the female.

Eugene on the other hand will have to spend the rest of the day trying to figure out why he slapped Emma and what it means. When he thinks about his action, he does not come up with a complicated reason, but instead he sighs, again letting out his breath, and when he does he thinks of Emma in very precise physical terms. He imagines "the rosy mole might be riding the pulse in her throat" (*CSEW*, 394). The difference between these images and his earlier thoughts is that these are real descriptions of actions he has seen her perform. They are memories, not hallucinations. After slapping Emma everything takes on material form. Even the abstract question "Why, in the name of all reason, had he struck Emma?" becomes embodied and disengaged from him, an actual presence, skirting through traffic "almost like a comedian pretending to be an old man" (*CSEW*, 394). Every time he tries to discover why he hit Emma, he is brought back to his physical sensations: "Why slap her today? The question prodded him locally now, in the back of one knee as nearly as he could tell. It accommodated itself like the bang of a small bell to the stiff pull of his shanks" (*CSEW*, 395). When Eugene tries again to ask the question, "Why strike her even softly?" (*CSEW*, 395), Welty has him think of answers that she puts in italics because they are so removed from the essence of Eugene's character. They are the words of macho male culture: "*Why not strike her? And if she thought he would stay around only to hear her start tuning up, she had another thing coming. Let her take care and go about her business, he might do it once more and not so kindly*" (*CSEW*, 395). These words, which would have meaning in another narrative, seem fragile and even ridiculous in here.

As Eugene awakens to the material world, he thinks that the eucalyptus trees seem bigger and that he can hear the beating hearts of birds. He feels himself holding back as he walks downhill. He even sees himself, his body reflected in the windows: "His head and neck jerked in motions like a pigeon's; he looked down, and when he saw the fallen and purple eucalyptus leaves underfoot, his shoes suddenly stamped them hard as hooves" (*CSEW*, 395). Not only does this description imply that Eugene has entered the animal world, it also suggests that he has entered a mythical masculinity in which fallen leaves in August symbolize the death of the fertility consort. Like a satyr or horse Eugene stomps his hooves in unison with these forces. In the *Odyssey*, Nestor is the friend of Odysseus whom Telemachus visits in order to gain information about his father. Nestor is a master charioteer, and after he has told Telemachus the story of his father, Nestor gives him blood mares, the best horses, to speed him on his journey. Thus the horse is the symbol for this chapter in Joyce's plan. In *Ulysses*, Joyce writes of Deasy that "he stamped on gaitered feet over the gravel of the path "(*UL*, 30).[11] Eugene stamps his feet hard as hooves in a much more direct connection to the horse, but the similarity between the two actions is still apparent.

In an attempt to account for his behavior, Eugene wanders into the discourse of romantic love, musing that he has struck Emma because he can no longer love Miss Dimdummie Dumwiddie, a woman with whom he once imagined having an affair. When Eugene sees Miss Dimdummie Dumwiddie's face before him, he realizes that he could see her name, "the same as read underneath, in the italics of poetry" (*CSEW*, 396). Throughout Chapter 2 and throughout his entire book, Joyce puts poetry in italics beneath his descriptions. Italicized poetry could even be considered a mark of *Ulysses*. By making such a direct link to Joyce at this moment, Welty indicates that she is transforming the narrative of dim, dumb women, which Joyce exploits in almost every portrayal of women in *Ulysses*, into a new textual fabric. As Eugene becomes more and more involved in this romantic narrative, he is stopped in his tracks by the butcher. In Welty's text Eugene cannot get off the hook (quite literally) by running off with another woman in a conventional mid-life crisis: "The butchers, stepped outside for a moment in their bloody aprons, made a pause for ladies sometimes, but never for men. The beeves were moving across, all right, and on the other side a tramp leaned on a cane to watch, leering like a dandy at each one of the carcasses as it went by; it could have been some haughty and spurning woman he kept catching like that" (*CSEW*, 396). The butchers may pause for ladies but never for men, because the men need to be stopped in their tracks by this brutal physical image in order to let them know they cannot keep butchering the female body. The interruption does not stop the tramp who can still only see the beeves as women's flesh.[12] By halting Eugene's narrative of Miss Dimdummie, the butcher keeps Eugene from projecting onto her his sexual fantasies and making her a piece of flesh rather than a human being with a mind and heart who has just died. The butcher tells Eugene he can continue by motioning to him with his knife. After this interruption Eugene knows that he cannot go to work: "And things were a great deal more serious than he had thought" (*CSEW*, 396). The butcher's knife is a symbol of danger, of war, of a serious encounter, of an exploitative romantic narrative thread that must be violently interrupted or cut.

At this moment Eugene reaches under his raincoat and touches his coat, his vest, and his silver pencil, the artifacts of his technological manhood. In touching these articles, he recognizes their materiality and he clings to one small revelation: "today he was not able to take those watches apart" *CSEW*, 396). In reaching under his raincoat, Eugene emulates the actions of a person exposing himself, like Mr. Voight in "June Recital," but instead of masturbating or revealing himself, Eugene reaches for a silver pencil—a diminutive and feminized phallus. Standing on the top of a steep hill, he searches in vain for his lost sexuality: "*She could still bite his finger, couldn't she?* and some mischievous, teasing spirit looked at him, mouthing joy before darting ahead. But he looked down at the steepness, shocked and almost numb. A passerby gave him a silent margin. The slap had been like kissing the cheek of the dead" *CSEW*, 396). As he descends into embodiment, feeling, and sensation, Eugene knows that somehow he and Emma have become so far removed from one another after Fan's death that Emma is living in the world of the dead and he has not realized this. His blow has met blackness, a wide-open eye. Eugene looks down into the underworld and the steepness shocks him, the distance he has to travel, how far down he has to go to make this journey into the underworld, where Emma has already ventured.

To descend into this world Eugene must change shapes and

take on new forms. In the third break in the text of "Music from Spain," Welty echoes Joyce's third chapter of *Ulysses*, which in the plan and in the text focuses on the Proteus section of the *Odyssey*. Joyce sets this chapter on the Strand at 11:00 A.M. Philology is the art, green is the color, tide is the symbol, and monologue (male) is the technic. In the *Odyssey*, Proteus had the ability to change shapes and he was the herdsman for Neptune, the god of the sea. In Chapter 3 of *Ulysses* and in the third subsection of "Music from Spain," there are numerous references to shape-shifting and to the sea. Eugene descends "with his head seeming to float above his long steps," and he sees, "Market [Street] had with the years become a street of trusses, pads, braces, false bosoms, false teeth, and glass eyes . . . of jewelry stores" (*CSEW*, 397).[13]

Like Odysseus entering the underworld, Eugene is seeing the carnage of modern society for the first time, the constructed body, the female body adorned, made to be less physical, less threatening. He notices for the first time, "'Nothing but Gold to Touch the Flesh.' It could all make a man feel shame. The kind of shame one had to jump up in the air, kick his heels, to express—whirl around!" (*CSEW*, 397) In order to represent his guilt Eugene returns to his own jumping, moving, expressive body to help him wake up to the sound of the man cracking crabs, to the caw of the tropical bird, to all colors of the flowers—and thus to the contrast between his job of repairing watches and the fertile prolific life surrounding him.

When he sees in "the flyblown window of a bookstore a dark photograph that looked at first glance like Emma (Emma, he could bet, still sat on at the table composing herself, as carefully as if she had been up to the ceiling and back) was, he read below, Madame Blavatsky" (*CSEW*, 397). Madame Blavatsky was founder of the Theosophical Society. Theosophy, as Peter Fingesten describes it, was "founded in New York in 1875," and "aimed at a spiritual revitalization of the West. Its anti-rationalism had a certain appeal for those dissatisfied with the intense materialism and scienticism of the late 19th century. Theosophy offered instead a mystic, oriental interpretation of life and evolution" (2). By confusing Emma and Madame Blatvasky, Eugene puts all women in the realm of the antiscientific. Eugene's confusion supports the notion that he is journeying away from social expectations on a spiritual journey led by women. Madame Blavatsky also appears in *Ulysses*.

Throughout the Proteus chapter of *Ulysses*, Joyce exploits associations with the sea,[14] and Welty makes this correlation when she has Eugene look at the amber red caviar in the shape of a large anchor: "'They are fish eggs, sir,' a young, smocked clerk said, 'and personally I think it's a perfect *pity* that they should be allowed to take them'" (*CSEW*, 398). This is the most direct statement of the problem Eugene must face. A society that takes the eggs from the fish, the young from the mother, is destroying itself. Fan has died. Eugene is upset that the clerk does not recognize him, but of course Eugene is still invisible, a no/body in this material universe. In Bertsinger's jewelry store there is a rhinestone Pegasus and a ruby swordfish. In the Greek myth involving these figures, Pegasus leapt from the Medusa's blood when Perseus cut off her head. Pegasus jewelry, by catching the horse in flight, is a co-optation of the Medusa's protest. When Eugene passes the jewelry store he is invisible; Bertie Junior does not see him because he is watching the more compelling fist fight, the physical struggle emerging louder than Eugene's mental musings. When Eugene notices the fish eggs, he bows to them, perhaps because he recognizes them for the first time as part of himself. While the eggs are like a mother's young, they are perhaps more directly connected to male sperm, captured and put behind glass.

As Eugene passes the jewelry store, he releases himself from repairing watches, and natural time asserts itself as the sun, "with a spurt of motion, came out. The streetcars, taking on banana colors, drove up and down, the line of movie houses fluttered streamers and flags as if they were going to sea. Eugene moved into the central crowd, which seemed actually to increase its jostling with the sunshine, like the sea with wind" (*CSEW*, 398). The sun, symbolically male, the spurt of motion, and the streetcars (shape-shifting by taking on banana colors and driving up and down) create a phallic and highly sexual scene. The spurt of motion is like sperm issuing forth, the banana suggests a phallus, and the driving up and down can be read as sexual. As soon as Eugene leaves the watches and jewelry, the aesthetic abstractions of his life, he enters the vitality of his masculinity on the mythic, symbolic, and material planes. As the sun spurts forth, the crowd increases its movement. The sun has a livening, fertile impact. The Proteus chapter of *Ulysses* ends with a ship at sea.[15] Eugene, the movie house, and the people in the crowd in "Music from Spain" also seem to turn at the end of this section into (again, a shape-shifting) ships at sea.

In *Ulysses* Chapter 4 Joyce introduces Leopold and Molly's relationship and focuses more on Molly than he does in other chapters. Likewise in "Music from Spain," Eugene thinks and talks more about Emma in this section[16] than he has previously.[17] As the fog lifts, memory returns to Eugene, and he begins to feel the extent of Emma's grief at Fan's death.[18] He sees images of Fan, how she looked, what she wore, her innocence, and her sexuality. There is a direct correspondence in this section with the paragraph in *Ulysses* in which Leopold's daughter Milly's birthday reminds him of his dead son Rudy: "She knew from the first poor little Rudy wouldn't live. Well God is good, sir. She knew at once. He would be eleven now if he had lived" (*UL*, 54). In "Music from Spain," Eugene remembers asking Emma to take a trip to Half Moon Bay and her refusing: "it had been his luck to mention it on the anniversary of Fan's death and she had slammed the door in his face" (*CSEW*, 399). Emma and Eugene have been married twelve years. Rudy would have been eleven. Fan could have been eleven. Emma and Eugene's marriage was eleven years old when Fan died.[19]

Like Odysseus, Leopold wants to see the world, and Eugene

also wants to travel. Eugene suggests to Emma that they take "a simple little pleasure trip" (*CSEW*, 399), and Leopold imagines visiting Milly and planning a trip (*UL*, 55). As he continues his inner journey, Eugene begins to long for "that careless, patched land of Mississippi winter, trees in their rusty wrappers, slow-grown trees taking their time, the lost shambles of old cane, the winter swamp where his own twin brother, he supposed, still hunted" (*CSEW*, 399). The lost shambles of old cane, the image of King MacLain in "Sir Rabbit," is the image of the dying fertility god in the winter and symbolizes Eugene's loss of fertility. It is too late for Eugene to bring his seed to bear on the earth again, to have another child with Emma or another woman.

This awakening in him, this longing, materializes before him in the words of the "hoarse voice from a pitch-black bar" calling, "*Open the door, Richard!*" (*CSEW*, 399).[20] The door, which Eugene locks behind him when he leaves Emma, must be opened. Any shut door will keep Eugene from descending as far as he must descend to regain passion. Eugene wants to "put out a staying hand" (*CSEW*, 399) to the Chinese girl he sees on the street, and in *Ulysses* Leopold wants to follow/stop the maid from next door (*UL*, 49). Eugene has entered the underworld of society where all of the marginal characters meet, and in this world he cannot stop the movement of others.

> When a stocky boy with a black pompadour went by him wearing taps on his shoes, some word waited unspoken on Eugene's lips. His chance for speaking tapped rhythmically by. He frowned in the street, the more tantalized, somehow, by seeing at the last minute that the stranger was tattooed with a butterfly on the inner side of his wrist; an intimate place, the wrist appeared to be. Eugene saw the butterfly plainly enough to recognize it again, when this unfamiliar, callused hand of San Francisco put a flame to a bitten cigarette. In blue ink the double wings spanned the veins and the two feelers reached into the fold at the base of the hand; the spots were so deep they seemed to have come perilously near to piercing the skin. (*CSEW*, 399–400)

The stocky boy breaks gender conventions with his tap shoes and pompadour cap, and Eugene wants to cross over to communicate with this sexually liminal figure but has no language to do so. In this musical world where communication takes place in rhythms—taps on shoes—this visual world where the communication takes place in symbols and gestures—lighting cigarettes and displaying butterfly tattoos—Eugene is at a loss. He has not yet learned this coded language. The butterfly, a symbol of resurrection, is tattooed on an intimate and vulnerable place on a man's arm, suggesting that this regeneration is about male sexuality and vulnerability. In order to experience the tantalizing power of this resurrection, one must share in the intimacy, in this erotic adornment of the male body. Eugene, "withdrawing one step in his thoughts" (*CSEW*, 400), realizes that no familiar person will do him any good in this place at this time. Eugene has already decided to seek a stranger before he even meets the Spaniard, but the only words he can think of to connect with this stranger are again macho clichés: *"Hi, mate. Just lammed the little wifey over the puss.—Horray!—That's what I did.—Sure, not a bad idea once ever so often. Take it easy"* (*CSEW*, 400). Because there is little tender language of male homoeroticism in literary discourse, it is almost impossible for Eugene to find words to express the feelings he experiences after seeing the butterfly tatoo. The language that does exist is coarse, while the sexuality itself is like the butterfly tatoo, sensual and regenerative.

As Eugene proceeds along the street, he realizes that "a plaster bulldog, cerise with blue rings around the eyes, which ordinarily sat in the ground floor window of a hotel between the drawn shade and the glass, had this morning been taken away" (*CSEW*, 400). Eugene misses the dog that, like one of the guardians of the gates of hell, has been removed. He can now enter the underworld. Interestingly enough the new guardian of this underworld is a female cat in a grocer's window. In the cat's eyes Eugene finds his own boldness. The tortoiseshell cat pillowed in apples in "Music from Spain" mirrors the cat in *Ulysses*.[21] In the

Ulysses scene the cat is female and all knowing. In "Music from Spain," Eugene sees himself as all knowing and realizes he might be able to understand what threatens and transforms the moral way. He might be entering into this erotic realm of tender tattooed men and women.

In the fifth subsection of "Music from Spain," Welty echoes Chapter 5 of *Ulysses*, which is based on Homer's Lotus Eaters. The scene is the bath at 10:00 A.M., the organ genitals, the art botany and chemistry, the symbol eucharist, and the technic narcissism. In the *Odyssey*, Homer writes, "They fell in, soon enough, with Lotus Eaters, who showed no will to do us harm, only offering the sweet Lotus to our friends—but those who ate this honeyed plant, the Lotus, never cared to report, nor to return: they longed to stay forever, browsing on that native bloom, *forgetful* of their homeland" (Book 9, ll. 91–96). In the *Odyssey* the Lotus Eaters are drugged and lethargic. Although their honey-drugged world is wonderful, it is in this place that the men lose the will to sail the ship home, or even to remember what home is. Joyce makes many references to lethargy throughout Chapter 5 of *Ulysses* (ll., 5, 9–10, 29–36, 474, 481–83). In "Music from Spain," Welty uses the Spaniard's lethargic presence as a counterpoint to Eugene's focused presence. Eugene moves as a person living in the modern world, with a brisk, businesslike stride, while the Spaniard is "going along measuredly and sedately before, the only black-clad figure on this Western street, head and shoulders above all the rest . . . he was quite provocatively slow, moving through this city street" (*CSEW*, 401). Eugene represents the future while the Spaniard, represents the past and death. Before Eugene sees the Spaniard he is walking down Market Street where bright mist bathes the street and hides the ferry building. The mist allows us to imagine that Eugene is indeed entering another dimension, a forgetful place beyond the structures of civilization, beyond buildings. The mist covers the modern constructions.

When the Spaniard reaches the curb, he almost walks under

the wheels of a car, as if he does not see or care about the industrial machinery that surrounds him. Eugene recognizes him as "the Spaniard he had heard play the guitar at Aeolian Hall the evening before. . . . Emma had come out with Eugene to a music hall, and it had turned out that this Spaniard performed, in solo recital . . . his failure to respect music was part of the past, a night with little Fan at the Symphony, her treat. When the music began the child had held out her little arms, saying Pierre Monteaux came out of *Babar* and she wanted him down here and would spank him" (*CSEW*, 401). The hall, the music, the Spaniard, and Fan are all in a female sphere, a world of the past, of children's literature, and of music,[22] where the abstractions of modern life do not rule. Emma leads Eugene into this sphere. She is his female guide; the Spaniard is his male guide.

As soon as Eugene has spotted his male guide, "a gate opened to Eugene. That was all there was to it. He did not have time to think, but sprang forward as if to protect his own" (*CSEW*, 401). In this moment of danger when the Spaniard is about to be run over, the gate that opens is the gate of intuition, physical, emotional response. As he runs to save the Spaniard, he loses his paper, his last hold on civilization, and as he runs he feels his toes pointing out behind him like Hermes or Perseus with his winged shoes and remembers that once he was known for his running. When he reaches the Spaniard, "He seized hold of the Spaniard's coat—which had him weighing it, smelling it, and feeling the sun warm on it—and pulled. So out of breath he was laughing, he pulled in the big Spaniard—who for all his majestic weight proved light on his feet, like a big woman who turns graceful once she's on the dance floor. For a moment Eugene kept him at tow there, on the safe curb, breathing his faint smoke-smell or travel-smell; but he could not think of that long Spanish name, and he didn't say a word" (*CSEW*, 401–2) Eugene's actions are the actions of someone who has been deprived of something for a long time and finally finds it. He luxuriates in every sensation surrounding the Spaniard. In fact, he is so in the world of his senses that he cannot say anything. He only laughs and breathes in all the smells he has hungered for. The Spaniard is like a big woman and he is light on his feet. He can dance. He can move. He is in his body. At the same time, Eugene is the artist, the lover, the one who has created this man: "Eugene drew both hands away lightly, as if he were publicly disclosing something, unveiling a huge statue" (*CSEW*, 402). Like Pygmalion, he has created his love. He even thinks after he sees the Spaniard: "Imagine him walking along here!" (*CSEW*, 401). The Spaniard is the perfect guide; by denying Eugene language, he forces him to remain in his body. At the same time, Eugene is the Spaniard's guide into the future, into life. He speaks English, he knows the city, he knows how to laugh at classical music.

As we descend with Eugene into his memories of the Spaniard's concert at the Aeolian Hall, Welty makes another break in the narrative, and we hear echoes of Chapter 6 of Joyce's *Ulysses*. Chapter 6 in the plan focuses on the Hades section of the *Odyssey* and is set in the graveyard at 11:00 A.M. The organ is heart, the art religion, the colors white and black, the symbol caretaker, and the technic incubism. The Hades section of *Ulysses* involves the funeral for Dignam. In Eugene's description of the Spaniard on stage, Welty writes, "As he reached the center front of the stage and turned gravely—he seemed serious as a doctor" (*CSEW*, 402). The term gravely and the seriousness of the doctor indicate life and death issues.[23] If the narrative of "Music from Spain" is about the estrangement of Eugene and Emma, the death of love brought about by the death of their daughter, then the Spaniard is the embodiment of that grief. The Spaniard is dressed in black, he has painted red fingernails like a touched-up corpse. He gravely plays serious melodies from far away. His foot rests on an oblong object like a child's casket, and he appears the day Emma emerges from public mourning.[24] He is the incarnation of their grief and the possibility of future fertility/virility. As Eugene's guide, the journey they take together is the journey back to physical bodies, the Spaniard from the past to the present, Eugene from the future to the present.

The music draws Eugene out of the everyday into a "vast present-time. The lapse must have endured for a solid minute or two, and afterwards he could recollect it. It was as positively there and as defined at the edges as a spot or stain, and it affected him like a secret" (*CSEW*, 403). This lapse is very much like the drugged forgetfulness that the Lotus Eaters experience. To experience life even for a minute or two as present is subversive and secretive because it undermines social expectations. The continuous present destabilizes the concepts of wife and future and makes people act in unpredictable ways, staining the textile of cultural expectations. The secret is sexual, making possible "the racing of the pulse, of the dark face by his" (*CSEW*, 403). Eugene feels "fleet of foot" and wonders, "Was it so strange, the way things are flung out at us, like the apples of Atalanta perhaps, once we have begun a certain onrush? With his hand, which could have stormed a gate, he touched the Spaniard's elbow. It responded like a swinging weight, a balance, in the calm black sleeve. Eugene's touch, his push, now seemed judicious; and he pushed forthrightly to propel the old fellow across the street at the next crossing" (*CSEW*, 403–4). Eugene experiences the Atalanta myth from the female perspective; he knows the desire that Atalanta felt for the golden apples, a desire so intense it forced her to pause in her race to pick them up and thereby lose to her suitor. The Spaniard is this golden ball flung in Eugene's path, which allows him to stop and experience his intense homoerotic desire. Even though he could have stormed a gate like a warrior, he meets the elbow, and finds the judicious touch, the balance, the calm, like a lover.

If we have any doubt that Eugene is the lover looking at his love, we need only return to the intertextual evidence. One of the most impressive connections between "Music from Spain" and *Ulysses* is the similarity between Eugene's description of the Spaniard and Molly's description of her possible lover, the guitar player in Chapter 18. In "Music from Spain," Eugene describes the Spaniard: "his head looked weighty too, long and broad together, with black-rimmed glasses circling his eyes and his hair combed back to hang behind him almost to his shoulders, like an Indian, or the old senator from back home" (*CSEW*, 402). In *Ulysses*, Molly thinks: "Yes there was something about poetry in it I hope he hasnt long greasy hair hanging into his eyes or standing up like a red Indian what do they go about like that for only getting themselves and their poetry laughed at" (*UL*, 637). If the Spaniard is Molly's long-haired poet/guitar player from Gibraltar, then he symbolizes romantic love, something to long for.

As the force that propels the Spaniard through the streets, Eugene is like the wind propelling a ship through the water. This image ends subsection six of "Music," and at the beginning of subsection seven the Spaniard and Eugene wait at a crossing for the light to change. Chapter 7 of *Ulysses* alludes to the Aeolus section of the *Odyssey*. The setting is the newspaper, the time noon, the organ lungs, the art rhetoric, the color red, the symbol editor, the narrative enthymemic. Aeolus is the keeper of winds. In the *Odyssey*, Odysseus's men open the bag of winds and send the ship off course. Many Aeolus references in "Music from Spain" are not included in subsection seven but are scattered throughout the text—they are literally blown off course. For example, there are two references to the Aeolian Hall in the previous subsection (*CSEW*, 402).[25]

As Eugene waits at the crossing, he sees under a street light a lady who has birthmarks that resemble butterfly shapes all over her visible skin.[26] From the one butterfly on the man's wrist to this image of the woman as butterfly, the symbols of resurrection have become more blatant and more difficult for Eugene to handle. He tries to whistle to indicate his nonchalance. The next embodied sign is a sideshow exhibit of a woman named Emma, who is enormously fat, and with a look in her eyes of, "They done me wrong." She is the guilt, the anger, what has gone wrong between men and women. Her intimate things, her underwear, are displayed where everyone can see them, as she is an object to be gazed at. This Emma represents the woman's body distorted, disfigured, used; a more direct example of the trusses and braces that shame Eugene in the first subsection. Whereas the Spaniard directly relates and empathizes with the fat Emma, Eugene does not even get the hint that there might be a message for him in the question, "Have I seen the real Emma?"

The eighth textual break in "Music from Spain" corresponds to Chapter 8 of *Ulysses*, the chapter called Lestrygonians in Joyce's plan. In this section Eugene and the Spaniard eat lunch, as does Leopold in *Ulysses*. In Joyce's plan the organ is the esophagus, the art architecture, the symbol constables, and the technic peristaltic. The *American College Dictionary* (1963) defines peristaltic as "the alternating waves of constriction and dilation of a tubular muscle system or cylindrical structure, as the wavelike circular contractions of the alimentary canal." This is a description of the act of digesting. Leopold and Eugene both change their minds about where to eat. Eugene chooses a restaurant on Maiden Lane because the cafeteria "had begun to be infested by those wiry, but unlucky, old men forever reading racing forms as they drank coffee" (*CSEW*, 405). In *Ulysses* the patrons of Davvy Byrnes's pub discuss the horse races (*UL*, 142, 146). In "Music from Spain" the guitar player orders in French, "and it was probably in French that he responded (like a worshiper in the Catholic Church) to the waiter" (*CSEW*, 406). In *Ulysses*, Joyce uses French especially in reference to food throughout this chapter (*UL*, 140, 143, 144) and uses many references to the Catholic church particularly in connection with food (*UL*, 139, 140, 142, 148). In "Music from Spain," Eugene is shocked at the amount of food the guitar player orders. In *Ulysses*, Leopold summons up a large amount of food in his mind (*UL*, 143). Eugene orders veal. Leopold imagines calves at slaughter (*UL*, 140). Eugene counts up his money. Leopold imagines how much money he has made.

Subsection nine of "Music from Spain" continues with Eugene and the Spaniard's lunch. This section corresponds to *Ulys-*

ses Chapter 9, called Scylla and Charybdis, which takes place in the library at 2:00 P.M. The organ is the brain, the art literature, the symbol Stratford/London, the technic dialectic. In *Ulysses*, Stephen is hanging out with his artist friends at the National Library. In "Music from Spain" this is the first time Welty refers to the Spaniard as the artist and she does so at least five times.[27] Everything the Spaniard does during lunch has an exaggerated physicality to it. He shakes the staircase when he walks in the restaurant, and he eats an enormous amount of food. As Eugene watches the Spaniard eat, he moves out of his body and into the future. He does not want to waste this time, but the only things he can think of doing with the Spaniard are conventional. He wonders, "Perhaps the Spaniard could produce a beautiful mistress he had somewhere, one he enjoyed and always went straight to, while in San Francisco" (*CSEW*, 407). Eugene tries to conjure up this image for the Spaniard by caressing the air—which indicates the lack of substance in his idea.[28] As Eugene becomes more embodied, the choices for him are either physical violence or sex; he knows no other options. The Spaniard looks right through Eugene's attempts to conjure up a woman. Eugene's only other thought is that they could go gambling. He cannot simply enjoy his food as the Spaniard is doing because he is living outside his body in the future. While Eugene is expounding his abstract aesthetic notions, the Spaniard is totally absorbed in "spitting out the bones" (*CSEW*, 409). There is nothing abstract about his actions.

Eugene thinks to himself what he would do if he came here for one day, if he were looking for his father: "on the track, say, of his old man? (God forbid he'd find him! Old Papa King MacLain was an old goat, a black name *he* had)" (*CSEW*, 407). King's black name comes from his sexual prowess. In condemning King, Eugene is taking a high moral tone about sexuality. In "The Wanderers," Welty describes King as chewing, cracking, and spitting out bones. There is a direct correlation between King MacLain and the Spaniard. In *Ulysses*, Stephen not only tries to conjure up a performance of *Hamlet*, but he puts forth his ideas on fathers and sons. In *Ulysses* references to father-son relationships occur quite often (*UL*, 155, 160, 170–171), and in "Music from Spain": "Eugene saw himself for a moment as the kneeling Man in the Wilderness in the engraving in his father's remnant geography book. . . . That engraving itself, he had once believed, represented his father, King MacLain, in the flesh, the one who had never seen him or wanted to see him" (*CSEW*, 409). The words "in the flesh" remind us that this is what Eugene desires—to actually see and touch his father, who had never wanted to see him. This lack of contact is the source of his wound, and the direct physical contact with the fatherlike Spaniard is the source of his healing.

Moving away from the pain of his father, Eugene retreats into an abstract reverie about San Francisco and his journey, about walls closing in and purities or transparencies.[29] Finally he realizes "the thing he thought of wasn't really physical" (*CSEW*, 408). The next line is, "Eugene slowly buttered the last crust of bread." Eugene almost makes it through the entire meal without thinking about or experiencing what he is eating. Like a prisoner of his mind, he returns to eat the last crust of bread. At this moment he enters another fantasy, but this time it is a fantasy grounded in physical appearance and leading into mythical memory. He speculates about the Spaniard's other side, his dark, secret underlife. Visions of the Spaniard—as the Sybil in the picture in Miss Eckhart's studio, of the Spaniard dancing with an alligator, of him with horns like a bull, of fire coming from his nostrils—all crowd into his mind and magnify his projected representation of this new companion. His mind is peopled with myths and stories, like Welty's. In Eugene's experience Welty mirrors her own journey as an artist in the writing of this story. The present moment is crowded with the past, and the future always competes to destroy the present. The past will come and overwhelm if it is not given thorough attention. It will quite literally make Eugene choke on his bread. The artist has visions of things as they used to be, might be, or are in some other reality, yet the artist also has to remain firmly in the sensations of the moment. Artists must be able to swallow that crust of bread. This section is about writing, just as Joyce focuses on the art of literature in the corresponding chapter of *Ulysses*.

When the past does come into Eugene's present, it returns in all its physical, sensual richness. He hears the music he used to play—"The Stubborn Rocking Horse" (*CSEW*, 408)—and he sees the mimosa flowers, blue at the base like flames, and his piece of music transformed into drops of light. He has a physical response to this transformation so that, rather than seeing some disconnected speculation, the memory actually enters his body and he feels "his forehead bead with drops and the pleasure run like dripping juice through each plodding finger, at such an hour, on such a day, in such a place. Mississippi. A humming bird, like a little fish, a little green fish in the hot air, had hung for a moment before his gaze, then jerked, vanishing, away" (*CSEW*, 409). With this vision Eugene has the experience of the artist, what Loch calls the nearness of missing things, the artist's eye catching sight of, then losing, catching sight of, then losing, over and over—the hummingbird almost, then gone.

Ulysses Chapter 10, called Wandering Rocks and set on the street at 3:00 P.M., describes an ordinary afternoon on the streets of Dublin. The organ is muscle, the art mechanics, the symbol citizens, and the technic labyrinth. The beginning of this subsection of "Music from Spain" reads: "They came out into the flat light of day and the noise, like a deception or concealment of rage, of the ordinary afternoon stir" (*CSEW*, 410). Welty mentions a streetcar roaring down a crowded street. The scene in *Ulysses* is set in the street and Father Commee rides a tram. After lunch the Spaniard and Eugene see a streetcar accident in which an older woman is killed. The woman trips and pitches forward as if, in this new fast-paced industrial world, she is an endangered species. Like Virginia Woolf's angel in the house, this moral lady on her high heels must die before the story of homoerotic passion can progress. The two young girls just say "Let's go" (*CSEW*, 410) and move on. No one saves the old woman.

In *Ulysses*, Paddy's death returns as a theme (*UL*, 182, 184, 195, 207), and the men discuss an accident that occurred in America, "Terrible affair that *General Slocum* explosion. Terrible, terrible! A thousand casualties. And heartrending scenes. Men trampling down women and children. Most brutal thing. What do they say was the cause. Spontaneous combustion" (*UL*, 196–97). In both texts man-made technology (mechanics) kills people. In both texts the incidents are accidents. In both texts at least one woman dies. The difference is in scale. In *Ulysses* the accident is a major explosion and many women and children die, whereas in "Music from Spain" there is just a little accident and only one woman dies. In *Ulysses* an ambulance passes (*UL*, 191). In "Music from Spain" a bystander wonders where the ambulance is and in the next line the motorman is blamed for the accident. In response to the destructive nature of the technological, Welty describes Eugene and the Spaniard as if they were riding on a raft, like Odysseus.[30]

In this chapter Joyce characterizes Bloom as having a touch of the artist (*UL*, 193). Eugene also begins to have a touch of the artist as he ponders why the Spaniard is so great. "When the man at last played very softly some unbearably rapid or subtle songs of his own country, so soft as to be almost without sound, only a beating on the air like a fast wing—then was Eugene moved" (*CSEW*, 411). The tenderness and subtlety of this image is remarkable, as if Eugene can now feel art emerging into form.

The next break in the "Music from Spain" echoes Chapter 11 of *Ulysses*, entitled "Sirens" in the plan and set in the Concert Room at 4:00 P.M. The organ is ear, the art music, the symbol barmaids, and the technic Fuga Par Canonan. Eugene and the Spaniard have stopped walking and have boarded a streetcar. The sirens in the *Odyssey* try to lure Odysseus from his course by enticing him with song. He makes his men strap him to the mast to keep him from following the song. He fills their ears with beeswax so they will not hear: "I carved a massive cake of bees-wax into bits and rolled them in my hands until they softened— no long task, for a burning heat came down" (*Odyssey*, Book 12, ll. 175–81). The sun is warming the streets in "Music from Spain," and "Eugene, with his head turned away from the Ne-gro's, tried to close his ears against the cries of the children, and read the tattered street signs to himself as they passed" (*CSEW*, 412). The cries of the children and the black female conductor calling out to her friends are the sirens' cry, and like Odysseus, Eugene tries to close his ears to the voices of women and chil-dren. The sirens sing in the *Odyssey*: "No life or earth can be/Hid from our dreaming" (ll. 189–90), whereas in "Music from Spain" it is Eugene who feels that he is falling into a dreamland: "Be-cause the very silence between the men was—at last—replete and dream-like, the hills were to Eugene increasingly like those stairs he climbed in dreams" (*CSEW*, 413).[31]

Eugene has to enter this dream world in order to retrieve the most painful memory: "'Your little girl,' Eugene remarked aloud, "said, 'Mama, my throat hurts me,' and she was dead in three days. You expected her mother would watch a fever, while you were at the office, not go talk to Mrs. Herring. But you never spoke of it, did you. Never did," (*CSEW*, 413). Eugene remem-bers that not only Emma but he himself did not do what they should have done; his mistake was that he did not say anything. He did not match his words with his feelings. Only now does he speak words out loud and in doing so reconnects the abstract and the physical. Fan dies because her throat hurts. What Eugene remembers is what was not spoken.

From this moment on, his memories and visions appear more quickly. Again Eugene remembers the line from the comedian he heard yesterday, "Open the door, Richard. *Ouvrez le fenêtre, Paul ou Jacques*" (*CSEW*, 414).[32] The sirens lure men to the rocks in the *Odyssey*, and in *Ulysses* there are several references to rocks (*UL*, 214, 221, 234). Not only are Eugene and the Spaniard moving towards the rocks at Lands End, but Eugene remembers a black man from his hometown who would walk into a record store when he was in trouble at home and ask them to play: "'Rocks in My Bed Number Two,' by Blind Boy Fuller" (*CSEW*, 414). The reference to rocks echoes back to *Ulysses* and the *Odyssey*, and in *Ulysses* the piano tuner is a blind boy (*UL*, 216). Eugene can see a "colored woman plying the keys" (*CSEW*, 414) of an upright piano but he cannot hear her. In *Ulysses*, Pat, the waiter, can not hear (*UL*, 225, 230). Both of these references are to Odysseus's plugging his mens' ears against the sirens' song.

In the middle of this scene, Eugene meets a little boy, as if he is coming face to face with himself: "'*I* don't get the sun in *my* eyes,' said a little boy, looking up at Eugene, who was holding one hand slanted before his face. 'You don't, sonnie?' said Eugene gently. With one hand he took away the other, as if the little boy had asked him to stop using it. The boy gave him a sweet, cocksure smile, which jumped with many suns in Eugene's vision" (*CSEW*, 414).

The boy has asked Eugene to stop shielding his eyes from the light of the sun, from the life-giving light, from the power of the Spaniard, the power of his father King MacLain, the power of masculine fertility, and the Spaniard, who plays ancient songs, who has died and come back to life many times, will show him how to do this. These two travelers are now walking directly toward the setting sun, toward death, allowing the sun to set and rise and to set again and rise again. It is interesting to note that the rebirth of the male is not a return to the feminine but a movement to a heightened awareness of, and willingness to accept, the full range of masculinity—both its projections and fantasies and its dreams and myths. At the same time, the Spaniard is teaching Eugene a masculinity that embraces and includes the feminine.

Eugene's attention to mazes and labyrinths corresponds to the section in the *Odyssey* in which Odysseus has to follow a complicated twisting route to get past the sirens. Eugene describes a complicated twisted vision from which he can see no escape:

Each rounded house contained a stair. Every form had its spiral or
its tendril, outward or concealed. Outside were fire-escapes. He
gazed up at the intricacies of those things; sea gulls were sitting at
their heads. How could he make a fire-escape if he were required to?
The laddered, tricky fire-escapes, the mesh of unguarded traffic,
coiling springs, women's lace, the nests in their purses—he thought
how the making and doing of daily life mazed a man about, eyes,
legs, ladders, feet, fingers, like a vine. It twined a man in, the very
doing and dying and daring of the world, the citified world. (*CSEW*,
413)

The citified world has twined Eugene in, causing him to confuse body parts and city parts, to equate the tricky fire escapes
and the mesh of traffic with women's purses and lace. He is at
once the traditional hero trying to escape from the actual female
body and the newly developed masculine character trying to
escape from the tangled distorted representations of the feminine.

The opening of the twelfth break in "Music from Spain" is a
composite of the opening to Chapter 12, the Cyclops chapter of
Ulysses.[33] Joyce's opening includes references to eyes, a hill, a
chimney sweep, and a church. Welty's opening—"They walked
on, until the sky ahead was brilliant enough to keep the eyes
dazzled. On the next hill two nuns in a sea of wind looked
destructible as smokestacks on a flaming roof" (*CSEW*, 414) includes references to eyes, a hill, smokestacks, and nuns. This is
the Cyclops chapter—the eye references in both texts allude to
the section in the *Odyssey* in which Odysseus destroys the Cyclops's only eye with a burning torch.[34] When Eugene describes
the two nuns in the preceding paragraph as destructible, he indicates that here, at the end of the earth, morality is vulnerable.[35]
The wino can sleep a peaceful sleep in a garden of Eden before
the fall.[36]

In this place where he will not be judged, Eugene can experience the emotion "that visited him inexplicably at times—the
overwhelming, secret tenderness toward his twin, Ran MacLain,
whom he had not seen for half his life, that he might have felt

toward a lover" (*CSEW*, 415). This is the moment of dramatic transition in the story. For the first time Eugene admits a secret tenderness, a vulnerability that he has not allowed us to see until this point, and he equates this tenderness directly with the feelings one might have for a lover, moving far beyond the powerful social taboos of homosexuality and incest. As Eugene thinks of Ran, rain falls. Ran, as we have seen in the preceeding chapter, is himself equated to rain—Ran/rain. He is potentially a fertility god. Everytime a character moves into a more liberated or fertile connection with themselves or their world in this collection rain falls (as it does on Virgie at the end of "The Wanderers"). Rain falls on Eugene and the Spaniard in this subsection, and rain falls on Leopold and Stephen in *Ulysses* Chapter 12 (*UL*, 252). In *Ulysses* it is an irritating rain from which the characters seek shelter. In "Music from Spain" it is "fine, caressing, 'precipitation,'" (*CSEW*, 415), both the mist of the day and the mist of sexual connection.

In Eugene's description of this rain, old age and youth cross in the image of the old Chinese gentleman and the little baby trying to hold onto the mist, as all dualities pollinate each other. In this rain, in the return to child selves, there is a merging and combining; the boys' and girls' legs are mixed up and the kites are jumping side by side. This is the opposite of a wasteland; it is instead a place in which sweet alyssum regenerates the air. The Aeolian breeze takes with it Eugene's dreams and desires, and he can see the Spaniard clearly without projection or need. Again Eugene draws breath as he did at the beginning of the story; again he returns to his body and can now see the Spaniard for what he is, both male/father with a barrel of a chest and female/child with little bearded animal faces and pink suspenders. This cross-fertilizing breeze, this pollinating of dualities opens the way for the possibility of love between man and man.

The thirteenth break in the text of "Music from Spain" invites comparison with Chapter 13 in *Ulysses* which Joyce labels "Nausicaa" in the plan and which is set on the rocks at 8:00 P.M. The organs are eye and nose, the art painting, the colors grey and blue, and the symbol virgin. The technic is tumescence and detumescence, or swelling and shrinking. It is evening in Welty's section and the men are walking on the rocks. Welty describes sights and smells, paints the setting like a painter, employs the blues and greys of the ocean, and exploits the idea of Eugene's virginity; Eugene swells and shrinks in the passion of his excitement as does the Spaniard. In the *Odyssey*, Nausicaa is the young virgin who finds Odysseus after he has been swept up on the shore. As she and her nymphs are doing laundry down by the water, he views her from his hiding place in the reeds. In *Ulysses*, Joyce turns this meeting between the young virgin and the older hero into the scene of Leopold's leering at Gerty on the beach and masturbating to his sexual fantasy of her. His gaze is one of voyeuristic appropriation although she also participates. In "Music from Spain" the entire section is taken up with a description of a cat looking at what turns out to be another cat in the bushes and Eugene's intense excitement as he watches this scene.

Eugene is now fully in the moment, actively watching, feeling, hearing what transpires before him. He feels the excitement of a cat and mouse, a snake, or whatever it might be as he watches this scene in the grass and twice he mentions the word "passion" in reference to the Spaniard.[37] The voyeuristic aspect of the scene as well as the facial expressions of the Spaniard connect this text to the masturbation scene in *Ulysses*, but the cat and its prey present the possibility of a new power dynamic. The narrative does not always have to depict cat and mouse and the cat does not always have to be in control (*CSEW*, 214–15).[38]

In *Ulysses*, Joyce refers to Leopold as a snake: "He was eyeing her as a snake eyes its prey" (*UL*, 295). If the whirring in the grass is a snake, it might be the cat's predator. If it is a bird, the cat will probably be attacking it. Welty deconstructs the predator hierarchy that makes Leopold's objectification of Gerty possible.[39] By making the adversary another cat, Welty creates a double, introducing a new sexual dynamic, the meeting of equals.

The cat and the other mirror the conventional relationship between Eugene and Emma, but the cat and the cat more fully mirror the homoerotic relationship between Eugene and the Spaniard. The reference to Paris—"he might have been over in Paris"—is another coded reference to homosexuality since Paris was thought to be a center of homosexual activity in the 1920s (*CSEW*, 416).

Eugene's description of the Spaniard's detachment and his connection of this detachment with passion reveal both the homoerotic nature of this passage and its direct connection to *Ulysses*. In *Ulysses*, Gerty notices while gazing at Leopold that she "could see that he had enormous control over himself. One moment he had been there, fascinated by a loveliness that made him gaze, and the next moment it was the quiet gravefaced gentleman, self control expressed in every line of his distinguished looking figure" (*UL*, 296). In her description of the Spaniard's face, "with its expression that might be solicitude still—and at the same time, meditation, amusement, sleepiness, or implacability when the whole was seen at such close quarters with the black circles, the shell rims, around the eyes—was directed for a round moment on Eugene" (*CSEW*, 415), Welty, as the artist watching and creating the Spaniard's face symbolically, returns the male-dominating gaze of Joyce's Leopold. Rather than male watching female, we find female author watching male, and male character watching male character, cat watching cat. When Welty describes the Spaniard turning his gaze from Eugene, his long black hair bobbing behind, she echoes Leopold's description of Gerty's hair (*UL*, 286).[40] The subject of the Nausicaa chapter is both Leopold's and Gerty's sexual excitement. This subsection of "Music from Spain" is about Eugene's and the Spaniard's sexual excitement.

When Eugene looks over at the Spaniard, he "was simply making a face over the lighting of another cigarette. The muscles of his face grouped themselves in hideous luxuriousness, rippled once, then all cleared. His lips were grape-colored, and the smoke smelled sweet" (*CSEW*, 417). Welty uses the word hideous in "June Recital" to describe the face Mr. Voight makes when he exposes himself to Virgie, Cassie, and Miss Eckhart in Miss Eckhart's studio. This is a literal description of the face of a person who is having an orgasm. The cigarette is a symbolic phallus, like the fireworks in *Ulysses*. Joyce mentions the "nice perfume of those good cigarettes" (*UL*, 287), and Leopold smells Gertrude's perfume.

In the fourteenth subsection of Welty's story there are references to both Chapter 13 and Chapter 14 of *Ulysses*. In the plan this section is called "Oxen of the Sun," And it is set in the hospital at 10:00 P.M. The organ is the womb, the art medicine, the color white, the symbol moth, and the technic embryonic development. In the first sentence of this section of "Music from Spain," Eugene and the Spaniard come to the end of the beach. In *Ulysses* Chapter 13 Leopold has come down to the beach and is looking at Gerty. The great emptiness that Welty describes reminds us of Eliot's *The Waste Land* and Steven's "The Idea of Order at Key West." In Chapter 14 of *Ulysses* men are waiting around in a hospital for a woman to give birth. They are supposedly doctors but it is more like a gathering of friends at the pub. The men are laughing and telling jokes. One of the most powerful images in Welty's fourteenth subsection is of a mechanical woman laughing on the beach.[41] Joyce's concept of a woman having difficulty giving birth and men sitting around pretending to be doctors doing nothing to help her but discussing womanhood and birth is certainly laughable. Welty's woman is possibly laughing at the whole premise of the chapter, and her laugh is also what is left out of Joyce's chapter; we hear nothing from the woman who is giving birth.

In *Ulysses* Chapter 13 all of the characters are on the beach waiting for the sunset, and in "Music from Spain" Welty writes: "in the pale expanse two middle-aged ladies in steadily threatened hats materialized; they looked at their watches: waiting for sunset" (*CSEW*, 417). In the symbology of *The Golden Apples* the sun is masculine; the ladies are waiting for the setting of masculine power. In the same paragraph Welty notes "a horse's bleached skull," and that "black smoke moved on the air, fading; the day's casual fires along the beach had gone out, and a ship was disclosed at sea" (*CSEW*, 417). Welty's inclusion of both the fire and the ship reveals how closely and directly she is following intertextul threads. Circe warns Odysseus's men, when they get to Helios's island, not to kill the sacred cows. Hungry for meat, they slaughter the cows anyway and cook them over fires on the beach. Terrified of Helios's wrath Odysseus puts to sea, and his men are drowned in a terrible storm. Welty's mention of the ship at sea and the casual fires indicates that she is consciously echoing the *Odyssey*. The fact that this subsection corresponds to Joyce's "Oxen of the Sun" suggests the complexity of the three-way intertextuality. A few sentences later the shuttered-down foodstands also reminds us that Odysseus's men left after eating hastily. This is the aftermath of the the senseless killing, and the horse's skull is another symbol of sacrifice and slaughter. Welty's horse's skull is bleached and we must assume bleached by the sun, by Helios. In addition, the sea onions scattered about let Eugene and the Spaniard know there has been a storm. In Chapter 13 Leopold calls the beach, "land of the setting sun this" (*UL*, 310) and Eugene calls the cliffs in San Francisco "Land's End."

Welty, like Joyce, describes the scene as a wasteland, but in "Music from Spain" it is out of this empty beach that the potential for something new emerges. Out of this wasteland Eugene begins to hear the laughter of the mechanical woman. She is a "shouting mechanical dummy of a woman," and she is the last vision of the female Eugene sees before entering the caves and rocks; her laugh is the final call of the socially constructed feminine. It must, like the lady in high heels, die. The ocean itself takes her laugh "supporting this one extra little chip," and "Eugene walked down to the sands where the wind beat the laughter to pieces and the ripping sound of his own hat filled his ears" (*CSEW*, 417). The natural sounds of wind and ocean destroy this manmade abomination. The Spaniard's immovable presence makes the aesthetic ladies withdraw as if they cannot wait for the sun to set in the presence of the sun himself. The only ones who remain are "a pair of lovers" who lie "close by the wall—motionless also" (*CSEW*, 418).[42] These lovers, are motionless, unchanging—the undying symbol of Western romantic love, the most formidable obstacle to Eugene's exploration of his unknown sexuality.

The Spaniard's tracks make a straight line to the ocean, cutting across all these others, including those of the wood gatherers, students, ladies, lovers, children, and dogs. The boys in Chapter 13 of *Ulysses* are building a sand castle. Tommy and Joey get in a fight and destroy the sand castle they have been building. Tommy has to pee and does so behind a pushcart. Welty conflates all of this information and writes: "The Spaniard looked affirmative, but first disengaged himself and made water toward the sea, throwing up a rampart, a regular castle, in the sand" (*CSEW*, 418).

The first sentence of the fifteenth break in "Music from Spain" alludes to "the black pits of fires" along the shore, a direct reference to the pits that result when the men cooked the cattle in the *Odyssey*. This chapter is called Circe in Joyce's plan and is set in a brothel at midnight. The art is locomotor apparatus, the symbol whore, and the technic hallucination. The locomotor apparatus appears as a velocipede in "Music from Spain"; Joyce mentions two men on bikes who pass Leopold. In *Ulysses* the entire chapter has a dreamy hallucinatory tone as does Welty's subsection fifteen. She even describes the boy as riding his velocipede "dreamily" (*CSEW*, 418). Although this scene is not set in a brothel, Eugene and the Spaniard are moving beyond the realm of conventional sexuality. The first two lines of *Ulysses* Chapter 15 is a dialogue between a Call and an Answer. The Call says, "Wait, my love, and I'll be with you." The Answer responds, "Round behind the stable." The Spaniard and Eugene follow a path "beyond the car barn [where] there was something of a road that followed along the cliff interminably, or once there had been" (*CSEW*, 418).[43] Out behind the stable or car barn is where lovers go, but these new lovers can only find something of a road not a clear path and it follows interminably. The Spaniard and Eugene go beyond where Eugene and Emma once had a picnic. The heterosexual love does not follow the path that Eugene will now take. Eugene and the Spaniard are walking into unknown territory. This territory is the love between men; it is the territory of socially unsanctioned acts. Whether Welty knew this or not, the paths around Land's End have traditionally been used as places for gay men to meet.

Throughout the brothel scene the whores and others accuse and interrogate Leopold. In this section of "Music from Spain," Eugene puts himself and the Spaniard on trial by accusing the Spaniard of hitting his wife. In "Music from Spain" the Spaniard's hands meet on top of his head to clamp his hat on, and his elbows bend outward. Welty describes this as "the lumpy pose of a woman, a 'nude reclining'" (*CSEW*, 419). Chapter 15 of *Ulysses* is set in a brothel with nudes reclining. In this chapter Marion refers to a powerful prostitute or Bartholomona, the bearded woman. In the last section of "Music from Spain" we hear that the Spaniard's name is Bartolome Montalbano. There are references to the femininity or androgyny of the Spaniard throughout the text. Rapture and seduction define the tone of the Circe chapter of *Ulysses*, and as Eugene breaths in the air out by Land's End, he defines it as "rapture" (*CSEW*, 419).

In the *Odyssey*, Circe changes the men into swine so that changes of appearance are central to this section. In "Music from Spain," Eugene "was aware that he jerked like a pigeon or rocked like a sailor, going down, or sagged like an old poodle, going up; it was all the same. Once he leaped, and almost without care" (*CSEW*, 419). Leopold, like Odysseus's men, constantly changes shape, dress, personality, gender, class: "*barefoot, pigeonbreasted, in lascar's vest and trousers, apologetic toes turned in, opens his tiny mole's eyes and looks about him dazedly, passing a slow hand across his*

*forehead. Then he hitches his belt sailor fashion and with a shrug of
oriental obeisance salutes the court, pointing one thumb heavenward"*
(*UL*, 378). At another point in the chapter he becomes a dog (*UL*,
433) and later he sees or appears as a Spanish dulcimer player:

> From left upper entrance with two gliding steps Henry Flower
> comes forward to left front center. He wears a dark mantle and
> drooping plumed sombrero. He carries a silver stringed inlaid dul-
> cimer and a long stemmed bamboo Jacob's pipe, its clay bowl fash-
> ioned as a female head. He wears velvet hose and silverbuckled
> pumps. He has the romantic Savior's face with flowing locks, thin
> beard and moustache. His spindlelegs and sparrow feet are those of
> the tenor Mario, prince of Canadia. He settles down his goffered
> ruffs and moistens his lips with a passage of his amorous tongue.
>
> Henry:
>
> (in a low dulcet voice, touching the strings of his guitar) There is a
> flower that bloometh. (*UL*, 422)

Like the Spaniard, Henry Flower is Spanish, plays a guitar,
wears dark clothes, and has long hair. The Spaniard smokes a
cigarette, not a pipe, and has silver buckles on his suspenders,
not his shoes, but the similarities are unmistakably present. Both
figures are lightfooted and have long hair. In subsection seven-
teen of "Music from Spain," the Spaniard presents a flower to
Eugene.

One of the most exciting intertextualities occurs not in the
final text of "Music from Spain" but in an earlier manuscript in
which Welty included in the last paragraphs of subsection six-
teen a reference to a love letter. A scrap of paper fluttered and
blew zig zag in the air, alighting on a rock at the Spaniard's heel.
It did not escape Dowdy's (Eugene's name in earlier versions) eye
and he picked it up; it was the upper left-hand piece of a letter,
neatly typed.

> Baby:
> I am
> can get w/it un

what I am doing
I do not know wh
if you did I didn
when to call at
thrilled when w
reading the let
way together.
You didn't tell m
You also told me
asked me whether
single detail of
arms ache when I
and how I wish you
       Incid

(ms. Mississippi Department of Archives and History and Humanities Research Center at University of Texas)

In *Ulysses*, Leopold has a letter from his mistress in his pocket throughout the book, a love letter telling him how much she misses him and how she wants to see him. This scrap of paper blown from Joyce's text, pollinates and transforms both itself and the text it has entered; Welty is acknowledging through Dowdy (Eugene) that the fragment of this letter is significant to him as a fragment, that he is actively involved in solving the mystery of lost love and eager to try to pick up the pieces of the old story. Dowdy (Eugene) is not quite ready to give up his hold on the conventional love story. If Welty had included this fragment, she would have been revealing that her text literally tears the conventional narrative of heterosexuality, the narrative of the toothy sweethearts, in half, making it incomprehensible. She would have been taking her text out of the closet. By removing it from the final versions, Welty does not let us see this process, only the finished textile.

The Spaniard has no problem walking on the path Eugene and he have chosen, but Welty describes Eugene's progress as "back-slidings" (*CSEW*, 419). This is not the kind of path Eugene is accustomed to following: "By now the path had grown wild and narrow" (*CSEW*, 419). Welty's description of the view is complex and especially important:

> The deepening sky was divided in half as it often was at this hour, by a kind of spinal cloud. Ahead, the north was clear and the south behind was thickened with white. Under the clear portion of sky the sea rushed in dark to greenness and blackness, the lips of the waves livid. ("Flounder, flounder in the sea," he heard his mother read.) Under the cloudy portion the sea burned silver and at moments entirely white, and the waves coming in held their form until the last minute and appeared still and limitless as snow. The beach and the city where they had walked were crossed with dust and mist, the scene flickered like the banners and flying sand of distant battle or a tumult in the past. Ahead, the extending rocks were unqualifiedly clear, hard, and azure. (*CSEW*, 419)

As Katie Rainey's body is divided lengthwise in "The Wanderers," the sky in this description is divided by a spinal cloud, representing a division of consciousness, one side emerging and the other still left in obscurity. It is not a cloud that cuts the head from the body as in the case of the Medusa but one that divides the body, replacing a culturally defined division with an experiential division. Interestingly enough the North is clear and the South—from which Eugene comes, from which the Spaniard comes, from which Welty comes—is thick with clouds. The future is clear but the past is cloudy; however, clear does not mean easy—this wild path is not easy to navigate. In the clear part, the northern part, the sea is dark, rushing, green, black, and angry—livid. The line that comes to Eugene's consciousness as he looks at this scene is a line from Grimm's fairy tale, "The Fisherman and His Wife."

In this fairy tale, a poor fisherman goes down to the sea one day and catches a magic flounder who speaks to him. The flounder tells him that it will grant him any wish he desires. His wife asks him to wish for a cottage, because they now live in a little fisherman's shanty. The fishermen does not want to wish for this but goes along with his wife, and the flounder grants his wish. This happens over and over again, the wife asking for greater and greater mansions and more and more power. Even when she becomes Empress she still wants to be lord of the heavens. At this point the flounder refuses and returns her to her hovel. The moral of the story is not to reach too high, but it is also a lesson to women not to overstep their bounds. The fisherman himself is always content. The rhyme that Welty alludes to reads:

Flounder, flounder in the sea
Come I pray thee here to me
For my wife
Good Ilsabil
will not as I'd
have her will

Another version reads :

"O man, O man!—if man you be,
Or flounder, flounder , in the sea—
Such a tiresome wife I've got,
For she wants what I do not."

The gist of both rhymes is that the fisherman's wife will not obey him. The fact that the voice from the past, from the South, from the mother, evokes this story indicates that what has not been fully resolved is the relationship between male and female.

This is also the story that Mrs. Ramsey reads to James in Woolf's *To the Lighthouse*. In the scene in *To the Lighthouse*, Mrs. Ramsey wonders what is happening to two lovers who have just walked off down the beach. She is also concerned about the fact that Mr. Ramsey might not let James go to the lighthouse the next day and that he will be terribly disappointed. The dual themes of the powerful domineering father who disappoints his little boy and the theme of the two sweethearts on the beach, the sexuality that must be controlled through marriage, are both woven into the fabric of Welty's narrative. In this section of "Music from Spain" the disappointed little boy is about to find the lost father, to take him once again in his arms. In the cloudy portion of Eugene's vision, the images are still, unchanging, frozen like snow, silver like a dream or make believe. The past through which they have walked on their journey is covered with mist and dust and represents a tumult or battle, but ahead is clear, hard, azure. From this point they enter the wilderness, the completely unknown land.

In this wilderness Eugene and the Spaniard lose the path and enter some rock caverns. This place is the opposite of a wasteland. Here, even the rocks live: "Here and there a boulder had lately fallen and lay in their path wet within its fissures as if it began to live, and secrete, and they had to climb around it, holding to brush. Where there were not rocks it was sandy and grassy and very wild. A fault of course lay all through the land" (*CSEW*, 419).[44] The two men climb around this vibrating representation of clitoral sexuality. Welty repeats the word wild and we know that this is a place where anything could happen, an earthquake for instance—"a fault . . . lay all through the land" (*CSEW*, 419). What appears solid and unchanging can change at any moment. Unlike the brothel section in *Ulysses*, in "Music from Spain," Eugene and the Spaniard are moving away from the degrading relationship between male and female, away from the world of fat Emma and corsets, away from social constructions of sexuality, away from the city. Stephen and Leopold walk further and further into the abstracted maze of the city, while Eugene and the Spaniard leave it behind. At the end of subsection fifteen Eugene is in an altered state. His body does not feel like his body: "When pain did not hurt, and the world did, things had got very strange—different" (*CSEW*, 419). This is a description of liminality. Eumaeus in the *Odyssey* is the keeper of Odysseus's swine and his herdsman. When the Phoenicians return Odysseus to his homeland, it is only when he meets Eumaeus that he knows he is indeed at home. Chapter 16 of Ulysses is the Eumaeus section. It is set in a shelter at 1:00 A.M. The organ is nerves, the art navigation, the symbol sailors, and the technic is narrative old. Navigation is the art in Joyce's plan because Odysseus finally finds his way home to Penelope. Eugene and the Spaniard walk, navigating their way together along the cliff by the ocean; Leopold and Stephen walk, navigating their way through the city streets.[45] As the sun sets Eugene confronts the Spaniard saying, "You heard me, all the time" (*CSEW*, 420).

Throughout the story we have been made to assume that the problem is the difference between English and Spanish, when in reality the problem is the difference between the language of the dominant conventional culture and the language of the artist— between the language of society and the language of love.[46] The Spaniard does not hear Eugene, does not respond to Eugene, because Eugene does not speak the language of the artist, of eyes, of touch, of smell, of bodily communication, of sensation. Eugene has been mouthing cliché after cliché. The Spaniard has been leading all along, looking at everything, involved with everything, like a lover. The Spaniard

> was peering at some blotched wild lilies that grew in the coarse grass there. He touched the tips of his fingers deliberately under the soft pale petals and examined their hairy hearts. Eugene was waiting behind him as he turned with a flower in his hand. All at once the Spanish eyes looked wide awake, and the man smiled—like someone waking from a deep dream, the sleep of a month. He put up his little flower, and regarded it.
>
> "*Mariposa*," he said, making each syllable clearly distinct. He held up the little wild waving spotted thing, the common mariposa lily. "*Mariposa?*" He repeated the word encouragingly, even sweetly, making the sound of it beautiful. (*CSEW*, 420–21)

Welty describes the inside of the lily as she would describe a woman's or a man's most intimate parts. In this language the examination becomes an affirmation of love. At this intensely sexual, sensual moment the Spaniard tries to connect to Eugene by speaking the word *mariposa*. In *Another Mother Tongue*, Judy Grahn suggests that "coming out from one world into another is reflected in the Spanish word for gay men, mariposa, the butterfly" (37). The Spaniard is thus communicating the passion he feels for Eugene, the transition or resurrection from the confining world of conventional love to the liberating world of free sexuality. He is literally coming out, but Eugene does not understand and has not yet found this voice in himself. When the Spaniard speaks he makes the word sound beautiful. He reminds Eugene that language expresses sexuality, that it is fertile, that it comes from the mouth and the tongue. Eugene cannot hear him.

He answers in the conventional language of heterosexual marriage: "'You assaulted your wife,' Eugene said loudly . . . . 'But in your heart,' Eugene said, and then he was lost. It was a lifelong trouble, he had never been able to express himself at all when it came to the very moment. And now, on a cliff, in a wind, to . . .'" (*CSEW*, 421). In an earlier manuscript version of this passage Welty completes the sentence "But in your heart . . . —you could kill a thing if it would not be, any more now for you . . . Calm as he was his tongue still stumbling." Eugene is thinking not about the Spaniard's offering of love and resurrection but about the possibility that he Eugene or the Spaniard as Eugene's other self could murder. Throughout Chapter 16 of *Ulysses*, Leopold speculates on whether the sailor who is telling the stories of faraway places is really a murderer. The possibility of losing his life lingers over the scene. As Eugene clings to the Spaniard on the edge of the cliff, he thinks about how one little push would send the Spaniard over the edge. On the edge of the cliff, Eugene's own mortality/morality is at stake. Facing the possibility of a forbidden sexuality, Eugene faces the possibility of all that is forbidden in society.

Both Stephen and Eugene experience a moment in which they cannot articulate their inner thoughts. Trying to answer Leopold, "'Couldn't,' Stephen contrived to get out, his mental organs for the moment refusing to dictate further" (*UL*, 518). The cliff and the wind make it impossible for Eugene to speak in the old form, but he cannot find the words in the new form. Eugene has truly reached land's end. All that is left for him is the expression of his physical body as he clings to the Spaniard "almost as if he had waited for him a long time with longing, almost as if he loved him, and had found a lasting refuge. He could have caressed the side of the massive face with the great pores in the loose, hanging cheek. The Spaniard closed his eyes. Then a bullish roar opened out of him" (*CSEW*, 421). Out of the deep comes the roar, the return to the source of language. His mouth is wide open like Easter's, and Eugene listens "to the voice that did not stop" and cannot imagine someone "laying himself altogether bare like that, with no shame, no respect" (*CSEW*, 421). It is the lack of shame and respect that allows the Spaniard to move out of the socially contricted world into this more primal existence—to lay himself bare. Eugene even recognizes it as a recital, because it is the deepest artistic expression, the sourcing, like Miss Eckhart's recital in the storm.[47]

This is both a moment of love and a moment of homecoming. This is Eumaeus's emotion for his long-lost master and yet it is much more. In Welty's text it is a tender and sexual moment between lovers.[48] When Eugene returns to hold the Spaniard after he loses his hat, "he could not budge him an inch" (*CSEW*, 422). Before the Spaniard takes hold of Eugene, he gets a strange sensation "as if he listened to sirens" (*CSEW*, 422). Not only does this reference echo back to the *Odyssey* and Odysseus strapped to the mast listening to the song of the sirens that drive him wild with a desire, but it is also the sensation Eugene feels when lying in bed with Emma. Both references have sexual connotations. When the Spaniard touches Eugene's arms, "it was a hold of hard, callused fingers like prongs" (*CSEW*, 422). When Leopold takes hold of Stephen's arms, he experiences a strange sensation also: "Yes, Stephen said uncertainly because he thought he felt a strange kind of flesh of a different man approach him, sinewless and wobbly and all that" (*UL*, 539,). As has been pointed out earlier, this entire chapter refers to Odysseus's homecoming. Both of these are descriptions of the skin and the touch of a very old man, a father who has been gone for a long time and is just now returning.

In the *Odyssey*, Odysseus returns home to his wife Penelope. Throughout Chapter 16 in *Ulysses*, Leopold has been showing an early, sexy picture of Molly to his friends in preparation for his return home and in hopes of renewed sexual relations with her. For a moment Eugene is also able to imagine such a reunion: "It was too bad that circling in his mind the daylong foreboding had to return, that he had yet to open the door and climb the stairs to Emma. There she waited in the front room, shedding her tears standing up, like a bride, with the white curtains of the bay window hanging heavy all around her" (*CSEW*, 423).[49] Eugene does not feel passion for Emma but instead sees her swathed in the heavy and oppressive conventionality of marriage. At the moment, Eugene has the strange sensation of having a round object as large as the world on his tongue. Eugene finds himself laughing, letting go: "The fog flowed into his throat and made him laugh" (*CSEW*, 422). As the Spaniard lifts him, the Spaniard frees him from the earth: "He was without a burden in the world" (*CSEW*, 423), and, whirled around, guilt leaves him and he "was brought over and held by the knees in the posture of a bird, his body almost upright and his forearms gently spread. In his nostrils and relaxing eyes and around his naked head he could feel the reach of fine spray or the breath of fog. He was upborne, open-armed. He was only thinking, My dear love comes" (*CSEW*, 423). At this moment all thought of Emma disappears. This is Eugene's real homecoming, his discovery of his own body, his own sexuality, and his release from social convention. This is his return to his love, this big father man. Eugene has become the bird, transcendent, but embodied, the Christ open-armed, the all forgiving, the body in the moment of sexual orgasm. Eugene thinks, "My dear love comes," and the Spaniard makes a loud emotional cry.

Even while he experiences this moment, he hears an echoing laugh and sees a man and a woman circling (the same word he uses to describe his image of marriage) over him like vultures: "Two big common toothy sweethearts stood there in its light, and the next moment vanished in the fog looking pleased with each other" (*CSEW*, 423). The sweethearts circling above descend like birds of prey and tell the Spaniard to put Eugene down. Eugene has been defeated by convention. His journey has been ended by the vision of the two sweethearts and their morals and ethics. He cannot enter the world of alternative sexual fulfillment, regeneration, and mythic rebirth without their demands interruptions. The sweethearts have a flashlight, indicating power and civilization; the Spaniard and Eugene make their way home by matchlight.

As he returns to earth, "his dangling heels, one of which had gone to sleep, kicked at the rock and then his feet stood on it. In the purple of night there was struck a little pasteboard match" (*CSEW*, 425). It is Eugene's heel, the vulnerable part of the hero Achilles, that has fallen asleep and left him susceptible to this intrusion; at the moment when he must be most conscious, he has been caught off guard. In *Ulysses*, Leopold speaks of the heel of Achilles, and Skin the Goat gives a long soliloquy on the subject.[50] One could read the reference to Eugene's heel as suggesting that Eugene's vulnerable point is heterosexual love. Grahn points out that purple—"the purple of night"—is traditionally a gay color that represents not only the coming together of female red and male blue, but the "radical transformation from one state of being to another. . . . Purple appears at twilight and at predawn. It stands in the gate between the land of the material flesh in one world and the land of the spirit or soul" (6). This subsection ends as the Spaniard strikes a match in the darkness. The Spaniard has tried to show Eugene the symbol of the *mariposa*, of the butterfly, of gay resurrection, but Eugene has not understood. It is not the Spaniard who is unable to comprehend, it is Eugene. Now they can only light one match after another in the darkness, and the Spaniard will light this match, not Eugene. The sweethearts win out in the end, and Eugene must return to his passionless relationship. He will return to Morgana and die of tuberculosis. Eugene is not so much defeated by women's self-sufficiency as by heterosexual conventionality.

The Spaniard is now wide awake. The sun has just gone down and the Spaniard as love, as the moon, is just waking up from the sleep of a month. The moon is on a monthly cycle and so are women. This lily growing at the side of the ocean is like the resurrected female whose laugh and body died in the image of the mechanical woman. In the beginning of the sixteenth subsection in "Music from Spain," the Spaniard lights matches and leads Eugene along the cliff paths. It is not, however, pitch black because the moon is emerging and racing ahead: "the world was not dark but pale" (*CSEW*, 424). The two men are stumbling along looking for their way back as did Leopold and Stephen in the first section of Chapter 17 in *Ulysses*. This chapter in Joyce's plan is called "Ithaca" and is set in the house at 2:00 A.M. The art is science, the symbol comets, and the technic catechism. Eugene and the Spaniard are walking and moving together, not separately like Stephen and Leopold.

When Leopold reaches the kitchen he too will light a match in order to see. Leopold and Stephen have been drinking coffee in the shelter, and Leopold makes them two cups of cocoa in his kitchen. The Spaniard and Eugene go to a small café and have two cups of coffee. While Stephen drinks his cocoa he is silent. While the Spaniard smokes he sits back and closes his eyes.

The form of this subsection is catechism, and the waitress asks Eugene and the Spaniard, "What kind of bread?" (*CSEW*, 425). Leopold makes fun of Molly's attempt at pronunciation, and the waitress makes fun of the Spaniard's desire for sugar and adds baby talk to her accent. She then turns to Eugene; "'Go to hell,' she said resonantly to Eugene. 'In my country I have a husband. He too is a little man, and sits up as small as you. When he is bad, I peek him up, I stand him on the mantelpiece'" (*CSEW*, 425).

In this subsection the waitress is transformed into a giant able to pick up her husband at will. In *Ulysses*, Joyce asks: "What homothetic objects, other than the candlestick, stood on the mantelpiece?" (*UL*, 581). This odd woman in the café is their guide back into society, but she does not speak English clearly. She speaks the creole language of the borderland—bringing together the language of convention and the language of sexuality. She is a strange woman who puts both Eugene and the Spaniard in their places; they are still children in her world. She speaks in a "resonant, brooding voice—there was something likeable and understandable about her, with her unbelievable accent" (*CSEW*, 425). This is the first woman they have talked to all day. She talks only about real things—milk, sandwiches, customers. The Spaniard and Eugene want milk and sugar, close to the milk and honey of the promised land, but this woman and this place are not the promised land. As if to confirm this point she tells Eugene to go to hell, almost as if she is telling him to go back to the land of the dead, land's end, and journey further. She tells him that he has not come far enough, that he is still a little man whom she could put on her mantelpiece. Eugene is broke, has no money for further journeying, and can only wonder about petty things like whether the Spaniard would ever have deigned to pay him.

Eugene leaves the Spaniard on the street corner as he goes home, and Leopold leaves Stephen on the street corner. The last image Eugene has of the Spaniard is of him "looking in the sky for the little moon" (*CSEW*, 425). The Spaniard is looking for the women's world, or he is himself the man in the moon and will return there. One of the oddest and most sexist sections of this *Ulysses* chapter is the passage about the moon which Joyce begins:

"What special affinities appeared to him to exist between the moon and woman? (*UL*, 576).

The most striking difference between subsection eighteen in "Music from Spain" and Chapter 18 of *Ulysses* is the fact that Molly is alone and Emma has a friend visiting—Mrs. Herring. Molly speaks of a fishwoman (*UL*, 631) and talks about getting potatoes for dinner. Emma is making chowder, which is made from fish and potatoes. In the beginning of Molly's narrative Molly thinks of what she would do if Leopold got sick: "Anything really the serious the matter with him its much better for them to go into a hospital where everything is clean" (*UL*, 608). Emma tells Eugene she will be burying him from pneumonia, and Eugene eventually dies of pneumonia. In *Ulysses*, Molly says that men always talk about being sick but "woman hides it not to give any trouble they do yes" (*UL*, 608). In "Music from Spain," Emma does not hide her burn: "Then, with a stamp of her foot, she showed him—and also Mrs. Herring, who was evidently seeing it for the second or third time—where the hot grease had splattered on her hand today" (*CSEW*, 426). Molly, in *Ulysses*, talking about how her skin is getting old, comments: "I thought it was beginning to look coarse or old a bit the skin underneath is much finer where it peeled off there on my finger after the burn its a pity it isnt all like that" (*UL*, 618). Emma is burned on the hand. Molly is burned on the finger. While Eugene thinks that the "wounded cry" he hears as he goes down the stairs in the morning is a response to his slap, Emma is actually crying out because she has been burned.

That Emma has heard nothing from Mr. Bertsinger suggests that Eugene's whole journey has existed in a separate textual plane, that Eugene has imagined everything he thought about Emma—even that he slapped her. Eugene should be the returning hero or wanderer, but Mrs. Herring has usurped his place. The two women are drinking wine in honor of Mrs. Herring's return from her trip as if she were Odysseus coming back from his journey. Emma rather than Eugene has a scar like Odysseus. When Odysseus returned he had to fight for Penelope against the suitors, but when Eugene returns, he cannot compete with Mrs. Herring. His only way of entering the conversation is to bring up the Spaniard; however, he does not have the poetic language to describe the events of the day: "'Saw Long-Hair, the guitar player, today, saw him walking along the street, just like you or me. What was his name, anyway?' he asked, as if he wondered now for the first time" (*CSEW*, 426).[51] Emma answers Eugene: "'Bartolome Montalbano,' Emma said and popped a grape onto her extended tongue. She added, 'I have the feeling he suffers from indigestion,' and drummed her breast while she swallowed.' . . . He's a Spaniard'" (*CSEW*, 426).

Like Molly, Emma can pronounce the Spanish. Molly wonders if she can get her "tongue round any of the Spanish como esta usted muy bien gracias y usted see I havent forgotten it all" (*UL*, 640). Emma can get her tongue both around the Spanish and a grape. Emma knows the Spaniard's name and claims to know the intimate detail that he suffers from indigestion. One might ask how she could know such a fact. Does Welty want us to think that Emma might be having an affair with the Spaniard? Has she fed him, her most loving act? She comes out of public mourning the night of his concert. She also repeats the obvious information that he is Spanish.[52] While she says all of this she is popping grapes into her mouth. Grapes are the Dionysian symbol of orgies. They represent fertility and sexual abandon.

Welty changed the ending of this story from the manuscript to the published text. The ending of the published text reads:

> "A Spaniard? There was a Spaniard at early church this morning," Mrs. Herring offered, "that needed a haircut. He was next to a woman and he was laughing with her out loud—bad taste, *we* thought. It was before service began, it's true. He laughed first and then slapped her leg, there in Peter and Paul directly in front of me home from my trip."

Eugene tilted back in his chair, and watched Emma pop the grapes in.

"That would be him," said Emma. (*CSEW*, 426)

We know that the teachings of Peter and Paul are among the most mysogynist and antihomosexual in the Bible. In Rom. 1:27, Paul writes: "And likewise also the men, leaving the natural use of the woman, burned in their lust one toward another; men with men working that which is unseemly, and receiving in themselves that recompence of their error which was meet."

Peter and Paul say that women should obey their husbands in every thing and that they should be silent in church. Emma recognizes Mrs. Herring's description. Emma knows the Spaniard. She laughs at the teachings of Peter and Paul, at everything in society that forces women and homosexuals into silence. Welty's earlier ending to "Music from Spain" reads:

> ". . . Peter and Paul directly in front of me home from my trip!"
>
> "That would be him," Emma said.
>
> Eugene tilted back his chair. He sipped the Burgundy with the two of them, and joined every time in their laughter.
>
> "*So* late," said Mrs. Herring.
>
> "*So* late," said Emma.
>
> Laughter.
>
> (ms. Mississippi Department of Archives and History and Humanities Research Center at University of Texas)

The manuscript version does not make clear the fact that the women are laughing at the teachings of Peter and Paul, but the repetition of the words "so late" indicates that Eugene has understood the joke so much later than the two women. The mechanical dummy of a woman on the beach is dead, and the living women have regained their voice and their laughter. Eudora Welty has the last laugh with her finely textured parody and critique of modernism.

7

Like the Tips of Wings Must Feel to Birds

The Charged Field of Dramatic Fiction in "The Wanderers"

Eudora Welty wrote "The Wanderers" after completing the other stories in *The Golden Apples* and after she had consciously decided to make the stories into a collection. In "The Wanderers" the collection doubles back on itself, writing itself again in the reading. The text pulls the threads of all the other stories together and insists on a meeting at the crossroads from which King MacLain, or for that matter any character, cannot run. Although this story is called "The Wanderers," it is about wanderers who come home, wanderers who cross one another's paths, even if only for a moment. In this story Welty brings the narrator Katie from "Shower of Gold" and the subject Virgie from "June Recital" into each other's orbits. She forces them to switch places. At the end of *One Writer's Beginnings*, Welty offers an insight into her work that helps explain "The Wanderers":

> It is our inward journey that leads us through time—forward or back, seldom in a straight line, most often spiraling. Each of us is moving, changing, with respect to others. As we discover, we remember, remembering, we discover, and most intensely do we expe-

rience this when our separate journeys converge. Our living experience at those meeting points is one of the charged dramatic fields of fiction.

I'm prepared now to use the wonderful word *confluence*, which of itself exists as a reality and a symbol in one. It is the only kind of symbol that for me as a writer has any weight, testifying to the pattern, one of the chief patterns of human experience. (102)

In "The Wanderers" the charged dramatic field is created precisely out of the coming together of characters and the dichotomies they represent—male and female, young and old, black and white, the past and the present, the dead and the living. Welty describes this confluence through the inner journey of Virgie—a journey that, as Welty reminds us, only occurs in relation to the community, in her connection to all of the other characters who inhabit her textual universe. In the last line of *One Writer's Beginnings*, Welty writes that "all serious daring comes from within" (104).

Critics often complain that there is no plot in Welty's works or in the works of other women writers, including the feminist modernists Virginia Woolf and Gertrude Stein. If we can percieve no plot in these texts, it is because we have come to identify plot with the narrative of heroic dominance. Heroic plot records a journey that is necessarily external, because it is based on fear, revenge, and escape—all of the emotions that depend on the existence of an "other," from which one can differentiate one/ "self." Fear paralyzes and sets a character in the defensive position of the thousand-eyed Argus. In such a position, there can be no internal movement and thus no change. The daring, the excitement, is in the subtle movements that take place in the inward journey. In "The Wanderers," Welty records Virgie's inward journey. There is no plot, only the charge of discovery. Welty reminds us throughout her fiction that the field becomes charged, not just when one individual tries to know another individual, but when one character has the same experience as

another or becomes that other for a moment, when Cassie becomes Mr. Voight, when Loch sees himself in Miss Eckhart,
when Nina wants to try for the fiercest secrets.

The first words of "The Wanderers" are spoken by Mrs. Stark
to her maid: "How come you weren't here yesterday?" (*CSEW*,
427). Although these are literally the words of Mrs. Stark asking
her maid, Juba, where she has been, they are symbolically the
words of the white woman writer asking herself, "Where was the
black woman character yesterday?" Mrs. Stark is old. It is Sep-
tember and she can feel October, winter and death, approaching.
She must look to the younger black women to help her. Mrs.
Stark plays solitaire on an inlaid board, but in her helplessness
she must break this isolation and reach across the racial boundary
to the black woman Juba. When Mrs. Stark asks Juba where she
has been, Juba replies, "Showin' my teef" (*CSEW*, 427). "Showin' my teef" can be a southern expression for visiting, but it can
also mean that Juba has new teeth that she has been showing her
sister. This expression also has greater mythological significance.
During the male initiation ceremonies that Jane Ellen Harrison
examines in *Themis*, it was common for an older male to knock
out a young boy's tooth, which would be kept by an elder or
someone in the tribe as a symbol of the masculine rebirth.[1] In
many societies people thought that teeth were sources of divination. Perseus gains divine power by stealing the tooth of the
Graeae. Juba's teeth, which will live on beyond her, represent
the future rebirth of an egalitarian world in which there are no
racial and class boundaries. Juba tells Mrs. Stark, "I was comin'
back. Sister's place a place once you get to it—hard time gettin'
out" (*CSEW*, 427). Juba has been gaining power from an all-
female, all-black sphere, but we have the sense that if she does
not "get out" she would lose herself there forever. Mrs. Stark
responds, "'You and all your sisters!' She rose and walked, with
her walk like a girl's, to the front door, looking down over the
hill, the burned, patchy grass no better than Katie Rainey's, and
the thirsty shrubs; but the Morgan sweet olive, her own grand-

mother's age, her grandmother's tree, was blooming. She murmured over her shoulder, 'I never had cause to set foot in the Rainey house for over five minutes in my life. And I don't suppose they need me now. But I hope I know what any old woman owes another old woman. It doesn't matter if it's too late'" (*CSEW*, 427). Mrs. Stark is an old woman, yet she walks like a girl, reminding us that any woman is all three aspects of the triple goddess simultaneously. Although the grass is burnt and the scrubs thirsty, indicating a lack of fertility, the Morgan olive tree, the tree representing the feminine side of the Morgana/MacLain dichotomy, is still blooming, connecting three generations of women. By acknowledging that she is not much different from Katie Rainey, Mrs. Stark crosses the class boundary, but she neglects to understand her dependence on Juba, a realization that would allow her to cross the racial boundary: "Only thing I can do for people any more, in joy or sorrow, is send 'em you" (*CSEW*, 427). She still thinks that she owns Juba, that she can order her around. Although Mrs. Stark seems to be angry about Juba's sisters, she understands sisterhood; she knows what any old woman owes another old woman, but she has not yet learned what an old white woman owes a young black woman.

Before she dies, Katie Rainey is trying to hold on to order, to control her environment, to keep things from converging. She is trying desperately to hold up her head, as Cassie did in "June Recital" to keep from drowning. We learn that Katie had a light stroke five years ago, while separating the cows and calves, and after this "she'd begun ordering things done by set times" (*CSEW*, 428). The attempt to separate the cows from the calves, to separate anything from anything else, but particularly the babies from the mothers, causes Katie to have a stroke—not to die, but to lose physical movement, to freeze. Against the nearness of death, against the fear of death, Katie tries to stop the progression, the beat of life, not with a metronome like Miss Eckhart, but by ordering Virgie to do things by set times.

When Miss Katie stands waiting for Virgie by the side of the road, "she still walked her narrow path, not yielding even to the kind sun" (*CSEW*, 428). Even though the sun, fiery and fierce in "Moon Lake," is now kind, the old woman does not let this fertility penetrate her body, but her attempt at protection is useless. Katie Rainey's home is no protected female sphere like "Moon Lake" or Juba's sister's place in the country. Her house sits right on the main road where the loggers drive by day and night to cut down trees in the Morgana woods. Her own daughter Virgie works "for the very people that were out depleting the woods, Mr. Nesbitt's company" (*CSEW*, 428). Her house is the point of intersection, the crossroads between the past and the future, conservation and progress, old and young: "Miss Katie couldn't spare her good hand to put up and shade her eyes; yet after you passed, you saw her in that position, in your vision if not in your sight (*CSEW*, 428). Although Miss Katie does not actually shade her eyes, our vision is of her shading her eyes, trying both to protect her image of herself and to see something in the sunlight at the same time. By making a distinction between vision and sight, Welty indicates that physical sight and inner vision are equally important, at once independent and interdependent. When we see through our eyes, we see what we are supposed to see; when we use our vision, we learn to see what we can know, the wider perspective. This is the duality that Diarmuid Russell calls "the meshing of two types of reality" (Kreyling, *Author and Agent*, 118), which we experience throughout *The Golden Apples* whether it is in the tension between dreaming and waking or between imagination and action. It is this meshing or bringing together of types of reality that allows Katie's character to become the text over whose dead body confluence can occur.

Every character in the text crosses paths in Katie's house. Every character converges in their response to her living, dying, and dead body. Most people who see Katie waiting by the side of the road laugh. Only the children and blacks take her for granted because, in Welty's vision, they see Katie as part of the town's constellation. On a mythic level she is the old woman at the turn in the road, Hecate watching the crossroads or Demeter looking for Persephone. The people watching her "were reminded vaguely of themselves, too, now that they were old enough to see it, still watching and waiting for something they didn't really know about any longer, wouldn't recognize to see it coming in the road" (*CSEW*, 429). One person's waiting reflects all people's waiting, the longing for something unrecognizable, unspeakable.

As Katie waits "she heard circling her ears like the swallows beginning, talk about lovers. Circle by circle it twittered, church talk, talk in the store and post office, vulgar man talk possibly in the barbershop. Talk she could never get near now was coming to her" (*CSEW*, 429). Even the talk that Katie does not want to hear, and could not hear even if she wanted to because it is whispered in the town where she no longer goes, comes to her on swallow wings. Katie knows that people talk about how Mr. Mabry leaves Virgie a bag of quail every day. She knows that they make Virgie's sexuality the topic of gossip, everyone's business, but this gossip is no longer secret. It has taken to the air, become the very air she breathes. There no longer are boundaries between the male barbershop and the female kitchen, the church and the street. In the twittering talk, Katie hears her husband's name, Fate, in place of Mr. Mabry. "Not Fate Rainey at all; but Mr. Mabry. It was just that the talk Miss Katie heard was in voices of her girlhood, and some times they slipped" (*CSEW*, 429). Katie imagines that she asks people where Virgie is, but she does not actually do this. She confuses the spoken and the unspoken, the present and the past, Virgie and herself, the natural sound of birds and the sound of gossip. In all of these slippings, there is a new knowledge breaking the accepted categories. In the act of slipping, of one thing becoming another, there is forgiveness and insight. This slippage, this blurring of distinct boundaries, opens up new possibilities. Katie cannot judge Virgie because she is, could be, has been Virgie. The love between Katie and Virgie exists in the space between the spoken and the not spo-

ken. It lives in the dynamic charged connection and separation of
I/not I.

> The day Miss Katie died, Virgie was kneeling on the floor of her
> bedroom cutting out a dress from some plaid material. She was
> sewing on Sunday.
> "There's nothing Virgie Rainey loves better than struggling
> against a real hard plaid," Miss Katie thought, with a thrust of pain
> from somewhere unexpected. Whereas, there was a simple line down
> through her own body now, dividing it in half; there should be one in
> every woman's body—it would need to be the long way, not the
> cross way—that was too easy—making each of them a side to feel
> and know, and a side to stop it, to be waited on, finally. (*CSEW*, 430)

When Katie Rainey thinks "there's nothing Virgie Rainey
loves better than struggling against a real hard plaid," she lets us
know that Virgie actively seeks difficult puzzles. Virgie will not
shy away from the task of piecing together any puzzle she comes
across, even the puzzle of her own life or her mother's life. In the
act of cutting cloth, a cutting that ends in the death of her mother, Virgie takes on the aspect of the third of the Fates, Atropos,
who cuts the thread of life with her shears. Earlier Virgie had
many characteristics of the second aspect of the triple goddess,
but at her mother's death, Virgie becomes the crone and moves
into the last phase of her life. Virgie is not only cutting the
thread, she is cutting up one pattern to make another. She is
struggling against the plaid—the chessboard of "June Recital,"
Mrs. Stark's inlaid board, and the difficult but symmetrical pattern that the world imposes on her, by piecing it into a new
form. This is exactly the action Welty takes in writing *The Golden
Apples*. Unlike Easter, or Cassie, or even Miss Eckhart, Virgie
confronts the system directly. Virgie's hard-to-match plaid is a
much more complicated arrangement than Easter's antic flower
pattern. At the same time Katie Rainey, watching Virgie, becomes the seamstress and the cloth as she turns the women's
bodies into a fabric that can be marked with a line lengthwise

rather than across the neck like Perseus or across the waist like a sexual object. Through her plaid, which cuts both ways, Virgie is trying to live in the world, to match up the fragments, the opposing realities of freedom and constraint, to make a dress that will fit her and that she can actually wear. She sleeps with men, she takes a job with the loggers, she butts her head directly against the wall.

As Virgie returns from working at the logging camp to milk the cows and cook the quail, it is as if she goes back in time. Miss Katie says, "'It's a wonder, though,' she thought. 'A blessed wonder to see the child mind'" (*CSEW*, 430). Katie treats Virgie like a child even though Virgie is forty years old and takes care of her mother. Katie's last clear feeling as she stands there, holding herself up, "was that she wanted to be down and covered up, in, of all things, Virgie's hard-to-match-up plaid" (*CSEW*, 430). In this last act Katie would let herself become the baby wrapped up in the swaddling of Virgie's—her daughter's—creation. In this moment of being waited on, Katie and Virgie would switch places; the daughter becomes the mother and the mother the daughter. Katie does not allow herself the second option, the letting go.

Instead she walks the length of the room, lies down in her bed, and asks Virgie to fan her. Virgie, who is working in her gown, comes in "with pins in her mouth and her thumb marked green from the scissors" (*CSEW*, 430) and stands over her mother, fanning her with the *Market Bulletin*. A person with a green thumb is someone who can make things grow, but with the pins in her mouth and the thumb marked green, Virgie also becomes the queen of the May or a nymph waiting on the queen as well as Welty pinning the text together. As Virgie fans, Katie silently tries to go over all of the flowers listed in the bulletin, to give them all their proper names. In Katie's list of flowers, we see at once the complexity of life and the convergence—not melting into sameness, but able to live with difference and let difference live.

A poetics of confluence is a poetics that allows and encourages the proliferation and constant interrelatedness of separate elements—both a constellation and a scattering of little lights. In the tradition of H. D.'s "Sea Rose"[2] and Gertrude Stein's "rose is a rose" Welty deconstructs the traditional image of the rose through proliferation. Welty has Katie name "Roses: big white rose, little thorn rose, beauty-red sister rose, pink monthly, old-fashioned red summer rose, very fragrant, baby rose. Five colors of verbena, candlestick lilies, milk and wine lilies, blackberry lilies, lemon lilies, angel lilies, apostle lilies. Angel trumpet seed. The red amarylis" (*CSEW*, 431). In the moment of her death, Katie holds on to the seeds of life, to the beauty and proliferation of difference. Language becomes not a means of dividing and separating but a way of loving. This is Katie's last struggle. She asks Virgie to keep fanning in order to keep the flame of her life burning. As Virgie fans she begins to think faster and faster. There is the crossroads between life and death, one of the charged fields of dramatic action; Katie is meeting life in all its richness and variety while she is at the same moment running toward death. She uses language to hold on to life and to enter death; in naming these flowers, she both honors life and comes closer to the earth that she will soon become. At her funeral, on her grave, in the earth above her, there will be flowers. Katie, confusing her own death with her mother's death, begins thinking, "And when Mama is gone, almost gone now, she meditated, I can tack on to my ad: the quilts!" (*CSEW*, 431). The list of quilts tells the story of Katie's life as it progresses from youth—"Double Muscadine Hulls"—to romance and dreams of escape—"Road to Dublin" and "Starry Sky"—to images of entanglements—"Strange Spider Web"—to children and neighbors—"Hands All Around"—and finally marriage—"Double Wedding Ring" (*CSEW*, 431). In this last moment, the last words of Katie's life, she is telling us of her attempt to get enough money to escape. We do not know what she had planned, but we do know that whatever Katie was saving money for, it was her secret and her life, something that she desired passionately, her protest.

Katie not only confuses herself with her mother, but she also slips into Virgie. As she lies there "carelessly on the counterpane. . . . She was thinking, Mistake. Never Virgie at all. It was me, the bride—with more than they guessed. Why, Virgie, go away, it was me. She put her hand up and never knew what happened to it, her protest" (*CSEW*, 431). Katie makes the mistake of thinking of Virgie as herself, but the exclamation "mistake" also refers to the mistake Katie might think she made in selling the bulbs and the quilts to get married, in giving up the money that would have been her source of independence. When she tells Virgie to go away, she means both that she needs Virgie to go away so that she can remember her own life accurately and that she wants Virgie literally to leave Morgana and escape the trap of the "double wedding ring." Katie's last words support the second reading. Katie Rainey's hand is her symbol of rebellion, but Virgie is also her symbol of rebellion. If Virgie is King MacLain's daughter—and it seems likely that she is, even if only metaphorically—then Katie Rainey protested her marriage and social convention when she gave birth to Virgie. Katie as the bride was not the spotless virgin, not the penniless girl, but a woman rich with her mother's quilts and possibly rich— pregnant—with Virgie. Virgie is Katie's protest in all ways. In naming her Virgie, "virgin," she protests the masculine definition of virginity. As a younger woman, she is Katie's protest, able to go places, live the independent life Katie gave up. Virgie can, and at her mother's funeral does, find King MacLain and look him straight in the eye. With her raised hand, Katie is planting seeds for the future, but she does not live to see what happens to Virgie, her protest. In the last moment Katie becomes the triple goddess, her own mother and her daughter in one, but she also recognizes the difference. Difference and integration coexist. Virgie lives. Katie dies with a vision of a "sunburst design, very lacy" (*CSEW*, 431).

At the moment of Katie's death, Welty shifts the narrative to Virgie's consciousness. In most heroic narratives, the text ends as the hero breathes his last breath, but in the intertextual poetics of community and continuity, death is simply part of the journey. Virgie picks up the thread of the narrative where Katie leaves off. When her mother dies, pins drop from Virgie's mouth and she holds her own head. Welty describes Virgie's reaction visually rather than through abstractions such as grief; if she allowed such clichés to enter the text at this moment, she would inevitably lose the complexity of Virgie's charged field of emotion. Instead we see the visual manifestation of Virgie's reaction rather than a necessarily flawed attempt at analysis; her mouth opens, as Katie's shuts. She holds her head as Katie's falls. The shadow that falls over her mother is the shadow not only of King Arthur's shield but of Perseus's mirror, which he uses to protect himself from the Medusa's eyes, to separate himself from the Medusa and from death. Virgie holds her head almost as if to make certain she has not been slain along with her mother.

The ungiving headboard conceals a motto whose content is less important than the fact that its message will never change. As Virgie looks at the bed she moves from seeing the ungiving headboard as a mirror—echoing the line "mirror, mirror on the wall" of the jealous queen in "Snow White," describing woman's conventional inheritance—to seeing the counterpane that covers her mother as an inherited personal pattern, a pattern beyond convention. Interestingly enough in this description we see the fragments of the witch—the allusion to the mirror on the wall echoing Snow White and the black shoes sticking up beneath the counterpane suggesting a dead witch. In death she merges back into the composite picture, the textured headboard, counterpane, painting on the wall, and the window. Her mother has become the social text that is simultaneously conventional and ungiving like the shield, and warm, knotty, inherited, and overworked like the counterpane. The headboard shadows her mother's body to the waist while the counterpane covers the rest. Katie has become textile or text for Virgie's story. Virgie does not describe her mother's dead body because there is no body, there is only text. She has become the difficult puzzle that Virgie will now piece together. The fragments of the composite character in cultural heritage called "witch" still remain as scars on the textured surface. Virgie can only see this tapestry because "she was not much afraid of death, either of its delay or its surprise" (*CSEW*, 431). She has moved beyond the fearful position of the girls at Moon Lake, of Miss Eckhart, and of Katie. As Virgie waits "nothing in the place of fear came into her head; only something about her dress" (*CSEW*, 431). The dress is Virgie's new outfit; it is the textile that will continue to be woven, cut, and pieced together. Virgie's gaze moves from the solid headboard, like the solid bust of Beethoven in Miss Eckhart's studio, to the textured counterpane, to the window where a hummingbird flies and flowers grow. Her gaze turns from images of stasis to images of change and growth. In Barthes's terminology she has turned the dead work into the living text. Against the enormity of death and change, the feeble human attempt to control time fails; the clock can jangle but it cannot strike. Outside, in the natural world, social time has no meaning; human life is part of a much grander movement. From the movement of the hummingbird and the sweet fig syrup, "a torrent of riches seemed to flow over the room" (*CSEW*, 432).

Virgie's vision expands to include the hummingbird, and it will eventually extend to embrace everything, even the community that has treated her so badly. This transition is difficult and must be accomplished through her mother's body. At this point, Katie's body has become the writing itself; she has evolved from storyteller/author in the first story to the textual body in the last story. At the gathering the day before the funeral, Cassie says to Virgie, "You know I know what it's like" (*CSEW*, 232), but we know that Cassie cannot know what it is like for Virgie precisely because Virgie herself does not "know what it's like." After Mrs. Morrison committed suicide, Cassie froze her emotions and reactions and never progressed beyond the moment of shock and grief. She wears black stockings and balances a "gold-rimmed coffee cup" (*CSEW*, 432) like an old lady herself. For Virgie death is not like anything; there can be no knowing because once Virgie knows what it is like, she will stop experiencing the moment. Virgie is experiencing, Cassie is knowing. Cassie's knowledge is false confluence, false understanding. Because Virgie is experiencing and not knowing, she moves among these people strangely and responds to Cassie's comment by promptly falling asleep; this is both the sleep of renewal, like Easter's sleep, and a direct rejection of the falsehood that Cassie is expressing. In her dream vision she sees herself like the swallows, circling the crowd: "Through their murmur she heard herself circle the room to speak to them and be kissed. She made the steps of the walk they had to watch, head, breasts, and hips in their helpless agitation, like a rope of bells she started in their ears" (*CSEW*, 432). In this dreamlike state Virgie sees an image of herself that is different from what people expect of her. Her movement around the crowd fills the room with a living body, agitated, sexual, waking people up with the sound of bells. These bells are church bells ringing for the dead but they are also the bells of celebration, of Virgie's loose, independent living. In the house of death, the body of life is not supposed to breathe. Virgie sees her body as agitated, alive.

As Snowdie MacLain lays out Katie's body, Virgie is distanced: "Always in a house of death, Virgie was thinking, all the stories come evident, show forth from the person, become a part of the public domain. Not the dead's story, but the living's" (*CSEW*, 433). These people are the swallows that have twittered about her and her mother, that have shunned them and judged them. Now Virgie must move amongst them. She does not judge or gossip but merely sees their stories written on their bodies. She cannot separate herself from them, and at the same time she realizes that the people around her are a script that she can read: "And didn't it show on Ran, that once he had taken advantage of a country girl who had died a suicide?" (*CSEW*, 433). Ran's story is now both part of her and separate, but Virgie not only sees other people's stories, she must endure the retelling of her own. Mr. Nesbitt takes her to his friend Mr. Thisbee and asks her, "who's your best friend in this town," and Virgie must respond, "You, Mr. Bitts" (*CSEW*, 433). It comes out now that Virgie has worked for Mr. Nesbitt for twenty years. "She never turned away until it was finished; today this seemed somehow brief and easy, a relief" (*CSEW*, 433). It is brief and easy, a relief because, if the stories are part of the communal consciousness, then they have less personal weight. Anything that Virgie holds on to, keeps inside herself, will impede her inner journey toward freedom. Virgie's narrative no longer has meaning because it is something that is known, not something in the act of becoming.

As Virgie begins to release the stories, she can extend into her own personal history to remember Miss Eckhart and her recital night. She can remember how she "was thirteen, waiting outside, on guard at a vast calming spectacle of turmoil, and saving it. A little drop spilled, she remembered it now: an anxiety which brought her to the point of sickness, that back in there they were laughing at her mother's hat" (*CSEW*, 434). The words "back in there" may refer to Miss Eckhart's studio years ago or to her mother's room now. We also realize that in the moment of connecting with her past self, with the little thirteen-year-old girl who would be so afraid of the fact that people were laughing at her mother, Virgie lets herself feel for the first time. For the first time in the collection, we know that Virgie is not just the tough little tomboy, the insensitive daughter, or the town whore.

At this moment of opening within Virgie, her mother's door opens, and Snowdie emerges. The women begin to pull on Virgie's arms and beg her to look at the body. Snowdie MacLain has finished laying Katie out, and all the women look at Katie "as they would bend over the crib of a little kicking baby" (*CSEW*, 434). The collection of stories has doubled back on itself so that Snowdie, who was Katie's subject—her baby—in "Shower of Gold," has now become the artist, and Katie is her subject and her baby. In the moment of physical contact with people who have never touched her before, Virgie repeats the words of Cu-chulain, of Narcissus, of Christ, and says "Don't touch me" (*CSEW*, 435). The words are both like and unlike the hero's words. As with the hero, these words are interpreted as the last rejection of a body that does not want to look death in the face, but they are also the words of self-protection from a body that has been neglected, talked about, hurt, and ostracized: "They were all people who had never touched her before who tried now to struggle with her, their faces hurt" (*CSEW*, 435). The hurt continues into the present as "Miss Perdita Mayo's red face looked over their wall. 'Your mama was too fine for you, Virgie, too fine. That was always the trouble between you'" (*CSEW*, 435). The women are, however, right about one thing: Virgie must let them lead her before she can move past the statement, "Don't touch me." Virgie has not yet fallen.

Virgie has not let go; "even their hands showing sorrow for a body that did not fall, giving back to hands what was broken, to pick up, smooth again. For people's very touch anticipated the falling of the body, the own, the single and watchful body" (*CSEW*, 435). For Virgie to fall means to give up the false heroic independence, the rebellious stance that has kept her strong all her life and allowed her to survive. Virgie's body does not fall to others' hands easily. She fights falling in the same way that Easter fought Loch's efforts to revive her. Virgie does not cry or fall when these ladies expect her to. She cries later, in the parlor, when they tell stories about her mother. They claim that Katie used to sell muscadines out by the road but that now the road goes the wrong way. Virgie weeps "because they could not tell it right, and they didn't press for her reasons" (*CSEW*, 435). The road in Virgie's story has not changed; it still stretches from Morgana to MacLain, from the feminine to the masculine, from the mother out to the world, but the world no longer sees the woman selling muscadines. The people who pass in fast trucks are not people who use words to talk about fertility, to ask about the seasons and what grows, but people who cut down trees.

What Katie had to bring together, the confluence that Katie had to achieve in a world that no longer cared for what she had to offer, was too much for her. It killed her.

As the neighbors go through the list of things that Virgie will inherit, they mention two interesting items, a "picture of the deer Miss Katie's mother hooked in Tishomingo with the mistletoe crown over the horns, and the oak leaves," and "the cloth doll with the china head and hands, that she used to let any and all play with" (*CSEW*, 436).[3] The picture of the deer includes the mistletoe, the oak, and the stag—all symbols of male resurrection and rebirth in Celtic mythology. These three icons tell the story of the ritual murder and rebirth of the male oak king which Frazer describes in *The Golden Bough* (812–23). Miss Katie thinks this picture is the prettiest thing in the world, but no one knows anymore what it signifies. The doll symbolizes the female who gives herself to any and all, either sexually or in her willingness to be used. Both of these inheritances Virgie must leave behind. These potential barriers to her growth are now small and insignificant. When all the guests from the first day's visit leave, Virgie feels, "As they went, they seemed to drag some mythical gates and barriers away from her view. . . . The world shimmered" (*CSEW*, 439).

When the guests leave, Virgie goes down to the Big Black River, the place where King pretended to drown himself and where Mr. Sissum actually did drown, removes her clothes, and steps into the river.

> She saw her waist disappear into reflectionless water; it was like walking into sky, some impurity of skies. All was one warmth, air, water, and her own body. All seemed one weight, one matter—until as she put down her head and closed her eyes and the light slipped under her lids, she felt this matter a translucent one, the river, herself, the sky all vessels which the sun filled. She began to swim in the river, forcing it gently, as she would wish for gentleness to her body. Her breasts around which she felt the water curving were as sensitive at that moment as the tips of wings must feel to birds, or antenna to insects. She felt the sand, grains intricate as little cogged

wheels, minute shells of old seas, and the many dark ribbons of grass
and mud touch her and leave her, like suggestions and withdrawals
of some bondage that might have been dear, now dismembering and
losing itself. (*CSEW*, 439–40)

Virgie does not use language that echoes conventional discourse; instead she speaks of her relationship to being itself, to
the act of living, which is at once sexual, sensual, embodied, and
without boundaries. This vision moves us beyond a poetics of
duality to an inclusive poetics of waves rippling from the center
to include the sky, the bank, the water, her body. It is the sunburst design, the lacy pattern, the point with strokes raying out.
In this vision, everything can be seen; there are no invisible
barriers. Virgie is swimming, not drowning, but she can only
swim because she lets herself "drown," that is, she treats the
water as she would her own body. Rather than hide from the sun
or the water, she simply moves into the water and becomes a
vessel like the river or the sky which the sun can fill, aware of
"the nebulous edges of her feeling and the vanishing opacity of
her will" (440). Virgie does not become Danaë; since she is willing to be filled by the sun she cannot be raped by it. Rape is an
act of violation. If there is no separation—"All was one warmth,
air, water, and her own body"—then she is the sun and cannot
be a victim of the sun.

As the boundaries drop, so do the fears. This falling away of
dichotomies allows for the emergence of a sexuality based on the
multiple pleasures of physical experience. As Virgie swims in the
water, she finds her sexuality in the love of her own moving body.
She swims "as she would wish for gentleness to her body," and the
sensitivity she feels in her breasts is like the "tips of wings must
feel to birds." In each moment she falls deeper into the natural
world, while the old stories recede. The sand, intricate as little
cogged wheels, reminds us of the goddess Nemesis and the minute shells of old seas—and thus again of Venus/Aphrodite—but
this time these feminine images are diminutive, not because they

are powerless but because Virgie no longer needs these external symbols of her power. At the same time the masculine symbols are reduced; they have lost their mythological significance. What were knotted, dangerous roots in "Moon Lake" become simply ribbons of grass and smooth fish in "The Wanderers." The bondage created by fear of male violence and of death is "dismembering and losing itself." Virgie is moving effortlessly through the water. As Virgie gives up holding her head or trying to learn through the head, her will vanishes. In this moment of confluence, memory or the stories of the living become only slight agitations. Virgie could turn into something else, know the fiercest secrets; in this state anything is possible. This is the greatest dramatic moment because it is unknown, completely unexpected. When she gets out of the water, the two little boys are not threatening. The Medusa's head and body are one. At this moment the moon is high in the sky and the thrush is singing.

When Virgie goes back to her mother's room, she sees her body body in a new way: "Only the black dress, the density of skirt, was stamped on it, like some dark chip now riding mid-air on blue lakes" (*CSEW*, 441). From the release Virgie has experienced in the river, she is able to see that in her death, Katie as the black dress, has become textile—no longer witch but the movement of witch, the power of witch to fly. If she is to continue to change and develop, Virgie must bring her experience of confluence in the natural world into the social world. The next morning Virgie continues her spiritual journey. She takes the sewing scissors and begins to cut the grass in the front yard. In this scene she returns again to the third aspect of the triple goddess who cuts the male grain in the fall so that it may come back to life in the spring: "it had all gone to seed" (*CSEW*, 441). Until this moment Virgie has cried only once. After the death of Maideen in "The Whole World Knows" and the resurrection of Easter in "Moon Lake," we have finally come to the point at which the goddess is actively cutting off the heads of the old grain god. The old male image, the bloody fist, the gun, the vision of domination, is dead, gone to seed. The roses of feminin/e/est rebirth are choked but alive, drawing drops of blood. Virgie weeps the tears of the earth mother who brings back the fertility consort in the spring and mourns the loss of her daughter Persephone in the fall. They are the tears of the daughter for the lost mother. They are the tears of the daughter for herself. Virgie's anger is the anger of the Medusa at the terror and violation of the vaunting hero, of Miss Eckhart at the world for denying her talent, of Mrs. Morrison who could have sung, of Jinny Love, of Snowdie MacLain. Virgie takes in the anger and tears of all of those she has forgotten, of the Snowdie MacLains and Miss Eckharts of the world. In this moment of connection to her female past, Virgie finds herself still "dimmed around Venus" (*CSEW*, 441). Venus is the only goddess in Greek mythology who was not raped by a god. She rises independently from the sea. Venus is also the goddess of love. For Virgie, Venus represents independent sexuality.

These moments of transcendent embodiment give Virgie the power to face the crowd at the funeral. The ladies at the house, "radiating once more from the kitchen" (*CSEW*, 441), are a point with strokes raying out, but it is not just Venus or Missie Spights or Snowdie whom Virgie must let in, she must face King Mac-Lain. King MacLain is now an old man and, as Virgie says the day before: "There was something terrifying about that old man—he was too old" (*CSEW*, 438). On the second day, however, Virgie does not find King so terrifying, and she actually has a long conversation with him about her mother. In her embodied connection to Venus and to the fertility goddess, her own mythological power has become as old and as powerful as his. King tells Virgie that he promised Katie he would get her anything in the world she wanted and she asked him for a swivel chair. He had the chair delivered the next day and she set it out by the road and sold eggs from it. He claims, "'I set her on a throne!,' 'Mr. King, I never knew the chair came from you,' Virgie said, smiling'" (*CSEW*, 444).

On one level King shows that he knows what Katie wants when he gives her the chair, but he does not really heal her wounds. He does, however, heal Virgie's wounds and give her a gift when he tells this story. She smiles when she hears that King gave Snowdie the chair because she makes another connection. Those twittering swallows, the neighbors, equate the quail that Mr. Mabry gives to Virgie with gifts in return for sexual favors. If King gave Katie this gift, Virgie can assume that there was something between Katie and King. If this was true, then her mother was not too fine for her. They were much more alike than she had thought. These gifts may have nothing to do with sexuality, but the exchange between the male and the female indicates a debt that Virgie can understand.

When Jinny Love, now married to Ran MacLain, comes to the funeral, she takes on the role of the married lady, and her iron mask mirrors the ironclad pattern in "June Recital" and the feminine mask the twins wear in "Shower of Gold." She insists that Virgie should get married, grimacing as she says so, trying "to drive everybody, even Virgie for whom she cared nothing, into the state of marriage along with her" (*CSEW*, 445). When she looks for a husband for Virgie "her eyes rested over Virgie's head on—Virgie knew it—Ran MacLain. Virgie smiled faintly; now she felt, without warning, that two passionate people stood in this roomful, with their indifferent backs to each other" (*CSEW*, 445). For Jinny at this moment, marriage has nothing to do with the passionate connection between Virgie and Ran, Echo and Narcissus, Morrigana and Cuchulain, Katie and King, Miss Eckhart and Virgie, Eugene and the Spaniard, Easter and Nina. Institutionalized love, marriages, and funerals have nothing to do with the experience of love and death. During the funeral service, which could have as easily been a wedding, Virgie is uninvolved. The only action she takes is to move her mother's old stick from the china jar, where someone had put it, to the rack where it belonged. She does not want death to be outside life, special or different. Virgie knows that death is life. Children are outside screaming and playing. People are cooking food. Nina Carmichael is pregnant. Brother Dampeer is taking up a collection for his church. The stories of the living are coming forward.

After her discussion with King, Virgie more clearly comprehends the deep relationship between herself and the MacLains. While the service goes on, King MacLain keeps eating pieces of ham and looking at Virgie from down the hall, then he "made a hideous face at Virgie, like a silent yell. It was a yell at everything—including death, not leaving it out . . . Then he cracked the little bone in his teeth. She felt refreshed all of a sudden at that tiny but sharp sound" (*CSEW*, 446). Virgie does not have to ask King MacLain to recognize her or see her as Miss Eckhart did. King not only sees Virgie but picks her out. She is his death. She is the fertility consort who will replace him. She is his equal, whether he knows it or not. Cuchulain finally turns to Morrigana to heal the deep wounds, the wounds that go down to the bone. King's bone cracking is like the Boy Scout's intrusion, but not so violent. The crack of the one is an embodied thing, something that breaks through the twittering gossip, the superficial love. It is solid and real, like the table itself. In the crack of the bone, Virgie hears death, connection, human contact, a piercing look that descends as far as she descends and moves beyond social concepts of right and wrong. When Snowdie tells Virgie that she cannot forgive herself for spending all her parents' money looking for King, Virgie wants to tell her "Forgive yourself, yes" (*CSEW*, 448). These simple words, which Virgie as yet cannot speak, are the words that embody the poetic tenderness and toughness of Welty's vision. A poetics based on community and confluence must start from the premise that everything is part of the vision. The most important point to remember is simply, forgive yourself, yes. Since the self is relational, this will mean forgiving everyone, certainly a demanding but dramatically exciting task.

When Virgie goes to the cemetery, the confusion of one person with another, which happens repeatedly in this story, occurs again. While Virgie claims to have hated Miss Eckhart, "more than once she looked for the squat, dark stone that marked Miss Eckhart's own grave; it would turn itself from them, as she'd seen it do before, when they wound near and passed. And a seated angel, first visible from behind with the stone hair spread on the shoulders, turned up later from the side, further away, showing the steep wings" (*CSEW*, 449). The stone angel is a monument to Mrs. Morrison. Unlike Virgie, Cassie is unable to let her mother's memory live in the world and tries to solidify the moment of death, to catch the symbol of death—the angel, the hair, the wings of movement in stone: "After being so gay and flighty always, Cassie's mother went out of the room one morning and killed herself. 'I was proud of it,' said Cassie. 'It took everything I had' (*CSEW*, 449). It is difficult to determine whether Cassie is speaking of being proud of her mother's committing suicide or of the monument she has erected for her. The problem is that Cassie has confused the two. Although Cassie could be proud of her mother's suicide—her mother took back the power over her own death from the vaunting hero in a way that Miss Eckhart could not—Cassie has chosen instead to be proud of the monument, the solid object that crystallizes death, thereby mirroring the action of Perseus when he used the Medusa's head to turn men to stone. As Virgie looks at the cemetery, she sees the grave of "some lady's stillborn child (now she knew it must have been that baby sister of Miss Nell Loomis's), the lamb flattened by rains into a little fairy table" (*CSEW*, 449–50).

The stillborn child is that which has not reached fruition in the woman's life, that which has not come to life, the unspoken in Virgie. Virgie is watching the world of the dead, but in this place she does not see death; she sees movement and change, the rains flattening the little lamb, the angel turning. As Virgie watches her mother's burial, she sees anything but a deadly or still scene; it is full of life.

. . . the earth grew immediately vivacious and wild as a creature. . . . The cornucopias were none of them perfectly erect but
leaned to one side or the other, edging the swollen pink mound,
monstrous, wider than it was long until it should "settle."

As the party moved away, one of the cornucopias fell over and
spilled its weight of red zinnias. No one returned to right it. A
feeling of the tumbling activity and promptitude of the elements had
settled over people and stirred up, of all things, their dignity; they
could not go back now. (*CSEW*, 451)

At the sight of the burial, life rushes forward with tumbling
activity, pregnant, aroused, swollen, monstrous. The frail humans try to maintain their dignity in the face of the elements, but
they cannot go back. They are part of the march forward, the
resurgence of life at the moment of death.

All that Virgie tries to hold on to is falling from her; the
division in the woman's body that Katie speaks of is disappearing. The vast separation between Miss Eckhart and Virgie is now
falling before Virgie. She sees what she must move toward: "Mr.
King MacLain, an old man, had butted like a goat against the
wall he wouldn't agree to himself or recognize. What fortress
indeed would ever come down, except before hard little horns, a
rush and a stampede of the pure wish to live?" (*CSEW*, 452).
Who would think earlier in the story that King MacLain would
be able to tear down Virgie's fortress? But of course he must.
The strongest male and the strongest female must butt up
against each other. He is too old to know what he is doing, but
she knows.

When the funeral party has finally gone home, Virgie returns
to herself again and this time descends even deeper. She thinks
about the hours spent milking the cows and how "she would
hunt, hunt, hunt daily for the blindness that lay inside the beast,
inside where she could have a real and living wall for beating on,
a solid prison to get out of, the most real stupidity of flesh, a
mindless and careless and calling body, to respond flesh for flesh,
anguish for anguish. And if, as she dreamed one winter night, a

new piano she touched had turned, after the one pristine moment, into a calling cow, it was by her own desire" (*CSEW*, 453).
The woman's art, the pristine piano, can never be far from the
cow that the woman's hands must milk. Virgie wills the piano to
become a cow, because only as a cow, only as a powerful symbol
of women's spirituality, only as the beast who gives us milk, only
in the real physical world can a woman begin to find the artist
within her. The only art that will speak the woman's voice will
be the art of stupidity—meaning lack of knowledge, meaning
lack of preconceived ideas—and thus the brilliance of the flesh.
The pristine piano says nothing to the woman artist. Virgie has
moved inside her own body, into the body of woman, where the
walls she beats against will not be the enemy of the hero or of
anything external. This very real, very exciting movement will
find response, find flesh for flesh, find the excitement of knowing a body, that which is careless, without care, mindless, without mind, and calling. It is the body that has been calling Loch,
Cassie, Miss Eckhart, Nina, and Virgie. For the first time Virgie
responds.

In the middle of the night, after the funeral, an old woman
who remembers Virgie from when she played at the movie the-
ater brings her a night-blooming cereus. Because this flower
symbolizes the separation between night and day, between sun
and moon, between the old and the young—a separation that
Virgie has moved beyond—Virgie is afraid of the flower and
throws it into the woods. The choice to tend the night-blooming
cereus, to live only in the world of the mothers at Moon Lake in
the little studio, is a choice that Virgie rejects. Virgie must take
the gift of the all-woman sphere, knowing it for the power that it
has, but she knows that the flower that will fade in the morning
is not this power. She knows that "from the eyes to the moon
would be a cone, a long silent horn, of white light. It was a
connection visible as the hair is in air, between the self and the
moon, to make the self feel the child, a daughter far, far back"
(*CSEW*, 454). The cone of light from the moon to the self, this is

the connection to the feminine past that Virgie can receive. She does not have to choose the fading cereus because the feminine world encompasses a much greater sphere now. She will never have to move back to her mother's house, to Miss Eckhart's stifling studio, or even to Moon Lake. Virgie can release everything and leave. She says, "I'll sell the cows to the first man I meet in the road" (*CSEW*, 454). Virgie gives the cows to the person most unlike herself. She is willing to give up everything in order to begin a life free from the restrictions of the past. Juba keeps trying to tell Virgie about ghosts, but Virgie does not want to listen to her. "'*Now!*' Juba said, by way of affirmation. 'However, this'n, your mama, her weren't in two pieces, or floatin' upside down, or any those things yet. Her lyin' up big on a stuff davenport like a store window, three four *us* fannin' her'" (*CSEW*, 455).

Even though Virgie keeps asking Juba not to tell her about ghosts, Juba continues: "I seen that Mrs. Morrison from 'cross the road in long white nightgown, no head atall, in her driveway" (*CSEW*, 455). Juba asks Virgie, "She die in pain?" and Virgie says "Pain a plenty" (*CSEW*, 455). In some ways King MacLain did heal Katie's wounds; she is not in two pieces—mind and body. She is a queen being fanned. Mrs. Morrison's wounds are not healed. She walks around like the Medusa with no head at all. Even though Juba's words are very revealing, Virgie has a reason for not wanting to hear about ghosts. Ghosts surround the spirit with more images and narratives that Virgie will have to endeavor to release; they keep the black chip from flying in the open sky. Ghosts are an attempt to hold on to the dead by binding them with the hopes, fears, and forms of the living.

After listening to Juba's stories, Virgie gives everything to Juba and her sister Minerva. Minerva is not only the Roman goddess of wisdom, she is also the goddess of the arts (*New Larousse Encyclopedia of Mythology*, 208). As soon as Virgie gives away her material possessions to the goddess of the arts, it begins to rain and she cries. In the story "The Lucky Stone," one of the little girls says that fairies cannot survive in the rain, that nothing make-believe ever happens in the rain. Virgie has to give up everything that will protect her from reality, from the body, from her own soul, even her childlike belief in fairy tales. There can be no make-believe in the place where Virgie is going. There is only rain, growth, and tears to bring renewal. Virgie can now cry and let Juba say softly, "That's right. Cry. Cry. Cry" (*CSEW*, 456), as if she is speaking to the triple aspect within Virgie. Virgie has grown into her name. She is now the virgin rain, virgin in the sense of newness, fertility—rain that is of the self and will give birth to the self, but a self that is not autonomous or alone, a self of the whole world, a single entire human being. Now Virgie can leave Morgana, or not leave Morgana. She is free to do as she pleases.

As she departs her mother's house and drives to MacLain, she sees Cassie Morrison, who has just planted the garden full of narcissus for her mother, spelling out her mother's name. "Across the front yard stretched the violet frame in which Mama's Name was planted against the coming of spring" (*CSEW*, 457). Virgie drives past Cassie's static vision, down the road seven miles to MacLain. Finally Virgie can return to her memory of Miss Eckhart, her artistic foremother: "When Miss Eckhart died, up in Jackson, Miss Snowdie had her brought here and buried in her lot. Her grave was there near to Eugene's. There was the dark, squat stone Virgie had looked for yesterday, confusing her dead" (*CSEW*, 458–59). Virgie returns to MacLain, which is no longer a male sphere but a place where she can move freely, a place where Miss Eckhart is buried and where Snowdie lives. In MacLain, not in Morgana, she finds the woman artist. In MacLain she finds "space itself," "the uncrowded water tank" (*CSEW*, 457), but she will not stay here. This is a place to stop and think, a stop on the road from Morgana to—? Virgie sees a man hurrying through the rain and thinks he looks womanly. Virgie sits on a stile in the rain and watches the men in her life move past her, Mr. Mabry, Eugene, all of her suitors, and finally King MacLain. She has not come to MacLain for these men; she has not made this long journey to return to men. Virgie Rainey has now, like her mother, become the text itself, the movement of meaning rather than the solid form. When Mr. Mabry marches by, she "sat up tall on the stile, feeling that he would look right through her—Virgie Rainey on a stile, bereaved, hatless, unhidden now, in the rain—and he did. . . . Then she was all to herself" (*CSEW*, 459). What Virgie realizes as she sees these men, as she recognizes that she will not go back to meet them, is that she is not really by herself. What comes into Virgie's mind when she thinks about being all to herself is nothing other than the picture of Perseus and the Medusa on Miss Eckhart's wall.

Virgie does not hate Miss Eckhart. In fact she loves Miss Eckhart and the two emotions converge in this passage. Although Virgie can absorb Miss Eckhart's gift of the Beethoven, she must at the same time believe in the Medusa as much as she believes in Perseus. So the melody comes in now with the beat of time. The Medusa and Perseus are endless, but with each doubling back, Virgie sees them differently, and we as critics see her description differently. The attempt to include both the Medusa and Perseus is a constant struggle; it means accepting Beethoven—the creative artist, the lost brother/lover and the dragon's blood—the vaunting hero's attack.

After cutting off the head of the Medusa, Perseus kills the dragon so that he can save and marry Andromache. The Cellini bronze of Perseus holding the Medusa's head reminds us of the image of separation, the dismembered body. It is this separation, "the horror in life and love," that Welty seeks to heal, and to do so Virgie must remember the blood of the Medusa and the blood of the dragon, as fully as she remembers Perseus's vaunting, the myth itself, Western literary culture, and Miss Eckhart's Beethoven. In touching the Beethoven and the dragon's blood with her fingers, Virgie transforms the myth and in doing so releases herself from Morgana and into the whole world. We have entered where the blood is, for now the blood is the whole mythical landscape, not the blood of the hero's death or the

blood streaming from the Medusa's head alone, but the blood of
the dragon, of creativity and renewal. Welty embodies and thereby releases the blood of disembodiment and rape to embody
once again the fertile menstrual blood of cultural renewal.

As Welty invites into her artistic vision all that constitutes
female as body, she finds the symbols and metaphors to transform not only the female from rape victim to conscious artist—
from the decapitated Medusa of male fiction in the picture of
Perseus over Miss Eckhart's piano to Venus, who defines her own
sexuality—but the male from disembodied warrior to father,
son, brother, lover. By including and thus mediating the dominant narrative of the male hero, by allowing the written word the
fluidity to transform meaning, Eudora Welty, instead of excluding the words of the fathers in some impossible surgery, writes
the female body through all of the words that have constituted
this body. This transformation is a much more lasting and radical change because it involves direct engagement, drowning and
resurrecting herself from the waters that would otherwise have
killed her. With this vision we can, as Virgie must, "believe in
the Medusa equally with Perseus" (*CSEW*, 460). It is at this
moment, when Virgie can see Miss Eckhart and what Miss
Eckhart gave her, that the old black woman comes up to Virgie.
This is one of the few times that Welty does not use the word
"nigger," and this is the first black character who is not in a
servile position. When she lets Miss Eckhart, the crone, the
magician, the queen, the voice of the lost artist back into her life,
she can begin to see everything else that she omitted. As Virgie
lets in the gift of artistic vision that Miss Eckhart made possible,
the Mississippi rain falls on both Virgie and the black woman.
They are equals. They both see the magnitude of this possibility.

> The rain of fall, maybe on the whole South, for all she knew on
> the everywhere. She stared into its magnitude. It was not only what
> expelled some shadow of Mr. Bitts, and pressed poor Mr. Mabry to
> search the street—it was air's and the earth's fuming breath, it could

come and go. As if her own modesty could also fall upon her now, freely and coolly, outside herself and on the everywhere, she sat a little longer on the stile.

She smiled once, seeing before her, screenlike, the hideous and delectable face Mr. King MacLain had made at the funeral, and when they all knew he was next—even he. Then she and the old beggar woman, the old black thief, were there alone and together in the shelter of the big public tree, listening to the magical percussion, the world beating in their ears. They heard through falling rain the running of the horse and bear, the stroke of the leopard, the dragon's crusty slither, and the glimmer and the trumpet of the swan. (*CSEW*, 460–61)

Virgie and the black woman have entered the mythological world of dragons and the natural world, the rainy world of all Mississippi, of everywhere. Virgie is now able to sit with the old black woman and hear the percussion. Welty brings the dragon to life. The collection ends with the trumpeting of the swan; swans trumpet only when they are about to die. The artist sings her own mortality, dying to live. It is only in this place without restriction, without separation, that creation can occur, that an old black woman can say to a middle-aged white woman, "Mornin."

8

Conclusion

By revealing the expansive intertextuality in *The Golden Apples*, the remarkable fluidity and inclusivity of Welty's imagination, we can begin to revise the traditional notions of Eudora Welty's place in the Western literary canon. Rather than being stereotyped and pigeonholed as a marginal or regional writer, she deserves to be recognized as a contributor to the most innovative literary movements of the twentieth century: she is a postmodern, feminist, experimental writer. At the same time, only by becoming aware of both the broad and the subtle distinctions between her voice and the voice of many of her contemporaries can we even begin to understand the magnitude of her accomplishment. As we read the intertextuality, the metaphoric allusions, the symbolic associations that resonate throughout this text, we are not simply watching the manueverings of a remarkably playful mind; we are instead participating in the emergence of a kind of literature that opposes the nihilistic, individualistic stance of early modernism and expresses value for the constantly evolving and fertile dynamic between individual and community, tradition and innovation, tragedy and comedy, written and oral cultures, and the technological and natural worlds.

One of the questions that critics often asked during the early stages of feminist literary theory was whether women wrote differently from men. While we can never answer that question without sinking into essentialist and reductionist definitions of women and writing, we can propose that those authors who weave the narrative threads of many different voices into the fabric of their texts, who choose the complexity of life over the simplicity of power, will often write differently, that is, from a position of difference. This participation in and commitment to difference will create the most passionate, multi-layered, and metaphorically resonate literature of any given time. Although Eudora Welty's expression of feminist difference is exceptionally daring and radically transformative, it is not the only such expression. Welty is following the work of many women writers including Gertrude Stein, Willa Cather, Virginia Woolf, and Zora Neale Hurston, and creating a tapestry that will eventually be extended and rewoven in the texts of Toni Morrison, Maxine Hong Kingston and hundreds of other women, whose voices are at once allusive and unique.

One need only look at the exceptional rennaissance of African American women writers in the past two decades to realize that occupying a position of difference, a position which is constantly in flux and subject to change at any moment, does indeed invite a much greater intertextual participation. Those who have lived with silence and hopelessness, who have heard the voices occupying both the margins and the centers, whose own voices have often been banned entirely, will have less to lose and more to gain by exposing themselves to all the possible varieties of human experience. This is the realm of the unfettered imagination, and few writers have dwelled in this textual space as fearlessly or as long as Eudora Welty has.

Those cultural dictators who wish to maintain hierarchy divert our focus back and forth between freeze frames of the abstract and the particular. They either allow us to see the com-

bination or the scattering but never the dynamic creative movement from one to the other. As the imagination begins to undo,
revise, and transform the dead into the living, the resulting text
is a complex and fascinating palimpsest, which requires attention
to detail and willingness to accept multiple interpretations. This
type of textual engagement is the most important contribution
that scholars can make to the creative artists who have brought
these texts to life. Many women writers works have gone unexplored, misunderstood, and misread because we have been looking only at the obvious, established narrative structures of their
texts; we have ignored or belittled as insignificant those subtleties
which we have not yet developed a language to describe. Once
we begin to recognize different narratives, different symbolic
transformations, we will find that texts carry meanings and sig-
nificances that we never before recognized. The detailed explication of difference, of the subtle emerging forms of discourse that
exist in the cross-pollination of masculinist and feminist texts,
has only just begun.

Finally, a recognition of the extent to which a text like *The
Golden Apples* can create such a dynamic transformation of exist-
ing stereotypes and conventional narratives forces us to revise
our fixed notions of canonicity, authorship, and convention. The
impulse of postmodernism has opened up previously closed discussions, texts, and discourses, exploring an exciting plurality,
but these discussions have not embraced fully enough a coherent
regeneration—a regeneration that will result in, not only the
deconstruction of old models or the establishment of new models, but also in the attention to the movement of structures, the
pulse of human e/motion—a regeneration that values both continuity and change, but not stagnation. The edifice of escape from
the mother on which the myth of heroic immortality was built is
unregenerative; it has been and will continue to be challenged
and transformed. Eudora Welty should be recognized as one
writer who is brave enough and brilliant enough, to follow the

minute shiftings, additions, subtractions, negotiations, translations, and associations of diverse elements required to challenge this myth, and to weave and become the text of *The Golden Apples*—a mystery of creation, which we will read over many a night.

— Notes —

CHAPTER 1

1. Critical works on mythology in *The Golden Apples*: Harry C. Morris, "Zeus and the Golden Apples: Eudora Welty"; Harry C. Morris, "Eudora Welty's Use of Mythology"; Louis D. Rubin, Jr., "The Golden Apples of the Sun"; Thomas L. McHaney, "Eudora Welty and the Multitudinous Golden Apples"; F. D. Carson, "The Song of Wandering Aengus: Allusion in *TGA*."

In Peggy Whitman Prenshaw, ed., *Eudora Welty: Critical Essays*: Robert L. Phillips, Jr. "A Structural Approach to Myth in the Fiction of Eudora Welty"; Merrill Maguire Skaggs, "Morgana's Apples and Pears"; Julia L. Demmin and Daniel Curley, "Golden Apples and Silver Apples"; Daniele Pitavy-Sougues, "Techniques as Myth: The Structure of *The Golden Apples*."

Other important essays: Elaine Upton Pugh, "The Duality of Morgana: The Making of Virgie's Vision; The Vision of *The Golden Apples*"; Naoka Fuwa Thornton, "Medusa-Perseus Symbolism in Eudora Welty's *The Optimist's Daughter*"; Joan Coldwell, "The Beauty of the Medusa: Twentieth Century."

2. See Peter Schmidt, *The Heart of the Story: Eudora Welty's Short Fiction* (Jackson: University Press of Mississippi, 1991).

3. T. S. Eliot discusses origins in terms of tradition, Harold Bloom as the anxiety of influence, Mikhail Bakhtin as heteroglossia, Michel Foucault as the culturally constructed product of discourse, Adrienne Rich in terms of re-vision, Sandra Gilbert and Susan Gubar as the anxiety of authorship, Edward Said as questions of beginnings, and Roland Barthes, Julia Kristeva, Johnathan Culler, and Michael Riffaterre in the language of intertextuality.

4. Adrienne Rich, in "When We Dead Awaken: Writing As Revision," writes that "entering an old text from a new critical direction—is . . . an act of survival. . . . We need to know the writing of the past, and know it differently than we have ever known it; not to pass on a tradition but to break its hold over us" (35). Rich recognizes the necessity of returning to old texts and looking again, but by assuming that one can consciously choose to break the hold of the past, Rich inescapably succumbs to the language, the structure she wishes to know differently. By thinking in terms of an identity called woman or female, she does very little to change the terms of the discourse of autonomy. The discourse is based on authority, on the power to refuse, to see, to know, and to

name—to create an identity that is autonomous, distinguished, and distinguishable from the inherited identity.

5. Barthes does not let the text have an integrity of its own but insists on grasping authorial control like a conquering warrior, claiming that "the work of commentary, once it is separated from any ideology of totality consists precisely in manhandling the text, interrupting it" (*S/Z*, 15).

6. Articles and books on Eudora Welty and feminism: Peggy Whitman Prenshaw, "Woman's World, Man's Place: The Fiction of Eudora Welty"; Elizabeth M. Kerr, "The World of Eudora Welty's Women"; Margaret Jones Bolsterli, "Woman's Vision: The Worlds of Women in *Delta Wedding, Losing Battles,* and *The Optimist's Daughter*; Merrill Maguire Skaggs, "Morgana's Apples and Pears"; Julia L. Demmin and Daniel Curley, "Golden Apples and Silver Apples"; Patricia Yeager, "The Case of the Dangling Signifier: Phallic Imagery in Eudora Welty's "Moon Lake" and "Because a Fire Was in My Head": Eudora Welty and the Dialogic Imagination"; Mary Anne Ferguson, "The Female Novel of Development and the Myth of Psyche"; Carol S. Manning, *With Ears Opening Like Morning Glories: Eudora Welty and the Love of Storytelling*; Louise Hutchings Westling, *Sacred Groves and Ravaged Gardens: The Fiction of Eudora Welty, Carson McCullers, and Flannery O'Connor*; Joan Coldwell, "The Beauty of the Medusa: Twentieth Century"; Ruth D. Weston, "The Feminine and Feminist Texts of Eudora Welty's *The Optimist's Daughter*"; Louise Hutchings Westling, *Eudora Welty*; Franziska Gygax, *Serious Daring from Within: Female Narrative Strategies in Eudora Welty's Novels*; Lucinda H. MacKethen, *Daughters of Time: Creating Woman's Voice in Southern Story*.

7. In Jocelyn Harris's introduction to *Jane Austen's Art of Memory*, she echoes Yeager's thesis: "I myself believe that Jane Austen took what she wanted from anywhere, not just from women, and not just from fiction either, and that her memory energized her art in a manner far more coherent than intertextuality. In spite of Freud and his followers, I detect no trace of anxiety in her, for to paraphrase Dryden on Johnson, she 'invades Authors like a monarch, and what would be theft in other poets, is only victory in her'" (90).

8. Barthes defines this distinction in his early work as the difference between a "readerly" (stagnant) text and a "writerly" (organic or fluid) text and in his later work as the difference between "work" and "text." The writerly text is what must be written. The readerly text is what can be read but not written: "The writerly text is perpetual present, upon which no consequent language (which would inevitably make it past) can be superimposed: the writerly text is ourselves writing, before the infinite play . . . is plasticized, by some singular system" (*S/Z*, 5). Accepting Barthes's premise here requires recognizing that one cannot read without writing, that the writerly text reconstitutes the reader as writer.

9. Welty recognizes the inseparability of the act of writing and the act of reading when she writes, "Only the writing of fiction keeps fiction alive . . . a society that no longer writes novels is not very likely to read any novels at all" (*The Eye of the Story*, 137).

10. The most creative and thorough exploration of the metaphoric and interpretive potentials of these allusions can be found in Vicki Mahaffey's "Part III. Multiple Authorities, Chapter 4. Text Styles, Textile, and the Textures of *Ulysses*." Mahaffey connects Penelope's and Molly's text with the materiality of cloth.

11. There are libraries throughout Virginia Woolf's *A Room of One's Own*. In fact, not being able to enter the library, which should be seen as a terrible discouragement becomes a moment of revelation and inspiration for the narrator of *A Room of One's Own*. She realizes that, because she is not allowed in the library, she is able to sit outdoors and learn from the natural world. In this position, she finds the spark that allows her to continue writing. In her trip to the British Museum, she finds herself amazed at the quantity of books men have written about women. Only by turning these works into text through writing does Woolf keep them from being a destructive and silencing force.

12. Throughout the text *CSEW* is used to indicate *The Collected Stories of Eudora Welty*.

CHAPTER 2

1. Barbara G. Walker, "Hecate," and "Crossroads," in *The Woman's Encyclopedia of Myths and Secrets*, 378–79 and 190–91; Sir James Frazer, *The Golden Bough*, 724.

2. This vision of woman as a blank page is very different from the one in the tradition that Susan Gubar describes, whereby men see the female as a receptive body that can be inscribed by male insemination or, in this case, by the masculine literary tradition (Susan Gubar, "'The Blank Page' and Issues of Female Creativity," 247).

3. Robert Graves, *The Greek Myths I*, 27, 28, 30, 53, 54, 55, 87, 127, 146.

4. Anne Ross, *Pagan Celtic Britain: Studies in Iconography and Tradition*, 204–34; Robert Graves, *The White Goddess: A Historical Grammar of Poetic Myth*, 384.

5. Jane Ellen Harrison, *Themis: A Study of the Social Origins of Greek Religion*; Graves, *The Greek Myths I and II*; Merlin Stone, *When God Was A Woman*; Marija Gimbutas, *The Gods and Goddesses of Old Europe: 6500–3500 B.C.*

6. In addition to the swan, Welty includes references to cats and cows, both symbolically connected to female power. "She went on keeping house, and gettin fairly big with what I told you was twins and she seemed to settle into her content. Like a little white Kitty in a basket, making you wonder if she

mightn't put up her paw and scratch, if anything was, after all, to come near" (*CSEW*, 8). In the image of the kitten, Welty includes both the settled, domestic picture of the expectant mother and the unsettling picture of a paw about to scratch. During the course of the story, the kitten develops into a full grown cat, and even a lion. Cats are traditionally female and sacred to the triple goddess; this is how they came to be thought of as mediums for witches. When Katie sees Snowdie next to the "little Jersey cow," she invokes the fertility spirits of the cow, which is also an ancient symbol of women's power, more powerful even than the cat.

7. Walker, "Eye" in *The Woman's Encyclopedia of Myths and Secrets*: "The idea of the 'evil eye' of the witches so terrified men during the Inquisition that they forced accused witches to enter the courtroom backwards" (294–95).

8. Harrisson, *Themis*; Graves, *The Greek Myths I and II*; Stone, *When God Was A Woman*; Marija Gimbutas, *The Gods and Goddesses of Old Europe: 6500–3500 B.C.*

9. Frazer, *The Golden Bough*: 341–76; Graves, *The Greek Myths I and II*, 118–48 passim, 84–226.

CHAPTER 3

1. Mrs. Morrison does not kiss Loch; instead she reminds him of his own human vulnerability by putting her hand on his pompadour cap and wobbling his scalp. The pompadour cap, a hairstyle named after the Marquise de Pompadour—the mistress of Louis XV—is "an arrangement of a woman's hair in which it is raised above the forehead" (*American College Dictionary*). Thus not only does Mrs. Morrison put her hand on the hero's sacred head, but he wears a hairstyle that puts his masculinity in question.

2. For works that discuss the tears of the earth mother see: Sir James Frazer, *The Golden Bough*. Jane Ellen Harrison, *Themis: A Study of the Social Origins of Greek Religion*; Robert Graves, *The Green Myths I and II*; see also Merlin Stone, *When God Was a Woman*; Marija Gimbutas, *The Gods and Goddesses of Old Europe: 6500–3500 B.C.*

3. *New Larrousse Encyclopedia Of Mythology*, p. 241. The horse-goddess emerges as another manifestation of the mother-goddess, a protectress of both the dead and the living.

4. Frazer, *The Golden Bough*: "Now an octennial cycle is the shortest period at the end of which sun and moon really mark time together after overlapping so to say, throughout the whole of the interval . . . every eight years the king's sacred powers needed to be renewed by intercourse with the god head, and that without such a renewal he would have forfeited his right to the throne" (326).

5. Harrison, *Themis*: "The marriage of the sun and the moon must clearly be

coeval with the reconstitution of the cosmos 'on a grander scale' associated with 'Pelops' and presumably this reconstitution meant the reform of the calendar by the introduction of the octennial period which is symbolized by this particular form of the sacred marriage" (229).

6. The word "lackadaisical" has special significance here. Not only does the word itself mean "sentimentally or affectionally languishing or listless," but it comes from the root "lack-aday," which means "a-lack," an exclamation of regret or dismay. If we go even further back, we come to "lack," which is a deficiency or absence of something. ("Lack" in the *American College Diction-ary*.)

7. Loch's observation evokes the words of Mrs. Ramsey in Virginia Woolf's *To the Lighthouse*: "Every door was left open. She listened. The drawing-room door was open; the hall door was open; it sounded as if the bedroom doors were open; and certainly the window on the landing was open, for that she has opened herself. That windows should be open, and doors shut—simple as it was, could none of them remember it?" (44). Every door in the MacLain house is open and every window tightly shut.

8. Frazer, in *The Golden Bough*, connects grasshoppers with fertility: "The Bataks of Sumatra have a ceremony which they call 'making the curse to fly away.' When a woman is childless, a sacrifice is offered to the gods of three grasshoppers, representing a head of cattle, a buffalo, and a horse. Then a swallow is set free, with a prayer that the curse may fall upon the bird and fly away with it" (627).

9. Sarah Orne Jewett, *The Country of the Pointed Firs and other Stories*. These two passages are descriptions of the woman writer entering the house of cult-ural transmission. The "tide is turning." This is "old life" stirring. "I spent many days there quite undisturbed, with the sea-breeze blowing through the small high windows and saying the heavy outside shutters to and fro. I hung my hat and luncheon basket on an entry nail as if I were a small scholar, but sat at the teacher's desk, as if I were a great authority" (18); "There was a silence in the schoolhouse but we could hear the noise of water on a beach below. It sounded like a strange warning wave that gives notice, of the turn of the tide" (26).

10. George Eliot, *Middlemarch*: "Your pierglass or extensive surface of pol-ished steel made to be rubbed by a housemaid will be minutely and multi-tudinously scratched in all directions; but place now against it a lighted candle as a center of illumination, and lo, the scratches will seem to arrange themselves in a fine series of concentric circles round that little sun" (258).

11. Virginia Woolf, *The Years*: " . . . She drew on her blotting paper; a dot with strokes raying out round it. Then she looked up. They were burning

weeds in the back garden; there was a drift of smoke; a sharp acrid smell; and leaves falling" (91).

12. Eudora Welty, *Losing Battles*: 'And then this morning' said Judge Moody, reaching again inside his coat and bringing out another crumpled envelope, 'in my box I found this. The envelope is one of my own, used over again. No letter inside, only a map she'd drawn me, showing how to get from Ludlow to Alliance and where she lived. That's when I gave up and started.'

"'I mailed it when I could and not before!' cried Miss Lexie.

"'And it's a maze,' he said, squinting down at the old bill on which a web of lines radiated from some cross-mark ploughed into center. 'Just a maze. There wasn't much right about her thinking any longer. I didn't try and go by it but I lost my own way on Boone County roads for the first time I can remember'" (303).

13. The rainbow, in matriarchal, classical, and Christian religions, is the bridge from the earth to the heavens, symbolized in the many colored necklace of the pagan goddess (Barbara G. Walker, "Rainbow," in *The Woman's Encyclopedia of Myths and Secrets*, 840). The rainbow, as bridge, is a perfect symbol of the woman artist's journey because it connects the earth to the heavens or, in Cassie's case, the past to the present.

14. Miss Eckhart is the witch, "crone, hag, the queen of the underworld, death, winter, the waning of the moon . . . Morgan, Persephone . . . the inevitable destruction or dissolution that must precede regeneration" (Walker, *The Woman's Encyclopedia of Myths and Secrets*, 187).

15. Walker, "Apple" in *The Woman's Encyclopedia of Myths and Secrets*: "Eve's fruit of knowledge used to be the goddess's sacred heart of immortality, all over the Indo-European culture complex. The goddess's many western paradises grew the apples of eternal life. The Celts call the western paradise Avalon, 'Apple land,' a country ruled by Morgan, the queen of the dead. Irish kings received the Goddess's magic apples of immortality and went to live with her under the sunset. King Aurthur was taken to Avalon by the Triple Goddess in person as three fairy queens. . . . Greeks said Mother Hera kept the magic apple garden in the west, where the Tree of Life was guarded by her sacred serpent. Graves points out that the whole story of Eve, Adam, and the serpent in the tree was deliberately misinterpreted from icons showing the Great Goddess offering life to her worshipper, in the form of an apple, with the tree and its serpent in the background. Similarly, Hellenes misinterpreted icons of the hero-victim receiving an apple from the Triple Goddess" (49–50).

16. *The Golden Apples* unveils itself as a whole and can be understood only by "making moments double upon themselves" (*CSEW*, 453). As the collection progresses Welty moves deep into the collective memory or mythology of the culture and thus further away from patriarchal attitudes and closer to what

many have called a matriarchal or matrilineal past. If we double forward or back to the story "Music from Spain," we find another clue to the riddle of the golden apples: "Was it so strange, the way things are flung out at us, like the apples of Atalanta perhaps, once we have begun a certain onrush?" (*CSEW*, 403). In this myth Atalanta, the young princess of a rich king, decides that she will not get married. When her father tells her she must marry, she replies that she will only marry if she can define the terms to pick the bridegroom. Her father agrees, and Atalanta announces that she will marry the man who can beat her at a foot race. Since Atalanta can run faster than anyone in the kingdom, she defeats all prospective candidates until the young suitor Melanion asks Aphrodite directly for her help. The goddess gives him three golden apples and tells him that, if he lets these apples drop during the race, Atalanta will not be able to resist stopping to pick them up. During the race each time Atalanta pulls out ahead of him, Melanion throws one of the apples and Atalanta cannot resist picking it up. She loses the race and has to marry the young prince.

What is peculiar about this myth is the fact that apples are a symbol of feminine not masculine sexuality. Melanion catches Atalanta not because she succumbs to him but because she cannot resist the temptation to repossess her sexuality: this is the secret—a woman's secret—that Aphrodite, the goddess of love, tells Melanion. Atalanta will lose to Melanion when she tries to retrieve the golden apples. Miss Eckhart fears Mr. Voight and Mr. Sissum because they overpower her; Virgie fears no man but tries to control them. True fertility occurs when there is no need for control, dominance, or power, but the first step is to move from fear to dominance as Virgie does. In "The Whole World Knows," Jinny Love does not play croquet with the men—or we might say that, unlike Atalanta, she does not run after the golden apples.

Describing Miss Eckhart after she has stopped teaching, Cassie says, "Yet she still had authority. She could still stop young, unknowing children like Loch on the street and ask them imperative questions, 'Where were you throwing that ball?' 'Are you trying to break that tree?'" (*CSEW*, 307). Not only does the first question refer to the Atalanta myth, but in *The Golden Bough*, Frazer writes that a hero's death takes place when a tree is broken because the hero's spirit is in the tree (126–56). According to the structure of this myth, Miss Eckhart would be the voice of the old goddess telling him with authority not to break the tree of his life. For the hero, Loch, would be bringing about his own death, as Narcissus does, by breaking the tree, the symbol of fertility.

CHAPTER 4

1. Carol S. Vance, "Pleasure and Danger: Toward a Politics of Sexuality:" "For some, the dangers of sexuality—violence, brutality, and coercion, in the

form of rape, forcible incest, and exploitation, as well as everyday cruelty and humiliation—make the pleasures pale by comparison. For others, the positive possibilities of sexuality—exploration of the body, curiosity, intimacy, sensuality, adventure, excitement, human connection, basking in the infantile and nonrational—are not only worthwhile but provide sustaining energy" (1).

2. It is important to reiterate that Eudora Welty had read *The Golden Bough* before she wrote *The Golden Apples*. In Prenshaw's *Conversations with Eudora Welty*, Welty tells interviewer Jan Nordby Gretlund that she read the one volume edition of *The Golden Bough* after college (224).

3. Sir James Frazer, *The Golden Bough*: "Amongst the Zulus and kindred tribes of South Africa, when the first signs of puberty show themselves while a girl is walking, gathering wood, or working in the field, she runs to the river and hides herself among the reeds for the day so as not to be seen by men. She covers her head carefully with her blanket that the sun may not shine on it and shrivel her up into a withered skeleton, as would result from exposure to the sun's beams. After dark, she returns to her home and is secluded in a hut for some time. In New Ireland girls are confined for four or five years in small cages being kept in the dark and not allowed to set foot on the ground" (690).

4. Robert Graves, *The Greek Myths I*: "The Cretan goddess had close associations with the sea. Shells carpeted the floor of her palace sanctuary at Cnossus. A triton-shell was found in her early sanctuary at Phaetus, and many more in late Minoan tombs, some of these being terracotta replicas" (50).

5. Robert Graves, *The White Goddess*: "The orgiastic oak-cult with which the dove goddess was concerned came at the summer solstice" (337); Frazer, *The Golden Bough*; "In another modern Greek story the life of an enchanter is bound up with three doves, which are in the belly of a wild boar. When the first dove is killed, the magician grows; when the second is killed, he grows very sick; and when the third is killed, he dies" (777).

6. Frazer, *The Golden Bough*; "In Moluccas, when the clove trees are in blossom, they are treated like pregnant women. No noise may be made near them; no light or fire may be carried past them late at night; no one may approach them with his hat on, all must uncover in their presence. These precautions are observed lest the tree should be alarmed and bear no fruit, or should drop its first fruit too soon" (132); "It is said that there are still families in Russia, Germany, England, France and Italy who are accustomed to plant a tree at the birth of a child. The tree, it is hoped, will grow with the child and it is tended with special care. The custom is still pretty general in the canton of Aargua in Switzerland; an apple tree is planted for a boy and a pear tree for a girl" (791).

7. "Now in the morning, as he returned to the city, he hungered. And when he saw a fig tree in the way he came to it and found nothing thereon, but leaves

only, and said unto it, Let no fruit grow on thee henceforward for ever. And presently the fig tree withered away. And when the disciples saw it, they marvelled, saying, How soon is the fig tree withered away! Jesus answered and said unto them, Verily I say unto you, if ye have faith, and doubt not, ye shall not only do this which is done to the fig tree, but also if ye shall say unto this mountain, Be thou removed, and be thou cast into the sea; it shall be done. And all things, whatsoever ye shall ask in prayer, believing, ye shall receive" (Matt. 21:18–22).

8. The biblical Esther had no father or mother: "And he brought up Hadassah, that is, Esther, his uncle's daughter: for she had neither father nor mother and the maid was fair and beautiful" (Esther 2:7).

9. Sir James Frazer, *The Golden Bough*: "Finally, a pretence is made of throwing Green George into the water, but in fact it is only a puppet made of branches and leaves which is ducked in the stream. In this version of the custom the powers of granting an easy delivery to women and of communicating vital energy to the sick and old are clearly ascribed to the willow" (147).

10. Robert Graves, *The White Goddess*: "The holding of the foot was doubtless protective, the heel being the one vulnerable point of sacred kings, witness the heel of Achilles pierced by Paris's arrow; the heel of Talus pierced by Medea's pin; the heel of Diarmaid pierced by the bristle of Behn Gulban Boar; the heel of Harpocrates stung by the Scorpion; the heel of Balder (in the Danish version of the myth) pierced by the mistletoe flung by the god Holder at the instigation of the king" (303).

11. "And he took his staff in his hand, and chose him five smooth stones out of the brook, and put them in a shepherd's bag which he had . . . . and his sling was in his hand: and he drew near to the Philistine" (1 Sam. 17:40).

"And David put his hand in his bag, and took thence a stone, and slang it, and smote the Philistine in his forehead, that the stone sunk into his forehead; and he fell upon his face to the earth." (1 Sam. 17:49.)

12. Barbara Walker. *The Woman's Encyclopedia of Myths and Secrets*: "The dead king's subjects were assured that 'the gods made a ladder for (him) that he might ascend to heaven on it.' The king's funerary inscription said, 'I set up a ladder to heaven among the gods'. . . . Priest kings in antiquity climbed soul ladders to meet the goddess on the occasion of their hieros gamos and also after death, when their souls returned to the Mother who bore them. Sometimes the ladder was perceived as a familiar passageway between the goddess in heaven and her consort the king on earth. Kosingas of Thrace controlled his subjects by threatening to ascend his special wooden ladder to the Great Goddess Hera, to complain to her of their conduct and invoke her wrath on them," (525).

13. Frazer, *The Golden Bough*; "Often the soul is conceived as a bird ready to

take flight. This conception has probably left traces in most languages and it lingers as a metaphor in poetry" (210).

CHAPTER 5

1. From Prenshaw's *Conversations with Eudora Welty*:
"Kuehl: Did you feel at all influenced by his [Faulkner's] presence?
Welty: I don't honestly think so. It is hard to be sure about such things. I was naturally in the deepest awe and reverence of him. But that's no help in your own writing. Nobody can help you but yourself. So often I'm asked how I could have written a word with William Faulkner living in Mississippi, and this question amazes me. It was like living near a big mountain, something majestic—it made me happy to know it was there, all that work of his life. But it wasn't a helping or hindering presence. Its magnitude, all by itself, made it something remote in my own working life" (79–80).
"Gretlund: During a press conference at Oxford, Mississippi, in l977, you were asked if you had been influenced by William Faulkner. You answered briefly, "Not any!" It is as simple as that?
Welty: Of course not! Gretlund: Are you simply fed up with the question?
Welty: I was sort of fed up with the question, and at a press conference how could I go into that? I think the answer is no. The answer is no because I think what was meant by the question is whether or not he had helped me in specific and personal ways. . . .
Gretlund: Have you consciously tried to avoid rewriting Faulkner?
Welty: No. I think that was what I was answering, too, when I said, "Not any!" It is not so self-conscious a process as that when you write. I think in the act of writing, "how I am going to handle something," and not "how would so-and-so have done it," or "I mustn't fall into this pitfall here." It is just trial and error on my own" (220).
2. See Peter Schmidt's discussion of "Asphodel" and *Absalom Absalom!* in *The Heart of the Story* (132–34).
3. "Like Father said down the long and lonely light-rays you might see Jesus walking, like" (*SF*, 47).
"It's always the idle habits you acquire which you will regret. Father said that" (*SF*, 47).
"Father said that constant speculation regarding the position of mechanical hands on an arbitrary dial which is a symptom of mind function. Excrement Father said like sweating" (*SF*, 47).
"In the South you are ashamed of being a virgin. Boys. Men. They lie about it. Because it means less to women, Father said. He said it was men who invented virginity not women. Father said it's like death: only a state in which

the others are left and I said, But to believe it doesn't matter and he said, That's what's so sad about anything: not only virginity and I said, Why wouldn't it have been me and not her who is unvirgin and he said, That's why that's sad too; nothing is even worth the changing of it and Shreve said if he's got better sense than to chase after the little sluts and I said Did you ever have a sister? Did you? Did you?" (*SF*, 48).

4. In *Sound and the Fury* Faulkner describes the little girl whom Quentin finds on his walk as "a little dirty child with eyes like a toy bear's and two patent leather pigtails" (76). In *The Sound and the Fury* the little girl is symbolic of all of Quentin's sexual fantasies and obsessions. In "The Whole World Knows," the men who are playing croquet in Jinny Love's backyard are playing with a little girl. "It was just a little Williams girl in pigtails" (*CSEW*, 382). Could this line be read: "It was just William's (William Faulkner's) little girl with pigtails"? Whether this is an accurate allusion or not, the "just" might still signify that this little girl is reclaiming her right to be just a little girl, not a projected male fantasy.

5. The reference to croquet, which is played with wooden balls, being Jinny's game, reminds us of the myth of the golden balls of Atalanta. In this myth Atalanta did not want to get married. She said she would marry only if her father let her set the terms of the engagement. Her compromise was that she would marry whoever could beat her in a foot race. She was in no great danger of having to get married because no one could run as fast as she could. Every suitor failed until one young man named Hippomenes threw golden balls onto the path in front of her. She could not keep her eyes off the golden balls and stooped to pick them up. At this point Hippomenes ran out in front of her, won the race, and married Atalanta. By continually returning the men to the croquet game it is as if Jinny is trying to remind them of their role in this myth.

CHAPTER 6

1. Albert J. Devlin, *Eudora Welty's Chronicle: A Story of Mississippi Life*: "A Joycean presence can be felt in 'Music from Spain' and 'The Wanderers.' The structure of Eugene MacLain's personal dilemma closely parallels that of Leopold Bloom. Each is a middle aged exile emotionally separated from his wife who mourns a dead child during a day of urban wandering" (204).

2. Louise Hutchings Westling, *Eudora Welty*: "Eugene wanders all day through San Francisco in 'Music from Spain' after a quarrel with his wife Emma, seeking adventure with a Spanish guitarist he and Emma had recently seen in concert and whom he has chanced to meet on the street and decided to show the town. Like Leopold Bloom in Joyce's *Ulysses*, Eugene grieves for a dead child and spends his time away from his wife in rather desultory activities

in his large city. By the end of the day he has spent his last penny and trudges home somewhat sheepishly. When he arrives, his wife is cheerfully engaged in conversation with a woman friend in the warm apartment full of the smell of hot chowder. He feels defeated by the women's self sufficiency and knows that they will not be impressed by his having spent the day with the famous guitarist. Since his little daughter's death, he and Emma have drifted farther and farther apart, so that he is clearly not essential to her anymore. By the end of the cycle, Eugene is dead of tuberculosis having returned alone to Morgana. There his 'light, tubercular body seemed to hesitate on the streets of Morgana, hold averted, anticipating questions' (CS, p. 458) His wife only sent a telegram when he died" (148–49).

3. However, Welty's own opposition to intertextual criticism is a daunting deterrent: "Well, you know, now I think I'd think twice before I threw around myths and everything so freely. I'm glad I did then because I used them as freely as I would the salt and pepper. They were part of my life, like poetry, and I would take something from Yeats here and something from a myth there. I had no system about it. But people write papers on these things and they just make things up." John Griffin Jones, 13 May l981, Prenshaw's *Conversations with Eudora Welty*, 331.

4. [12._____.1948] EW,[Jackson], to J[John Robinson], [Berkeley, California] at the Mississippi Historical Society.

5. Manuscript

6. When Eugene leaves the house, "he pulled the apartment door locked behind him" (*CSEW*, 393). In the final manuscript Welty changes the word from "shut" to "locked." We know that in "June Recital," Loch thinks about how uninteresting the world would be if people always locked doors. In Welty's creative universe, the locked door is symbolic of a lack of connection. In *Ulysses*, "Stephen, taking his ashplant from its leaningplace, followed them out and, as they went down the ladder, pulled to the slow iron door and locked it" (*Ulysses*, 15; hereafter cited as *UL*). Buck Mulligan sighs repeatedly. Eugene sighs. It is a grey foggy day in both stories. Stephen is at the sea. Eugene eventually walks to the sea.

7. Allusions to catechism and questions in "Music from Spain": "Why, in the name of all reason, had he struck Emma? His act—with that, proving it had been a part of him—slipped loose from him, turned around and looked at him in the form of a question" (*CSEW*, 394); "A quarrel couldn't even grow between him and Emma. And she would be unfair, beg the question, if a quarrel did spring up; she would cry" (*CSEW*, 395); "Why strike her even softly?" (*CSEW*, 395); "*Why not strike her?*" (*CSEW*, 395); "Why slap her today?" (*CSEW*, 395); "But couldn't it be his reason for hitting her, and not hers?" (*CSEW*, 395);

"Should he suspect? She had died, was that the story?" (*CSEW*, 396); "It was out of the question—that was all of a sudden beautifully clear—that he should go to work that day" (*CSEW*, 396); "*She could still bite his finger, couldn't she?*" (*CSEW*, 396); "What would Mr. Bertsinger Senior, down at the shop, have to say about this, Eugene wondered, what lengthy thing?" (*CSEW*, 396).

8. References to school in "Music from Spain": "She was stronger than he was, 150 pounds to 139, he could inform old Mr. Bertsinger Senior, who liked to press for figures" (*CSEW*, 394); "Eugene was walking down the habitual hills to Bertsingers', Jewelers, and with sharp sniffs that as always rather pained him after breakfast he was taking note of the day, its temperature, fog condition, and prospects of clearing and warming up, all of which would be asked him by Mr. Bertsinger Senior who would then tell him if he was right" (*CSEW*, 394); "The world was the old man's subject, but he knew yours" (*CSEW*, 396).

9. Leopold thinks, in Chapter 4 of *Ulysses*, that he "might manage a sketch. By Mr. and Mrs. L.M. Bloom" (*UL*, 56). In addition to these references there are at least seven others allusions to *Ulysses* in this section of "Music from Spain." Eugene remembers that Bertsinger likes a humorous remark. Stephen tells a joke that his students do not understand and then thinks: "A jester at the court of his master, indulged and disesteemed, winning a clement master's praise" (*UL*, 21). Eugene talks about Mr. Bertsinger's pressing for figures. One of Stephen's students is practicing figures (*UL*, 23). Emma takes things in slowly, and one of Stephen's students learns slowly. Eugene has the paper "pinned there by his right arm," (*CSEW*, 396). Deasy "pins" the sheets of his essay for the paper: "He came to the table, pinning together his sheets" (*UL*, 27). But one of the strongest pieces of evidence comes from the manuscript. In editing her manuscript Welty cut a section that read: "He met the postman at the usual corner and the postman said the usual—'Letter for Mrs. Dowdie only'—from her fat sister'" (Manuscript, 2–3). In Chapter 4 of *Ulysses* when Leopold leaves the house, he finds the mail on the floor: "Two letters and a card lay on the hallfloor. He stooped and gathered them. Mrs. Marion Bloom. His quickened heart slowed at once. Bold hand. Mrs. Marion" (*UL*, 50). Leopold is troubled by the exclusion of his name. He immediately thinks that Molly is having an affair. Although Emma's letter includes Eugene's original name, Dowdie, in the manuscript, it is from Emma's sister and "for Mrs. Dowdie only." Leopold and Eugene would have found the letter at the same moment in the two stories if Welty had left this sentence in.

10. Reference to eating in *Ulysses*: "I could quite easily get him to make it up any time I know how Id even supposing he got in with her again and was going out to see her somewhere Id know if he refused to eat the onions" (*UL*, 612).

11. Horse references in "Music from Spain": "It accommodated itself like the

bang of a small bell to the stiff pull of his shanks" (*CSEW*, 395); "*She could still bite his finger, couldn't she?*" (*CSEW*, 396).

12. In both *Ulysses* and "Music" there are references to butchers in this Nestor section. In *Ulysses*, Stephen, imagining the horse races in the pictures above Mr. Deasy's desk thinks: "Dicers and thimbleriggers we hurried by after the hoofs . . . past the meatfaced woman, a butcher's dame" (*UL*, 27). In the *Odyssey*, Nestor sacrifices a cow to the gods for Telemachus's safe journey. In Chapter 4 Leopold makes repeated references to butchers, knives, and animal organs.

13. An odd shape-shifting connection between the two texts is that the Proteus chapter of *Ulysses* is full of references to teeth (Chapter 3: ll. 186, 232, 493, 494–98) including "Toothless Cinch the Superman." The third subsection of "Music" has several references to teeth, including the mention of false—teeth the "No Toothless Days" sign on page 397. Interestingly enough the toothless character in Welty's story is a woman, not a superman.

14. References to the sea in "Music from Spain": "He passed the health food store where the shark liver oil pellets were displayed" (*CSEW*, 397); "A sailor in the penny arcade was having his girl photographed in the arms of a stuffed gorilla" (*CSEW*, 397); "Eugene could hear all day as he worked at his meticulous watches the glad mallet of the man who cracked the crabs" (*CSEW*, 397); "Bertsingers' did carry its brand of the rhinestone Pegasus and ruby swordfish, its tray of charms" (*CSEW*, 397); "When Eugene set his eyes on an arrangement of amber-red caviar in the shape of a large anchor, 'They are fish eggs, sir,' a young, smocked clerk said, 'and personally I think it's a perfect *pity* that they should be allowed to take them'" (*CSEW*, 398); "The streetcars, taking on banana colors, drove up and down, the line of movie houses fluttered streamers and flags as if they were going to sea. Eugene moved into the central crowd, which seemed actually to increase its jostling with the sunshine, like the sea with wind" (*CSEW*, 398).

15. "He turned his face over a shoulder, rere regardant. Moving through the air high spars of a threemaster, her sails brailed up on the crosstrees, homing, upstream, silently moving, a silent ship" (*UL*, 42).

16. References to Emma in "Music from Spain": "he had suggested to Emma that they take a simple little pleasure trip—modestly, on the bus—down the inexpensive side of the Peninsula; but it had been his luck to mention it on the anniversary of Fan's death and she had slammed the door in his face" (*CSEW*, 399); "It was womanlike; he understood it now. The inviolable grief she had felt for a great thing only widened her capacity to take little things hard. Mourning over the same thing she mourned, he was not to be let in. For letting in was something else. How cold to the living hour grief could make you! Her eye was quite marblelike at the door crack" (*CSEW*, 399); "There had been a time, too,

when she was a soft woman, just as he had been a kind man, soft unto innocence—soft like little Fan" (*CSEW*, 399); "*Hi, mate. Just lammed the little wifey over the puss*" (*CSEW*, 400).

17. The Calypso chapter of the *Odyssey* is the point at which Odysseus wakes up to the fact that he does not want to stay forever on the goddesses' island. Chapter 4 of *Ulysses* includes Molly waking up. Subsection four of "Music from Spain" begins with the tramp waking up. Molly and Leopold's discussion of "Metempsychosis" (*UL*, 52) raises the question of transformation. Eugene watches the tramp with the chickens as "he stood as if flattered by their trans-formation" (*CSEW*, 398).

18. One of these memories is of Emma and her hairpins, a paragraph that directly echoes but expresses the opposite sentiment as a passage in Joyce's Chapter 18. Eugene remembers: "Pretty soon, with her middle finger she would start touching her hairpins, one by one, going over her head as though in finishing her meditations she was sewing some precautionary cap on" (*CSEW*, 394). Molly, remembering her friend's reaction to her sexual fulfillment, recalls "afterwards though she didnt like it so much the day I was in fits of laughing with the giggles I couldnt stop about all my hairpins falling out one after another with the mass of hair I had youre always in great humor she said yes because it grigged her because she knew what it meant" (*UL*, 612). What it meant was that Molly was having good sex. Emma's precautionary cap is a cap against such enjoyment, against sex.

19. When Eugene remembers Fan, he thinks of how her hair met under her chin "like a golden rain hat," and he remembers her standing with her back to the fire. "There had been a time, too, when she was a soft woman, just as he had been a kind man, soft unto innocence—soft like little Fan, and he saw the child at bedtime letting her hair ripple down and all around, with it almost meeting under her chin like a little golden rain hat, and he wanted to say, 'Oh, stay, wait.' Just as the other thing was there too: Fan from the age she could walk to it was standing with her back to the fire (they kept an open fireplace then) and with that gesture like a curtsey was lifting up her gown to warm her backside, like any woman in the world" (*CSEW*, 399).

In Chapter 18 of *Ulysses*, Molly remembers standing in front of the fire as a child: "I yes I had the big doll with all the funny clothes dressing her up and undressing that icy wind skeeting across from those mountains the something Nevada sierra nevada standing at the fire with the little bit of a short shift I had up to heat myself I loved dancing about in it then make a race back into bed. Im sure that fellow opposite used to be there the whole time watching with the light out in the summer and I in my skin hopping around I used to love myself then" (*UL*, 628).

In *Ulysses* Chapter 4, Leopold mentions golden hair (*UL*, 50), raincoats and rainhats (*UL*, 46, 56), and an open fire (*UL*, 45) toward which the cat turns her backside (*UL*, 55).

20. Leopold passes a pub in *Ulysses* and smells the "flabby gush of porter. Through the open doorway the bar squirted out whiffs of ginger, teadust, biscuitmush" (*UL*, 47).

21. Eugene watches the cat close her eyes. Leopold's cat closes her eyes (*UL*, 45–46). Eugene observes, "As the cat opened her eyes again he had a moment of believing he would know anything that happened, anything that threatened the moral way, or transformed it, even, in the city of San Francisco that day" (*CSEW*, 400). Leopold also watches his cat, thinking, "They call them stupid. They understand what we say better than we understand them. She understands all she wants to. Vindictive too. Cruel. Her nature. Curious mice never squeal. Seem to like it. Wonder what I look like to her. Height of a tower? No, she can jump me" (*UL*, 45).

22. References to music in *Ulysses*: (Chapter 5: l. 1, 5, 7, 9–10, 29–36, 474, 481–83). Eugene and Emma go to a music hall. Molly sings in music halls. Fan says she want to spank Pierre Monteaux. In Martha's letter to Leopold, she says she wants to punish him (*UL*, 63, 64). Welty changes "she would like to play with him" to "spank him." The Spaniard is black-clad and Leopold is black-clad for the funeral. The reference to a bullfighter and Spain connects the story not only to Molly's comments on bullfighters but also to Hemingway's novels. Eugene sees that "bright mist bathed this end of the street" (*CSEW*, 400), and Leopold goes to take a bath at the end of the section. The scene in the plan is also a bath. Eugene's paper flies away from him and Leopold is about to throw away his paper. Throwing away a paper is giving up the past and the social world, forgetting how to return home, like the men in the *Odyssey*. Eugene's last image of the Spaniard in this subsection is of a man unperturbed, like the Lotus Eaters: "The artist, who now smoked a cigarette, was wholly as imperturbable, if not quite as large bodily, as he had seemed on the Aeolian Hall stage the evening before" (*CSEW*, 402).

23. As the Spaniard lowers himself to begin to play, he puts his foot on "an oblong object covered in black cloth" (*CSEW*, 402). This is a description of a child-sized coffin.

24. References to hats in the Hades chapter of *Ulysses*: Chapter 6: ll. 37, 39–40, 59, 129, 173–74, 234. Emma looks at Eugene "from under the brim of the blue hat in which she had that night emerged from public-mourning" (*CSEW*, 403). The mention of public mourning connects the hat back to death—resurrection from the underworld.

25. Welty consciously added the name Aeolian Hall to her final manuscript. In Chapter 7 Joyce mentions Madame Blavatsky: "That Blavatsky woman

started it" (*UL*, 115). In subsection three of "Music from Spain," Eugene sees a dark photograph of someone who at first looks like Emma but "was, he read below, Madame Blavatsky" (*CSEW*, 397). The third reference that has been blown off course is the reference to twins from Chapter 7 of *Ulysses*, "two men dressed the same, looking the same, two by two" (*UL*, 114). In *The Golden Apples* this appears in the eleventh break in the text: "At a corner two old fellows, twins, absurdly dressed alike in plaid jackets, the same size and together still, were helping each other onto the crowded step of a streetcar" (*CSEW*, 412).

There is still evidence, however, of a one to one correspondence between subsection seven of "Music from Spain" and Chapter 7 of *Ulysses*. There are numerous references to wind in subsection seven of "Music from Spain": "An enlarged photograph showed the side-show Emma—enormously fat, blown, her small features bunched like a paper of violets in the center of her face" (*CSEW*, 405); "But the Spaniard, cocking his head at Emma's full-sailed manifestation, simply pointed to his own breadth" (*CSEW*, 405); "'Come on. I'm inviting you, all right. We'll eat,' Eugene said, and tipping his finger to his companion's elbow turned him right around" (*CSEW*, 405). This last image is much like a sailboat being turned. In Joyce's plan and in *Ulysses* it is noon. In subsection seven of Welty's "Music from Spain," "It was midday" (*CSEW*, 405).

26. In "Music from Spain," Eugene notices that the woman with the butterfly birthmarks on her skin "had the look of waiting in leafy shade" (*CSEW*, 404). In *Ulysses* in the section Joyce calls "Erin, Green Gem of the Silver Sea," he writes: "'*Mid mossy backs, fanned by gentlest zephyrs, played on by the glorious sunlight or'neath the shadows cast o'er its pensive bosom by the overarching leafage of the giants of the forest*" (*UL*, 102).

27. "Eugene had been easily satisfied of one thing—the formidable artist was free" (*CSEW*, 406). "He was glad to feel himself in the role of companion and advisor to the artist" (*CSEW*, 406); "It was more probable that the artist remained alone at night" (*CSEW*, 407); "Suppose he was still in the process of leaving Mississippi—not stopped here, but simply an artist, touring through" (*CSEW*, 407); "for it was natural to suppose, supposed Eugene, that the solidest of artists were chameleons" (*CSEW*, 408); "What did Eugene MacLain really care about the life of an artist, or a foreigner, or a wanderer, all the same thing—to have it all brought upon him now?" (*CSEW*, 409).

28. In *Ulysses*, Stephen tries to conjure up a performance of *Hamlet*. In "Music from Spain," Eugene also tries to conjure up a woman and a bouquet of roses before the Spaniard.

29. Eugene imagines "the walls of whatever room it was that closed a person in in the evening, would go soft as curtains and begin to tremble. If like the curtains of the aurora borealis the walls of rooms would give even the illusion of

lifting—if they would threaten to go up" (*CSEW*, 408). In contrast, Stephen imagines a "strong curtain" (*UL*, 175).

30. The reference in "Music from Spain" to passengers on a raft echoes Odysseus's journey on the raft and a line from *Ulysses* Chapter 10: "A skiff, a crumpled throwaway, Elijah is coming, rode lightly down the Liffey, under Loopline bridge, shooting the rapids where water chafed around the bridge-piers, sailing eastward past hulls and anchorchains, between the Customhouse old dock and George's quay" (*UL*, 186–87).

31. Throughout Chapter 11 of *Ulysses*, we hear the sound of the blind piano tuner's tapping cane: (ll. 933, 951, 989, 1010, 1037, 1075, 1084, 1100, 1119, 1138, 1166, 1186, 1190, 1208, 1218, 1223, 1234, 1273, 1281). In "Music from Spain," Eugene describes the ladies coming down the hills in San Francisco: "Here came the old woman down the hill—there was always one. In tippets and tapping their canes they slowly came down to meet you" (*CSEW*, 413). One of the women in *Ulysses* snaps her garter on her ample thigh, and Welty adds to "Music from Spain" a description of Emma's concern with her fat legs. Bloom makes reference to Rudy's death, and Eugene expresses his feelings about Fan's death.

32. This phrase echoes the French phrase *"Sonnez la cloche!"* in *Ulysses* on page 219.

33. "I was just passing the time of day with old Troy of the D. M. P. at the corner of Arbour hill there and be damned but a bloody sweep came along and he near drove his gear into my eye. I turned around to let him have the weight of my tongue when who should I see dodging along Stony Batter only Joe Hynes" (*UL*, 240).

34. There are many references to eyes and blindness in *Ulysses* (Chapter 12: ll. 3, 207, 251, 700, 802, 806, 973, 1045, 1089, 1194, 1237, 1265, 1296, 1664, 1800, 1854). In the twelfth subsection of "Music from Spain," there are five references to eyes in two short pages, including: "The Spaniard threw him a dark glance" (*CSEW*, 414); "Eugene's eyes nearly closed and he half fainted upon the body of the city, the old veins, the mottled skin of pavement. Perhaps the soft grass in which little daisies opened would hold his temples and put its eyes to his" (*CSEW*, 415); "An open-eyed baby in his cart extended his little hands and held his thumbs and forefingers tight-shut: a hold on the bright mist" (*CSEW*, 415).

35. In this chapter in *Ulysses*, the whores accuse Leopold of all sorts of wrongdoings.

36. Welty's reference to burning and the sun that bedazzles alludes to this incident, as might the references to smokestacks and chimneys. Welty's description of the drunk lying asleep in the anemones echoes Joyce's description of Bob

Boran sitting drunk and asleep in a corner, away from the others, and his description of Breen: "Cruelty to animals so it is to let that bloody pover-tystricken Breen out on grass with his beard out tripping him, bringing down the rain" (*UL*, 263). Both of these images mirror the picture of the Cyclops asleep from the wine in the *Odyssey* and support Joyce's technic—giganticism—in his plan. In keeping with this technic and the Cyclops image, Welty's section has references to beards—"It waved the wispy white beard of an old Chinese gentleman who was running with the abandon of a school child for the car, which waited on him" (*CSEW*, 415)—and to the Spaniard's being like a giant or at least large. Like a giant would treat an adult, or a parent a child, animal, or plaything, "Eugene was half-lifted across the street. Then the Spaniard, still with a look of interest, made a gesture of examining him, patted him and straightened him up, gave him a little finishing shake, a cuff" (*CSEW*, 415). As the two travelers walk toward the setting sun, "the Spaniard rather unexpec-tedly lunged forward, swung his big body around, and gazed for himself at the world behind and below where they had come. He tenderly swept an arm. The whole arena was alight with a fairness and blueness at this hour of afternoon; all the gray was blue and the white was blue—the laid-out city looked soft, brushed over with some sky-feather. Then he dropped his hand, as though the city might retire; and lifted it again, as though to bring it back for a second time. He was really wonderful, with his arm raised" (*CSEW*, 414). The descrip-tions of the Spaniard's actions are the descriptions of a hero or ruler controlling his world, or a giant in a land of little people. In this image we watch the vaunting arm of the hero go up and down as the sun will go up and down. The city is brushed over with a softness like a painting. The Spaniard with his arm raised is wonderful, not terrifying or threatening or in any way dangerous.

37. The most obvious scene including a cat in *Ulysses* is in Chapter 4 when Leopold spends a long time watching his cat, but there are also general refer-ences to cats in Nausicaa (*UL*, 306), and Joyce compares women to cats twice in this chapter: "O yes, it cut deep because Edy had her own quiet way of saying things like that she knew would wound like the confounded little cat she was" (*UL*, 297) and "those girls, those girls, those lovely seaside girls. Fine eyes she had, clear. It's the white of the eye brings that out not so much the pupil. Did she know what I? Course. Like a cat sitting beyond a dog's jump" (*UL*, 304).

38. The Spaniard is a foreigner, and Gertie thinks Leopold is a foreigner: "She could see at once by his dark eyes and his pale intellectual face that he was a foreigner, the image of the photo she had of Martin Harvey" (*UL*, 293).

39. Eugene keeps throwing a stone at the cat, an act of violence, and he throws a stone at the whirring in the grass. Eugene has started this journey with the Spaniard because he hit Emma. In Chapter 13 Gerty "knew it was that

the man who lifts his hand to a woman save in the way of kindness, deserves to be branded as the lowest of the low" (*UL*, 290). Welty does not brand Eugene as the lowest of the low, but she makes the issue the central problem of her text, not a side issue.

40. Not only are there many references to gazes throughout *Ulysses* Chapter 13 (ll. 105–7, 188, 242, 495–6, 563, 652, 912), but the gaze is so intense in *Ulysses* that it causes Leopold to have an orgasm. In "Music from Spain," Welty refers to the possibility of the gaze erupting into fire, specifically the cat's gaze: "her face made a burning-glass of looking" (*CSEW*, 416). In *Ulysses*, Joyce writes, "Glass flashing. That's how that wise man what's his name with the burning glass. Then the heather goes on fire. It can't be tourists' matches. What? Perhaps the sticks dry rub together in the wind and light. Or broken bottles in the furze act as a burning glass in the sun. Archimedes. I have it! My memory's not so bad" (*UL*, 309). Welty writes of the cat's gaze, "She crouched rigid with the devotion and intensity of her vision, and if she had caught fire there, still she could not, Eugene felt, have stirred out of the seizure. She would have been consumed twice over before she disregarded either what she was looking at or her own frenzy" (*CSEW*, 416). Joyce also refers to the flame caused by the gaze: "She felt the warm flush, a danger signal always with Gerty MacDowell, surging and flaming into her cheeks . . . His eyes burned into her as though they would search her through and through, read her soul. . . . Her woman's instinct told her that she had raised the devil in him and at the thought a burning scarlet swept from throat to brow till the lovely colour of her face became a glorious rose" (*UL*, 292, 293, 295). Welty writes that the cat "seemed to have womanly eyebrows" (*CSEW*, 416), and Joyce comments on women's eyebrows: "Why have women such eyes of witchery? Gerty's were of the bluest Irish blue, set off by lustrous lashes and dark expressive brows" (*UL*, 286). Eugene throws a rock at the cat. Leopold throws the ball and it rolls toward Gerty. Gerty throws the ball back to the boys in what Leopold sees as a provocative manner.

41. The laughing woman mentioned earlier is echoed by Gertie in Chapter 13 (*UL*, 287, 297), and all of the men laugh in Chapter 14 except Stephen and Leopold (*UL*, 319). An additional reference to laughing occurs in Chapter 14 of *Ulysses*: "Thereat mirth grew in them the more and they rehearsed to him his curious rite of wedlock for the disrobing and deflowering of spouses" (*UL*, 321).

42. Joyce writes of "Master Francis Beaumont that is in their *Maid's Tragedy* that was writ for a like twining of lovers" (*UL*, 322).

43. As Eugene and the Spaniard make their way over the rocks Eugene sees the wind as a fortification that keeps him from falling over the cliff. In *Ulysses*, Leopold imagines falling over a cliff—"Fall from cliff" (*UL*, 448).

44. In *Ulysses*, Joyce writes that Leopold says "(*undecidely*) All now? I should not have parted with my talisman. Rain, exposure at dewfall on the searocks, a pecadillo at my time of life" (*UL*, 431).

45. In the first sentence of Chapter 16 Leopold hands Stephen his hat and bucks him up much in the same way that the Spaniard did to Eugene in subsection twelve. In "Music from Spain" the Spaniard sees rats, and in *Ulysses* the sailor mentions Chinese people cooking and eating rats (*UL*, 514). There is a also an entire section on drowning in *Ulysses*: "So then after that they drifted on the wreck of Daunt's rock, wreck of that illfated Norwegian barque . . . breakers running over her and crowds and crowds on the shore in commotion petrified with horror" (*UL*, 521). In "Music from Spain," Eugene recognizes, "There had evidently been, without their knowing it, a loss of the wish to go back. Perhaps this wish had expired. Eugene, who had once nearly drowned, remembered his discovery of the death of volition to stay up in the water. Such things were always found out no telling how long after it was too late" (*CSEW*, 420). This passage refers to both the possibility of drowning, which Odysseus almost experiences in the *Odyssey*, and Odysseus's near loss of the volition to return home both with Calypso and the Lotus Eaters.

46. Leopold talks frequently about his wife, particularly about her being Spanish, and things Spanish in general: "Spaniards, for instance, he continued, passionate temperaments like that. . . . It comes from the great heat, climate generally. My wife is, so to speak, Spanish, half that is. Point of fact she could actually claim Spanish nationality if she wanted, having been born in (technically) Spain, i.e. Gibraltar. She has the Spanish type. Quite dark, regular brunette, black. I for one certainly believe climate accounts for character. That's why I asked you if you wrote poetry in Italian. . . . It's in the blood, Mr. Bloom acceded at once. All are washed in the blood of the sun" (*UL*, 520–21).

Welty's text mentions the Spaniard or Spanish twenty times in six pages, more than in any other section. She also describes the sun as "wetter than water, then not so much a bright body as a red body" (*CSEW*, 420).

47. In the Spaniard, Eugene says he finds "a lasting refuge" (*CSEW*, 421), and we can remember that in Joyce's plan, the place is a shelter and that Stephen and Leopold spend their time in a shelter.

48. As Eugene listens to the voice that did not stop, his "hands waited nerveless moment after moment, while his ears were beaten upon, his whole body, indeed" (*CSEW*, 421). Nerves are the organ in Joyce's plan, and throughout this subsection Eugene is nervous and anxious. Later Welty mentions stress.

In *Ulysses* there is an interesting passage that corresponds to this moment in "Music from Spain:" "Rhododendrons several hundred feet above sealevel was a favourite haunt with all sorts and conditions of men especially in the spring when young men's fancy, though it had its own toll of deaths by falling off the cliffs by design or accidently, usually, by the way, on their left leg, it being only about three quarter's of an hour's run from the pillar" (*UL*, 513).

At this moment the Spaniard loses his hat and Eugene goes after it. Leopold recounts a story of having picked the hat of Parnell, the Irish leader who fell from the country's graces when he had an affair. Leopold also says about Parnell: "Though palpably a radically altered man he was still a commanding figure though carelessly garbed as usual with that look of settled purpose which went a long way with the shillyshallyers till they discovered to their vast discomfiture that their idol had feet of clay after placing him upon a pedestal which she, however, was the first to perceive" (*UL*, 534).

49. In *Ulysses*, Joyce relates at least four scenes of men thinking about a homecoming with a woman. First Stephen thinks back to his family hearth: "There was no response forthcoming to the suggestion however, such as it was, Stephen's mind's eye being too busily engaged in repicturing his family hearth" (*UL*, 507). In Stephen's image is his sister.

The sailor thinks about his home: "—That's right, the sailor said. Fort Camden and Fort Carlisle. That's where I hails from. I belongs there. That's where I hails from. My little woman's down there. She's waiting for me, I know. *For England, home and beauty*. She's my own true wife I haven't seen for seven years now, sailing about" (*UL*, 510).

Leopold remembers all the different writers who write on the subject of a man returning to his loyal wife.

50. Reference to the heel of Achilles in *Ulysses*: "England was toppling already and her downfall would be Ireland, her Achilles heel, which he explained to them about the vulnerable point of Achilles, the Greek hero, a point his auditors at once seized as he completely gripped their attention by showing the tendon referred to on his boot. His advice to every Irishman was: stay in the land of your birth and work for Ireland and live for Ireland. Ireland, Parnell said, could not spare a single one of her sons" (*UL*, 523).

51. "I suppose he was as shy as a boy he being so young hardly 20 of me in the next room hed have heard me on the chamber arrah what harm Dedalus I wonder its like those names in Gibraltar Delapaz Delagracia they had the devils queer names there father Vilaplana of Santa Maria that gave me the rosary Rosales y OReilly in the Calle las Siete Revueltas and Pisimbo and Mrs. Opisso in Governor street O what a name Id go and drown myself in the first river if I had a name like her O my and all the bits of streets Paradise ramp and Bedlam ramp and Rodgers ramp and Crutchetts ramp and the devils gap steps well small blame to me if I am a harumscarum I know I am a bit I declare to God I

dont feel a day older than then I wonder could I get my tongue round any of the Spanish como esta usted muy bien gracias y usted see I havent forgotten it all" (*UL*, 640).

52. Molly repeatedly refers to long-haired men (*UL*, 609, 633). She tries to remember the name of her old boyfriend (*UL*, 626) and speculates on Daedalus's name and on the names of other acquaintances (*UL*, 640). In addition, she prides herself on not having forgotten her Spanish.

CHAPTER 7

1. Jane Ellen Harrisson, *Themis: A Study of the Social Origins of Greek Religion*: "Such rites as circumcision and knocking out of teeth would thus find a new and simpler meaning. Bones and sinews decay, but a tooth lasts on and would serve, if carefully guarded, as an imperishable bit of the old body, as a focus for reincarnation, a stock of vital energy for the use of the disembodied spirit after death" (272–73); see also, Sir James Frazer, *The Golden Bough: A Study in Magic and Religion*, 43–46.

2. Hilda Doolittle, "Sea Rose" in *Selected Poems of H.D.*: "Rose, harsh rose / marred and with stint of petals, / meager flower, thin, /sparse of leaf, /more precious / than a wet rose, / single on a stem—/ you are caught in the drift. / Stunted, with small leaf, / you are flung on the sand, / you are lifted in the crisp sand that drives in the wind. / Can the spice-rose, / drip such acrid fragrance / hardened in a leaf?"(15).

3. Anne Ross, *Pagan Celtic Britain: Studies in Iconography and Tradition*: "The stag figures prominently in the vernacular tradition. Deer frequently entice heroes to the realms of the gods, as does the boar, and there are many legends concerning the hunting of a magical deer which leads the hunters into unexpected and sometimes symbolic situations. . . . In its iconographic appearance then, the stag seems to have been revered as the symbol and companion of the antlered god, Cernunos, while its role in the vernacular tradition is largely that of an other world animal, luring the living into the realm of the gods, or facilitating the fulfillment of some prophecy by allowing itself to be hunted and eaten, no doubt, like the other world pigs, to rise up alive and whole afterwards" (338).

Works Cited

American College Dictionary. C. L. Barnhart ed. New York: Random House, 1963.

Anzaldua, Gloria. "Tlilli, Tlapadli: The Path of the Red and Black Ink," in *Borderlands, La Frontera, the New Mestiza*. San Francisco: Spinsters/Aunt Lute, 1987.

Arnold, Marilyn. "When Gratitude Is No More: Eudora Welty's 'June Recital.'" *South Carolina Review*, 13, no. 2 (Spring, 1981).

Barthes, Roland. *Mythologies*. Trans. Annette Lavers. New York: Hill and Wang, 1972.

———. *S/Z*. Trans. Richard Miller. New York: Hill and Wang, 1974.

———. "From Work to Text" in *Textual Strategies: Perspectives in Post-structuralist Criticism*. Ithaca: Cornell University Press, 1979.

Bloom, Harold, ed. *Eudora Welty: Critical Views*. New York: Chelsea House, 1986.

Bolsterli, Margaret Jones. "Woman's Vision: The Worlds of Women in *Delta Wedding*, *Losing Battles*, and *The Optimist's Daughter*." In *Eudora Welty: Critical Essays*, ed. Peggy Whitman Prenshaw. Jackson: University Press of Mississippi, 1979.

Brinkmeyer, Robert H., Jr. "An Openess to Otherness: The Imaginative Vision of Eudora Welty." *Southern Literary Journal* 20, no. 2 (Spring 1988).

Brown, Abbie Farwell. "The Lucky Stone." *St. Nicholas: An Illustrated Magazine for Young Folks* (41, no. 1) (Nov. 1913 to Apr. 1914).

Bryant, J. A., Jr. *Eudora Welty*. Minneapolis: University of Minnesota Press, 1968.

———. "Seeing Double in *The Golden Apples*." *Sewanee Review* 82 (Spring 1974).

Burland, C. A. *Myths of Life and Death*. New York: Crown Publishers, 1974.

Butler, Judith. *Gender Trouble: Feminism and the Subversion of Identity*. New York: Routledge, 1990.

Carson, F. D. "The Song of Wandering Aengus: Allusion in *TGA*." *Notes on Mississippi Writers* 6, no. 1 (Spring, 1973).

Chopin, Kate. *The Awakening*. 1899. New York: Avon Books, 1972.

Cixous, Hélène. "Castration or Decapitation?" Trans. Annette Kuhn. *Signs: Journal of Women in Culture and Society* 7 (1981).

———. "The Laugh of the Medusa." In *New French Feminisms: An Anthology*, ed. Elaine Marks and Isabelle de Courtivron. New York: Schocken Books, 1981.

Caldwell, Joan. "The Beauty of the Medusa: Twentieth Century." *English Studies in Canada* 11, no. 4 (Dec. 1985).

Cousar, Franklin. "Recurring Metaphors: An Aspect of Unity in *The Golden Apples*." *Notes on Contemporary Literature* 5 (Sept. 1975).

Daniel, Robert W. "The World of Eudora Welty." In *Southern Renascence: The Literature of the Modern South*, ed. Louis D. Rubin, Jr., and Robert D. Jacobs Baltimore: Johns Hopkins University Press, 1953.

———. "Eudora Welty: The Sense of Place." In *South: Modern Southern Literature in Its Setting*, ed. Louis D. Rubin and Robert D. Jacobs. Garden City, N.Y.: Doubleday, 1961.

DeKay, Charles. *Bird Gods*. New York: A. S. Barnes, 1898.

De Lauretis, Teresa. *Alice Doesn't: Feminism, Semiotics, Cinema*. Bloomington: Indiana University Press, 1984.

Demmin, Julia L., and Daniel Curley. "Golden Apples and Silver Apples." In *Eudora Welty: Critical Essays*, ed. Peggy Whitman Prenshaw. Jackson: University Press of Mississippi, 1979.

Desmond, John F., ed. *A Still Moment: Essays on the Art of Eudora Welty*. Metuchen, N.J.: Scarecrow Press, 1978.

Derrida, Jacques. *Writing and Difference*. Trans. Alan Bass. Chicago: University of Chicago Press, 1978.

Devlin, Albert J. *Eudora Welty's Chronicle: A Story of Mississippi Life*. Jackson: University Press of Mississippi, 1983.

———. *Welty: A Life in Literature*. Jackson: University Press of Mississippi, 1987.

Dinnerstein, Dorothy. *The Mermaid and the Minotaur: Sexual Arrangements and Human Malaise*. New York: Harper and Row, 1976.

Dollarhide, Louis, and Ann J. Abadie, eds. *Eudora Welty: A Form of Thanks*. Jackson: University Press of Mississippi, 1979.

Doolittle, Hilda. *Selected Poems of H.D.* New York: Grove Press, 1957.

Dunn, Joseph. *The Ancient Irish Epic Tale Tain Bo Cualnge*. London: David Nutt, 1914.

Eliot, George. *Middlemarch*. 1964. New York. Signet Classics, 1964.

Eliot, T. S. "Tradition and the Individual Talent." *Selected Essays: 1917–1932*. New York: Harcourt, Brace, 1932.

Else, Gerald. *The Origin and Early Form of Greek Tragedy*. Cambridge: Harvard University Press, 1965.

Evans, Elizabeth. *Eudora Welty*. New York: Frederick Unger, 1981.

————. "Eudora Welty: The Metaphor of Music." *Southern Quarterly* 2 (Summer 1982).

Farwell, Marilyn. "Toward a Definition of Lesbian Literary Imagination." *Signs: Journal of Women in Culture & Society* 14 (1988).

Faulkner, William. *The Sound and the Fury*. 1929. New York: Random House, 1956.

Ferguson, Mary Anne. "The Female Novel of Development and the Myth of Psyche." *Denver Quarterly* 17, no. 4 (Winter 1983).

Fingesten, Peter. "Spirituality, Mysticism, and Non-Objective Art." *Art Journal* 21, no. 1 (Autumn 1961).

Fisher, Elizabeth. *Woman's Creation: Sexual Evolution and the Shaping of Society*. Garden City, N.Y.: Anchor Press/Doubleday, 1979.

Foucault, Michel. *Discipline and Punish: The Birth of the Prison*. New York: Vintage Books. 1979.

————. "What Is an Author?" in *Textual Strategies: Perspectives in Post Structuralist Criticism*. Ithaca, N.Y.: Cornell University Press, 1979.

Frazer, Sir James. *The Golden Bough: A Study in Magic and Religion*. 1922. Abridged Ed. New York: MacMillan, 1963.

Friedman, Susan. "Creativity and the Childbirth Metaphor: Gender Difference and Literary Discourse." *Feminist Studies* 13, no 1 (Spring 1987).

Fuss, Diana. *Essentially Speaking: Feminism, Nature, and Difference*. New York. Routledge. 1989.

Gimbutus, Marija. *The Gods and Goddesses of Old Europe: 6500–3500 B.C.* Berkeley: University of California Press, 1982.

Glucksman, Paul H., comp. *Dictionary German/Deutsches Wortenbuch*. Ed. Herbert Rodeck and T. C. Appelt. Chicago: Follet, 1966.

Grahn, Judy. *Another Mother Tongue*. Boston: Beacon Press, 1984.

Graves, Robert. *The Greek Myths I and II*. New York: Penguin Books, 1960.

————. *The White Goddess: A Historical Grammar of Poetic Myth*. New York: Farrar, Straus and Giroux, 1948.

Gilbert, Sandra, and Susan Gubar. *The Madwoman in the Attic: the Woman Writer and the Nineteenth Century Literary Imagination*. New Haven: Yale University Press, 1974.

Gubar, Susan. "'The Blank Page' and the Issues of Female Creativity." *Critical Inquiry* (Winter 1981).

————, and Sandra Gilbert, eds. *The Norton Anthology of Literature by Women: The Tradition in English*. New York: Norton, 1985.

Gygax, Franziska. *Serious Daring from Within: Female Narrative Strategies in Eudora Welty's Novels*. Westport: Greenwood Press, 1990.

Hamilton, Edith. *Mythology*. 1940. New York: New American Library, 1969.

Harris, Jocelyn. *Jane Austen's Art of Memory*. Cambridge: Cambridge University Press, 1989.

Harrison, Jane Ellen. *Mythology*. Boston: Marshall Jones, 1924.

———. *Religion of Ancient Greece*. London: A Constable, 1905.

———. *Themis: A Study of the Social Origins of Greek Religion*. 1912. Gloucester, Mass.: Peter Smith, 1974.

Herbert, George. "The Flowre," in *The English Poems of George Herbert*. London. J. M. Dent and Sons, 1974.

Herrmann, Christine. *The Tongue Snatchers*. Lincoln: University of Nebraska Press, 1989.

Homer. *The Homeric Hymns*. Trans. Charles Boer. Chicago: Swallow Press, 1970.

———. *The Iliad*. Trans. Robert Fitzgerald. Garden City, N.Y.: Anchor Press/Doubleday, 1975.

———. *The Odyssey*. Trans. Robert Fitzgerald. Garden City, N.Y.: Doubleday, Inc., 1963.

Hughes, Langston. *Montage of a Dream Deferred*. New York: Holt, 1951.

Hyginus. *The Myths of Hyginus*. Humanistic Studies, no. 34. Trans. and ed. Mary Grant. Lawrence: University of Kansas Publications, 1960.

Irigaray, Luce. "Ce sexe qui n'en est pas un" in *New French Feminisms*. New York: Schocken Books, 1981.

———. "And the One Doesn't Stir Without the Other." Trans. Helene Vivienne Wenzel. *Signs: Journal of Women in Culture and Society* 7, no. 1 (1981).

———. "When Our Lips Speak Together." *Signs: Journal of Women in Culture and Society* 6, no. 1 (1980).

Jackson, Kenneth Hurlstone, trans. *A Celtic Miscellany*. 1951. New York: Penguin Books, 1971.

Jardine, Alice. *Gynesis: Configurations of Woman and Modernity*. Ithaca: Cornell University Press, 1985.

Jewett, Sarah Orne. *The Country of the Pointed Firs and Other Stories*. 1896. Garden City, N.Y.: Doubleday and Co., 1956.

Joyce, James. *Ulysses*. 1922. New York: Random House, 1986.

Kerr, Elizabeth M. "The World of Eudora Welty's Women." In *Eudora Welty: Critical Essays*, ed. Peggy Whitman Prenshaw. Jackson: University Press of Mississippi, 1979.

King, William. *Heather Gods and Heroes*. Cardondale: Southern Illinois University Press, 1965.

Klien, Ernst. *A Comprehensive Etymological Dictionary of the English Language*. New York: Elseview, 1966.

Kreyling, Michael. *Author and Agent*. New York. Farrar, Straus, Giroux. 1991.

————. *Eudora Welty's Achievement of Order*. Baton Rouge: Louisiana State University Press, 1980.

Kristeva, Julia. "An Interview with Julia Kristeva." In *Intertextuality and Contemporary American Fiction*, ed. Patrick O'Donnell and Robert Con Davis. Baltimore: John Hopkins University Press, 1989.

Langdon, Stephen. *The Epic of Creation: Enuma Elish*. Oxford: Clarendon Press, 1923.

Lewalski, Barbara K., and Andrew J. Sabol, eds. *Major Poets of the Earlier Seventeenth Century*. New York: Odyssey Press, 1973.

Lorde, Audre. "The Master's Tools Will Never Dismantle the Master's House." *Sister Outsider: Essays and Speeches*. Trumansburg, N.Y.: The Crossing Press, 1984.

MacKethan, Lucinda H. *Daughters of Time: Creating Woman's Voice in Southern Story*. Mercer University Lamar Memorial Lectures, no. 32. Athens: University of Georgia Press, 1990.

Mchaffey, Vicki. "Part II. Multiple Authorities, Chapter 4. Text Styles, Textile, and the Textures of *Ulysses*," in *Re-authorizing Joyce*. Cambridge: Cambridge University Press, 1988.

McDonald, W. U., Jr., ed. Eudora Welty *Newsletter* 1, no. 1 (Winter 1977) and 10, no. 1 (Winter 1986).

McHaney, Thomas L. "Eudora Welty and the Multitudinous Golden Apples." *Mississippi Quarterly* 26 (Fall 1973).

Mannin, Ethel. *The Wild Swans and Other Tales Based on the Ancient Irish*. London: Jarrolds, 1952.

Manning, Carol S. *With Ears Opening Like Morning Glories: Eudora Welty and the Love of Storytelling*. Westport: Greenwood Press, 1985.

Manz-Kunz, Marie-Antoinette. *Eudora Welty: Aspects of Reality in Her Short Fiction*. Bern: Francke Verlag, 1971.

Marrs, Suzanne. *The Welty Collection: A Guide to the Eudora Welty Manuscripts and Documents at the Mississippi Department of Archives and History*. Jackson: University Press of Mississippi, 1988.

Messerli, Douglas. "Metronome and Music: The Encounter Between History and Myth in *The Golden Apples*." In *A Still Moment: Essays on the Art of Eudora Welty*, ed. John F. Desmond. Metuchen, N.J.: Scarecrow Press, 1978.

Miller, Owen. "Intertextual Identity." In *Identity of the Literary Text*, ed. Mario S. Valdez and Owen Miller. Toronto: University of Toronto Press, 1985.

Morris, Harry C. "Eudora Welty's Use of Mythology." *Shenandoah* 6, no. 2 (Spring 1955).

————. "Zeus and *The Golden Apples*: Eudora Welty." *Perspective* 5 (Autumn 1952).

Murray, Gilbert. *The Rise of the Greek Epic.* Oxford: Clarendon Press, 1907.

New Larousse Encyclopedia of Mythology. London: Hamlyn, 1959.

O'Donnell, Patrick, and Robert Con Davis, eds. *Intertextuality and Contemporary American Fiction.* Baltimore: John Hopkins University Press, 1989.

Ovid. *The Metamorphoses.* Trans. and ed. Horace Gregory. New York: New American Library, 1958.

The Oxford English Dictionary, 2nd ed., prepared by J. A. Simpson and E. S. C. Weiner. Oxford: Clarendon Press. 1989.

Pei, Lowry. "Dreaming the Other in *The Golden Apples,*" *Modern Fiction Studies* 28 (1982): 415–33.

Phillips, Robert L., Jr. "A Structural Approach to Myth in the Fiction of Eudora Welty." In *Eudora Welty: Critical Essays,* ed. Peggy Whitman Prenshaw. Jackson: University Press of Mississippi, 1979.

Pitavy-Sougues, Danièle. "Techniques as Myth: The Structure of *The Golden Apples.*" In *Eudora Welty: Critical Essays,* ed. Peggy Whitman Prenshaw. Jackson: University Press of Mississippi, 1979.

———. "Watchers and Watching: Point of View in Eudora Welty's 'June Recital.'" *Southern Review* 19, no. 3 (Summer 1983).

Plutarch. *Plutarch's Lives* I, trans. Bernadotte Perrin. 1914. London: William Heinemann Ltd., 1982.

Prenshaw, Peggy Joyce Whitman. "A Study of Setting in the Fiction of Eudora Welty." Ph.D. dissertation, University of Texas at Austin, 1970.

———. "Woman's World, Man's Place: The Fiction of Eudora Welty." In *Eudora Welty: A Form of Thanks,* ed. Louis Dollarhide and Ann J. Abadie. Jackson: University of Mississippi Press, 1979.

———, ed. *Conversations with Eudora Welty.* Jackson: University of Mississippi, 1984.

———, ed. *Eudora Welty: Critical Essays.* Jackson: University Press of Mississippi, 1979.

———, ed. *Thirteen Essays: Selected from Eudora Welty's Critical Essays.* Jackson: University Press of Mississippi, 1983.

Pugh, Elaine Upton. "The Duality of Morgana: The Making of Virgie's Vision The Vision of *The Golden Apples.*" *Modern Fiction Studies* 28, no. 3 (Autumn 1982).

Randisi, Jennifer Lynn. *A Tissue of Lies: Eudora Welty and the Southern Romance.* New York: University Press of America, 1982.

Rich, Adrienne, "Transcendental Etude," in *Dream of a Common Language.* New York: W. W. Norton, 1978.

———. "When We Dead Awaken: Writing As Revision," in *On Lies, Secrets, and Silences.* New York: W. W. Norton, 1979.

Robinson, Marilynne. *House-keeping*. New York: Bantam Books, 1980.

Ross, Anne. *Pagan Celtic Britain: Studies in Iconography and Tradition*. New York: Columbia University Press, 1967.

Rose, H. J. *A Handbook of Greek Mythology Including Its Extension to Rome*. London: Methuen, 1928.

Rouse, Sarah Allman. "Place and People in Eudora Welty's Fiction: A Portrait of the Deep South." Ph.D. dissertation, Florida State University, 1962.

Rubin, Gayle. "The Traffic in Women: Notes on the 'Political Economy' of Sex. " In *Towards an Anthropology of Women*, ed. Rayna R. Reiter. New York: Monthly Review Press, 1975.

Rubin, Louis D., Jr. "Art and Artistry in Morgana Mississippi." *Missouri Review* 4, no.3 (Summer, 1981).

———. "The Golden Apples of the Sun." *The Faraway Country: Writers of the Modern South*. Seattle: University of Washington Press, 1963.

Said, Edward. *Beginnings: Intention and Method*. New York: Basic Books, 1975.

Sandards, N. K., trans. *The Epic of Gilgamesh*. New York: Penguin Books, 1960.

Schmidt, Peter. *The Heart of the Story*: *Eudora Welty's Short Fiction*. Jackson: University Press of Mississippi, 1991.

Scholes, Robert. "Uncoding Mama: The Female Body as Text," in *Semiotics and Interpretation*. New Haven: Yale University Press, 1982.

Sedgwick, Eve Kosofsky. *Epistemology of the Closet*. Berkeley: University of California Press, 1990.

Shakespeare, William. *A Midsummer Night's Dream* in *William Shakespeare*: *The Complete Works*, ed. Alfred Hurbage. Baltimore: Penguin Books. 1969.

Showalter, Elaine, ed. *The New Feminist Criticism: Essays on Women, Literature, and Theory*. New York: Pantheon Books, 1985.

———. "Feminist Criticism in the Wilderness." *Critical Inquiry* (Winter 1981).

Skaggs, Merril Maguire. "Eudora Welty's 'I' of Memory." In *Critical Essays* on *Eudora Welty*, ed. W. Crelly Turner, and Lee Emily Hardin. Boston: G. K. Hall, 1989.

———. "Morgana's Apples and Pears," In *Eudora Welty: Critical Essays*, ed. Peggy Whitman Prenshaw. Jackson: University Press of Mississippi, 1979.

Slater, Philip E. *The Glory of Hera: Greek Mythology and the Greek Family*. Boston: Beacon Press, 1971.

Smith, Homer W. *Man and His Gods*. Boston: Little, Brown, 1952.

Smith, William. *Smith's Bible Dictionary*. New York: A Jove Book, 1977.

Squire, Charles. *Celtic Myth and Legend, Poetry and Romance*. London: Gresham Publishing Co., 1920.

Stone, Merlin. *Ancient Mirrors of Motherhood: A Treasury of Goddess and Heroine Lore from Around the World*. Boston: Beacon Press, 1984.

————. *When God Was a Women*. New York: Harcourt, Brace, Jovanovich, 1976.

Tapley, Philip A. "The Portrayal of Women in Selected Short Stories by Eudora Welty." 2 vols. Ph.D. dissertation, Louisiana State University, 1974.

Thornton, Naoka Fuwa. "Medusa-Perseus Symbolism in Eudora Welty's *The Optimist's Daughter*. *Southern Quarterly* 23 no. 4 Summer 1985.

Thomas, Joyce Carol. *Marked By Fire*. New York: Avon, 1982.

Tyler, Anne. *A Visit with Eudora Welty*. Privately published, 1980.

Vance, Carol S. "Pleasure and Danger: Toward a Politics of Sexuality." In *Pleasure and Danger: Exploring Female Sexuality*, ed. Carol S. Vance. Boston: Routledge, 1984.

Vande Keift, Ruth M. *Eudora Welty*. New York: Twayne, 1962.

————. *Eudora Welty: Revised Edition*. Boston: Twayne Publishers, 1987.

Vickery, John B., and J'nan M. Sellery, eds. *The Scapegoat: Ritual and Literature*. New York: Houghton Mifflin, 1912.

Walker, Barbara G. *The Crone: Woman of Age, Wisdom, and Power*. San Francisco: Harper and Row, 1985.

————. *The Woman's Encyclopedia of Myths and Secrets*. San Francisco: Harper and Row, Publishers, 1983.

Webster, Hutton. *Primitive Secret Societies: A Study in Early Politics and Religion*. New York: MacMillan, 1908.

Welty, Eudora. *The Bride and the Innisfallen and Other Stories*. 1955. New York: Harcourt, Brace, Jovanovich, 1980.

————. *The Collected Stories of Eudora Welty*. New York: Harcourt, Brace, Jovanovich, 1980.

————. *The Eye of the Story: Selected Essays and Reviews*. New York: Random House, 1979.

————. *The Golden Apples*. New York: Harcourt, Brace, 1949.

————. *Losing Battles*. New York: Random House, 1970.

————. *One Writer's Beginnings*. The William E. Massey, Sr., Lectures in the History of American Civilization. Cambridge: Harvard University Press, 1984.

————. *The Optimist's Daughter*. New York: Random House, 1972

.————. *On Short Stories*. New York: Harcourt, Brace, 1954.

————. *The Wide Net and Other Stories*. 1943. New York: Harcourt, Brace, Jovanovich, 1971.

Westling, Louise Hutchings. *Eudora Welty*. Totowa: Barnes & Noble Books, 1989.

————. *Sacred Groves and Ravaged Gardens: The Fiction of Eudora Welty, Carson McCullers, and Flannery O'Connor*. Athens: University of Georgia Press, 1985.

Weston, Jessie L. *From Ritual To Romance*. 1920. Garden City, N. Y.: Doubleday, 1957.

Weston, Ruth D. "The Feminine and Feminist Texts of Eudora Welty's *The Optimist's Daughter*." *South Central Review* 4, no.4 (Winter, 1987).

Williams, John. *English Renaissance Poetry: A Collection of Shorter Poems from Skelton to Jonson*. New York: W. W. Norton, 1963.

Wolkstein, Diane, and Samuel Noah Kramer. *Inanna, Queen of Heaven and Earth: Her Stories and Hymns from Sumer*. New York: Harper and Row, 1983.

Woolf, Virginia. *The Pargiters*. London: Hogarth Press. 1977.

———. *A Room of One's Own*. 1929. New York: Harcourt, Brace, 1957.

———. *The Three Guineas*. New York: Harcourt, Brace, 1938.

———. *To the Lighthouse*. New York: Harcourt, Brace and World, 1927.

———. "Professions for Women" in *Women and Writing*. Ed. Michele Barrett. New York: Harcourt, Brace, Jovanovich, 1979.

———. *The Years*. 1937. New York: Harcourt, Brace, 1965.

Wright, Harold Bell. *The Recreation of Brian Kent*. Chicago: Book Supply Company. 1919.

Wright, Richard. *Native Son*. New York: Harper and Row, 1966.

Yeager, Patricia. "Because a Fire Was in My Head: Eudora Welty and the Dialogic Imagination." *PMLA* 99, no. 5 (Oct, 1984).

———. "The Case of the Dangling Signifier: Phallic Imagery in Eudora Welty's 'Moon Lake.'" *Twentieth Century Literature*, 28, no.4 (Winter, 1982).

Yeats, W. B. *Mythologies*. New York: MacMillan, 1959.

———. *Selected Poems and Three Plays of William Butler Yeats*. 1931. Ed. and intro. M. L. Rosenthal. New York: Collier Books, 1962.

Index